ANSCR

ANSCR

THE ALPHA-NUMERIC SYSTEM FOR
CLASSIFICATION OF RECORDINGS

This book deals with classification of sound recordings of all types, whether on plastic disc or on tape (reel to reel, cartridge, cassette) or in any other physical format. It is a classification system devised specifically for sound recordings and is called the Alpha-Numeric System for Classification of Recordings. It is referred to herein by its acronym

"ANSCR"
pronounced "answer"

CAROLINE SAHEB-ETTABA

ROGER B. MCFARLAND

BRO-DART PUBLISHING COMPANY
WILLIAMSPORT, PENNSYLVANIA · 1969

To

LEILA, CHEDLY, ROBERT AND SANDI

PREFACE AND ACKNOWLEDGMENTS

The saying "There is nothing new under the sun" is true of library reference works as well as other less esoteric creations. The *ALPHA-NUMERIC SYSTEM FOR CLASSIFICATION OF RECORDINGS (ANSCR)* is "new" in its concept and comprehensiveness, but has behind it many years of tried and proven principles gleaned from many sources, and practiced by many dedicated librarians and audio-visual professionals. This distillation of ideas makes it impossible to acknowledge the original sources of many of the basic concepts which make the ANSCR system so workable.

There are many persons though whose contributions to ANSCR are known and can be gratefully acknowledged. We express special acknowledgment to the following:

William J. Speed, Director of the Audio-Visual Department, Los Angeles Public Library, who has spent many years encouraging the growth of library audio-visual collections, and who has been instrumental in formulating many of the ideas basic to successful recordings classification. His ideas have proved invaluable to the development of the ANSCR system;

Wesley A. Doak, Assistant Audio-Visual Director, Los Angeles Public Library, who supplied continued encouragement and active assistance in the early phases of ANSCR's development. His background in specific music areas was gratefully drawn upon during difficult stages of research;

Ronald F. Sigler, Coordinator of Audio-Visual Services, Los Angeles County Public Library System, who was able to provide much professional guidance and technical advice through his knowledge of library services.

For using ANSCR in their recordings collections we are grateful to Joleene Bock and June Bacon, Rio Hondo Junior College (Calif.); Florence James, Fullerton (Calif.) Public Library; and the staff of the Rosemead Regional Library, Los Angeles County Public Library System.

Appreciation is expressed to the many educators, librarians, and audio-visual professionals who took time from their demanding schedules to review ANSCR and give evaluative responses. Included among these are Martha Boaz, Dean, University of Southern California, School of Library Science; Joan Clark, Consultant, New York State Library; Natalie Coltman, Bucks County Public Library (Pa.); Edgar Cook, Bro-Dart Professional Services; Harriet Covey, Los Angeles County Public Library; Theodore Hines, Professor of Library Science, Columbia University; Eileen Hoy, Bro-Dart Professional Services; Sydney Marcu, New York Public Library; George L. Mayer, New York Public Library; Mayrelee Newman, El Centro Junior College (Texas); Richard Pfefferle, Nassau County Library System (New York); Vivian Prince, Professor of Library Science, University of Southern California; Janice Richards, Los Angeles County Public Library; Norman Seldes, Oceanside Public Library (New York); Rudi Weiss, Westchester Library System (New York).

We also wish to thank the following: Jack Berlin, William Courtney, Joseph Ilg, Myrna Johnson, Robert Johnson, Frances Makepeace, Norbert Moniz, Jack Russell, and David Wilt.

The ANSCR System would not have progressed from idea to reality, nor would the thousands of hours in research have been possible without the active assistance and encouragement of Arthur Brody, George Bonsall, David G. Remington, and Wayne E. Day.

There are many others who have been involved in various stages of ANSCR's development. We thank them for their efforts. We are especially grateful to each of our families for their continued patience and unvarying support.

Caroline Saheb-Ettaba
Roger B. McFarland

TABLE OF CONTENTS

TABLES

INTRODUCTION

The only good reason for creating a classification scheme is if there is a need for one. Two questions are asked repeatedly by librarians: "Do recordings need to be classified, and is a separate classification scheme necessary for recordings?"

The purpose of classifying any material is to enable the user to find what he wants as quickly and efficiently as possible. This is often easier said than done since users vary in their orientation, and materials vary in their form and content. But experience has shown that classification by logical arrangement of material is the most direct method of helping large numbers of people locate what they need.

Although anything from nails to supermarkets may be classified, it is customary in library work to think of classification in terms of books. Few librarians argue with the concept of book classification although they may not agree on the type of classification. In physical as well as intellectual terms, books are suited to systematic arrangement because they stand upright on shelves, and their spines provide a convenient place for placing identifying symbols.

From their inception, libraries have collected printed materials other than books, and the physical differences of such materials have always posed problems in storage and arrangement. It is impractical to house pamphlets, periodicals, pictures and maps on the same shelves with books, so these materials must be stored separately in boxes, racks or drawers. Once they are physically separated from the books, the classification symbol no longer serves as a unique location device, and the question arises whether the same book classification symbols should be used on these materials, if only in the interest of uniformity.

Because the scope and emphasis of these "non-book" materials tend to be narrower than those of books, and their usage is more specialized, many libraries do not attempt to incorporate them into the hierarchical book classification, but are content with a simpler arrangement, usually by direct subject heading. This practice is an implicit admission that one unified system of classification in the library does not serve the best interests of materials whose use and composition differ from books.

Although sound recordings have long since passed the novelty stage, libraries on the whole have been slow or reluctant to add them to their collections. Several reasons are advanced to explain this, such as the technical problems of handling and storage, the cost of equipment necessary for their use, and the rapidity of technological change which seems to outdate or outmode recordings too swiftly. That libraries have been slow to accept recorded material has only served to exaggerate the problems of handling, storage and arrangement which undeniably exist. The approach to these problems has been piecemeal rather than comprehensive, thereby preventing the establishment of uniform and realistic standards. Individual librarians have had to face and resolve their problems independently, and many have done so with remarkable imagination and resourcefulness. Unfortunately, most of their solutions have had little effect beyond the confines of their own libraries, while the lack of coordinated study and evaluation has produced a bewildering diversity of methods, at the cost of too much duplicated time and effort.

Two distinctive patterns may be seen in all these independent efforts. First, the physical shape and maintenance requirements of recordings have made it practical procedure to house them separately from books. Second, the rising popularity of library recordings collections has caused their size and number to rapidly increase. The increase in size of collections, along with open stack shelving arrangements, has made classification imperative. The recognition of this fact is attested to by the multitude of classification systems which are in use in library recording collections throughout the country. It is interesting to note that for classifying recordings, more "home made" schemes are used (schemes invented by individual librarians for their own collections) than schemes which attempt to use adaptations of present book schemes, such as Dewey or LC.

The failure of the book classification scheme to adequately classify recorded materials for the user is because book schemes are designed for arranging books, and recordings are not books. It is possible to use a recording as a book substitute by having someone read aloud, but the act of reading is in itself a performance, and interposes between the author and the "reader" an interpreter. PERFORMANCE is the unique characteristic of the recording, and SOUND is the unique function. A "valid" recording in the creative sense is one in which both elements are fully exploited. For example, plays and monologs, both designed to be spoken, are especially suited to recordings, as are discussions and open debates. Other areas in which the recording excels are dramatized documentary (an art form perfected in radio broadcasting) and transcriptions of sounds, such as bird calls, yodeling, train whistles, and music. It is lamentable that because recordings are so perfect a vehicle for music performance, and the wealth of recorded music is so great, many people think solely of music when referring to recordings. Some librarians will classify only music recordings, and leave other types of recordings in nondescript order or classed within a book scheme.

Librarians who work with recordings and with the public recognize the need for classification of their materials. The existence of many independent class schemes for recordings only indicates that an adapted book classification does not answer the librarians' needs, the public's needs, nor the needs of the recordings. Proponents of a single class system for use in the library often ignore the fact that the class number is primarily a locating device, and loses its effectiveness when collections are housed separately because of size or shape. Assuming that proper cataloging is performed for all library materials, it is the purpose of the subject heading, and not the class number, to bring together all related subject materials, regardless of size or shelving location. This factor is particularly important in American libraries, where use of classed catalogs is extremely rare, and even shelflists are not always accessible to the patron.

As more and more libraries come to accept the sound recording as a necessity, rather than an adjunct or luxury, the need for uniform standards becomes more urgent. Classification and cataloging standards for sound recordings must be comparable in quality to those used for books if maximum use is to be made of them by the library public. But such standards must be tailored, not adapted, to the special characteristics of recordings. Reference tools are necessary to establish and maintain standards, and the ANSCR scheme was developed to serve as such a tool. ANSCR was created because sound recordings are a distinctive medium of communication, and their classification must be based on the qualities and limitations which distinguish them from other media.

In concept and form, ANSCR contains much of the basic logic found in the numerous, independent class schemes already in existence. It differs from these, however, in that it provides not only an arrangement of subject categories, but a formula for establishing a unique class number for each recording. Unlike other classification schemes, ANSCR was not created for any individual recordings collection, but was conceived for collections in libraries of any size or type, with particular application to the browser oriented or open stack collection. Because ANSCR is the first comprehensive recordings class system to be made available in book form, with complete and detailed instructions on its use and formation, any library may adopt ANSCR for its own use in the knowledge that revisions and updating of the system will be forthcoming whenever warranted by growth and development within the field of sound recordings.

PART ONE

ORGANIZATION OF THIS BOOK

This book is divided into two separate parts, each part having a very different structure and purpose. Part One explains the ANSCR System, and describes its organization and application. All the basic concepts of the ANSCR System are discussed, as well as the philosophy underlying these concepts. Part One must be read in its entirety because with this information the reader is able to begin at once to classify recordings in the ANSCR System.

Part Two contains numbered lists of rules and definitions. These rules are divided and arranged so that each set of rules applies to a particular aspect of the ANSCR System. Part Two is a reference tool to be consulted whenever a particular definition is required, or to resolve specific problems or questions. These rules are detailed and comprehensive since they are intended to cover every possible problem or exception which the classifier may encounter. Because of the wealth of detail, Part Two is meaningful only if the reader has a thorough understanding of the information given in Part One.

CHAPTER ONE

CLASSIFYING A RECORDING

The ANSCR System is designed to be used quickly and easily for classifying all recorded materials. It is based on three concepts: a *list of subject categories*, a *Basic Rule* for classifying, and a *unique class number* for each recording. Using these concepts as guidelines, a recording is classified as follows.

1. Examine the album cover or tape box. These give so much information about the recording that it is usually possible to decide immediately in which subject category the recording should be placed.

2. Check the physical structure of the recording. (In the case of a disc, examine the disc itself. If the recording is on tape, read the information regarding number of minutes of play per selection.) This examination helps to determine if the correct subject category has been chosen according to the *Basic Rule of Classification*.

3. Consult the rules in Part Two for the category selected. These rules will confirm whether or not the category is correct for the recording, and will also explain how to form a unique class number for the recording.

With a list of the subject categories in hand, and a knowledge of the Basic Rule, the reader will discover that he can already select the category for many recordings just on the basis of the recording itself and his own experience. The Basic Rule is given in the next paragraph, and the list of subject categories is on page 7.

BASIC RULE OF CLASSIFICATION

Discs

If the first work on side one of the disc occupies one-third or more of the space on side one, the recording is classed according to the type or form of this first work. If the first work on side one does not occupy one-third or more of the space on side one, the entire recording is examined for general content in order to determine its classification.

4

Tapes

If the first work on side one of the tape occupies one-third or more of the time on side one, the recording is classed according to the type or form of this first work. If the first work on side one does not occupy one-third or more of the time on side one, the entire recording is examined for general content in order to determine its classification.

The Basic Rule exists because one recording cannot be shelved in more than one place. This being the case, some principle of classification must be established in order to select a category for the recording. The principle or Basic Rule of classification in the ANSCR System is based on *physical measurement* of the recording.

In practice, this means that if the first work on side one of a disc is a concerto, and the concerto occupies one-third or more of the space on side one, the recording is classed in category EC (CONCERTOS), whether or not all or any of the following works on the same recording are also concertos. If the first work on side one falls short of occupying one-third of the space, then examine all the works on the recording to determine a general subject content.

Physical measurement is a very useful tool in classifying recordings of classical music because record companies frequently put two, three, or more works of major importance on a single recording. It is impossible to class each work on the recording, and little would be gained by dropping all these recordings into a general or miscellaneous category. The Basic Rule solves this problem simply and directly for the classifier: The first work decides the classification, and the remaining works are retrieved through the catalog.

So far as popular music recordings are concerned, the Basic Rule has no significance. It is not the individual selections on a popular music recording which interest the classifier so much as type of music all these selections represent. Therefore, the Basic Rule is not applied to recordings of popular music, and the categories for these recordings are always determined on the basis of their general content.

CHAPTER TWO

THE CATEGORIES

The most important decision the classifier must make is to select the correct category for the recording. Once the proper category is selected, the formation of the unique class number will be determined by the rules of that category. Therefore, the reader must study the following carefully, since the categories, their heading, their intended content, and their arrangement into a functional scheme are discussed at length. (For daily reference in classification work, the classifier will find exact definitions and individual examples in chapter I of Part Two.)

The Alpha-Numeric System for the Classification of Recordings, (ANSCR), was developed uniquely for sound recordings. The scheme is composed of twenty-three major categories, each of which is represented by a letter of the alphabet. Four of the major categories are split into subdivisions, so that in the complete scheme there are thirty-six subject areas or categories into which sound recordings may be organized. The chart on the opposite page lists these thirty-six categories and their representative letters.

The first and most obvious feature in this scheme is that there is no mnemonic relationship between the alphabetical letter which represents a category and the heading of the category. For example, the letter "B" is the symbol for Operas, not the letter "O." A mnemonic approach requires the use of contrived headings if all available letters are to be used, and the arrangement of the subject areas or categories would be determined solely by alphabetical progression. An example of a mnemonic system might be imagined as follows: B–Band Music, C–Chamber Music, D–Dance Music, E–Ethnic Music, F–Foreign Music, G–Guitar Music, and so forth. This mnemonic approach puts the headings in alphabetical order, but is hardly true classification, since a classed arrangement is based on characteristics of the material being classed, not on the tools or symbols of the arrangement.

The ANSCR scheme should be studied in physical terms, by

THE ANSCR CLASSIFICATION SCHEME

A   Music Appreciation—
History and Commentary

B   Operas: Complete and
Highlights

C   Choral Music:

D   Vocal Music

E   Orchestral Music:
   EA   General Orchestral
   EB   Ballet Music
   EC   Concertos
   ES   Symphonies

F   Chamber Music

G   Solo Instrumental Music:
   GG   Guitar
   GO   Organ
   GP   Piano
   GS   Stringed Instruments
   GV   Violin
   GW   Wind Instruments
   GX   Percussion
         Instruments

H   Band Music

J   Electronic,
Mechanical Music

K   Musical Shows and
Operettas: Complete and
Excerpts

L   Soundtrack Music:
Motion Pictures and
Television

M   Popular Music:
   MA   Pop Music
   MC   Country and
         Western Music
   MJ   Jazz

P   Folk and Ethnic Music:
National

Q   International Folk and
Ethnic Music

R   Holiday Music

S   Varieties and Humor:
(Comic Monologs, Musical
Satire, Comedy Acts, Etc.)

T   Plays

U   Poetry

V   Prose

W   Documentary: History
and Commentary

X   Instructional:
(Dictation, Languages,
"How to . . .", Etc.)

Y   Sounds and Special Effects

Z   Children's Recordings:
   ZI   Instructional
   ZM   Music
   ZS   Spoken

visualizing a collection of recordings which is on shelves or in bins arranged by categories A to Z. Within the shelf or bin arrangement, dividers are separating the recordings by category. On these dividers are printed both the alphabetical letter which represents the category and the full name or heading of the category. One such divider (or shelf label, if more appropriate) is labeled MUSICAL SHOWS AND OPERETTAS so that all the recordings of musical shows may be located at sight by the browser who may not know that the letter "K" represents MUSICAL SHOWS AND OPERETTAS.

Careful examination of the scheme will reveal the logic underlying the arrangement of the thirty-six categories. Categories containing like subject matter are grouped together, and there is a theoretical progression from one category to another. Categories B, C, and D, for instance, are all for recordings of vocal music. Category B is designated for operas, the largest and most complex form of vocal art. Category C is for works performed by groups of voices and category D is for works recorded by solo voices. Therefore, these three categories progress from the largest vocal form to the smallest, and by being juxtaposed, enable the browser to locate all recordings of vocal music in one general shelf area.

The next three categories, E through G, are for recordings of instrumental music, arranged by size of the instrumental group. The orchestra is first since it is the largest instrumental group, involving every known musical instrument (if so desired) in any quantity. The letter "E" represents orchestral music. But because the category has been divided into four subcategories, the letter "E" is never used alone, but always in combination with another letter.

Category E is subdivided because of the special user interest in three types of orchestral music: ballet, concertos, and symphonies. A separate sub-category is provided for each of these, and a fourth sub-category, EA, is designated for all other types of orchestral music. This separation by sub-category of all orchestral music enables the browser to go directly to the type of recording which interests him.

8

Recordings of chamber groups follow orchestral music, and are represented by the letter "F." Although any of the instruments used in the orchestra may be present in a chamber group, the total number of instrumental players is limited to nine by the definition of category F.

The last category in this series is for recordings by solo instruments. The letter "G" indicates solo instruments in general, and is never used alone since this category is divided into seven sub-categories. Four of the sub-categories refer to specific instruments: the guitar, the piano, the organ and the violin. The remaining three sub-categories refer to groups of instruments; i.e., wind instruments, stringed instruments, and percussion instruments.

The sub-category divisions in category G are a direct reflection of patron interest and quantity of available recordings. The four specific instruments are versatile and highly adaptable to solo performance, as well as extremely popular. Since a great deal of music is written or arranged for the violin, the piano, the organ, or the guitar, many recordings feature these instruments in solo performance. The demand for such recordings is always heavy. Classifying these recordings into separate sub-categories makes them more accessible to the browser.

A separate sub-category for every known musical instrument is unwarranted since the amount of written and recorded solo music for many instruments is almost negligible. An excessive number of sub-categories becomes clumsy, especially if created solely for reasons of artistic uniformity rather than practical utility. Therefore, the recordings of all other solo instruments are grouped by instrumental choir. Classed in category GS, for example, are recordings of solo works performed on the cello, viola, double bass, harp, or any other stringed instrument, except the violin, which has its own category (GV).

The physical relationship of categories E, F, and G permits the browser to locate instrumental music in one general area on the shelves, and by their order and organization, is led from the largest instrumental group to the smallest.

Categories H and J are also for recordings of instrumental music, but differ from the preceding three categories in that the

9

type of instruments used to play the music is the significant characteristic, rather than the *number* of instruments.

Category H is for recordings of music played by marching and concert bands. The band came into existence because of the military's need for an instrumental group which could play and walk simultaneously. This required portable instruments which could be heard easily in the open air, a description fitting most wind and percussion instruments. The present day band may be mobile or stationary, but is still composed principally of wind and percussion instruments.

It is customary to think of "band music" as music in a march tempo, but nothing prohibits a band from playing any form of music provided it is written or arranged for wind and percussion instruments. The heading BAND MUSIC for category H is to be interpreted as any recording of music played by a band, since the philosophy of the ANSCR System is to classify the recording, not the specific work of music. An orchestral symphony, for example, is classed in category H if it is arranged for and played by a band. The same holds true for recordings of band medleys of show tunes, folks songs, opera overtures, and so on.

It is important to understand the use of the word "band" in category H. Only marching and concert bands are to be classed as "bands." Other types of instrumental groups which describe themselves as bands, such as dance bands, jazz bands, rock bands, jug bands, string bands, etc., are not classed by the instrumental composition of the group, but according to the style of music which they perform. (These styles of music will be pointed out in the discussion of categories K through R.)

The heading for category J is ELECTRONIC AND MECHANICAL MUSIC. Like band music, electronic music is distinguished by the types of instruments which produce it. It is impossible to discuss electronic music in terms of number of players or instruments, since these have no bearing on the end product, neither can synthesizers, tape recorders and ring modulators be equated to solo piano, string quartet or full orchestra. Category J is for recordings of music produced by means other than conventional musical instruments, although the production of such music may conceivably incorporate the use of standard instruments as well as human voices to achieve certain effects. The same philosophy of classification applies in this category as in category H. For example, a musical work written for piano, but produced on an electronic synthesizer is classed in category J, because the performance determines classification, not the musical composition.

Common sense must be used in application of the word "electronic." A number of standard instruments may be amplified by electronic means (such as the guitar and organ) just as the human voice may be amplified by the microphone, but the use of such instruments does not make the music played "electronic music." If applied in this sense, any recording of music could be termed "electronic" in view of the engineering techniques and devices employed to produce sound recordings. "Electronic music" is a recognized field of creative music, and classifiers should view this category in that light.

Categories B through J divide recordings by type or size of performing groups; i.e., the chorus, the vocal soloist, the orchestra, the band, the electronic device. The six categories which follow (K through R) have a different orientation.

POPULAR MUSIC CATEGORIES

The characteristics of categories K through R which are considered in classifying are style of performance and style of music. All six categories contain what can best be described as "popular music," and by extension, it can be said that categories B through J concern "classical music." (See footnote.)

NOTE: "Classical music" and "popular music" are terms which music specialists deplore, because they consider the current usage inaccurate and divisive. There is little doubt, however, that these terms are part of our contemporary language, and convey concepts which are understood and accepted by most people.

The term "classical music" is used to describe what people consider to be "art music," or music created solely for purposes of artistic expression (meaning, in other words, without commercial intent). It is always written music, and, as such, its interpretation and performance are determined to a fairly definitive degree by the composer. The "classical" composer is an individual with extensive academic training in the art and science of music, and the successful performers of his music must be highly skilled artists who have received years of formal music instruction. The most firmly rooted belief regarding classical music is that the listener himself should have a considerable musical knowledge in order to understand and enjoy it.

Popular music, by contrast, is more casual and spontaneous. The degree of formal musical training is less exacting so far as its creation and performance are concerned. It is designed primarily for mass consumption, thereby demanding no special musi-

The initial step in establishing categories for popular music is to single out areas of special interest. These can be identified by certain characteristics which equal the music in importance. For example, foreign folk music is easily recognized as an area of special interest since to most people the cultural and linguistic aspects inherent in the performance are of equal importance with the music. Holiday music is another area of special interest because of its particular frame of reference and seasonal use. Motion pictures and musical shows are certainly special areas, since each is a creative art form of considerable length, containing many elements in addition to music. As can be seen on the chart of the ANSCR scheme, separate categories are assigned for each of these areas; i.e., categories K, L, Q, and R.

Once the special interest areas are determined, there remains an enormous body of past and contemporary music which is characterized principally by its style of performance. Unlike classical music, where works rarely lose their identification with their composer, works of popular music rarely retain this identification, and are usually associated with the performer or style of performance. The performers' constant quest for public attention makes the field of popular music complex and volatile as they seek to distinguish themselves by unusual styles of singing and playing. Many of the trends in popular music flourish

---

cal knowledge on the part of the listener. Much popular music is essentially functional, and is used for social dancing, communal group singing, holiday festivities, light entertainment, or simply to accompany daily tasks, such as the work songs of early folk literature, or the "easy listening" music piped into factories, stores and offices.

In its narrowest usage, "popular music" refers to the current best sellers, but in its broadest sense it is "music of the people," or music which is part of the cultural pattern of peoples' daily lives. Therefore, a square dance tune, a blues melody, a gospel hymn or a Christmas carol are as much "popular music" as is a song from *Hello, Dolly!* or a Paul McCartney ballad.

These descriptions of "popular" and "classical" music are not formal definitions, but only broad summations of general beliefs. Specialists in all areas of music can object to any of the points named, and do so with justification. The technical accuracy is less important than the fact that non-musicians tend to think of music in these separate terms, and their interests and tastes are oriented accordingly. Recognizing this fact, the ANSCR scheme has arranged the various categories so that recordings of like and related interest are grouped together for the convenience of the general public. So far as the ANSCR scheme is concerned, the descriptions given above of "classical" and "popular" music are to be considered the ANSCR definitions, and are to be used in understanding and applying the concepts of the ANSCR System. For this reason, quotation marks are not used around the terms classical or popular.

briefly, only to fade away or blend with other trends to form a new style. Occasionally, trends which have disappeared entirely reemerge at a much later date under another name.

It is impossible to categorize each style of popular music because style and nomenclature change very rapidly; so much so that to attempt narrow classification of popular music is a disservice to the general public because the lack of standardized definitions requires many arbitrary, personal judgments on the part of the classifier. The lines of distinction between blues, rhythm and blues, rock, folk rock, pop rock, jazz rock, hard rock, soft rock, swing, be bop, cool jazz, Dixie jazz, to mention only a few, are largely a matter of personal taste and interpretation. In many cases, the names differ more than the music, and a single performance may incorporate the qualities of more than one style. Therefore, the role of classification should be to provide reasonable arrangement, but to avoid fragmentation of the materials.

In the ANSCR scheme there are two main categories for such music: category M, called Popular Music, and category P, Folk and Ethnic Music. The distinction is based on age, since folk music is the pop music of the past. The myth that whole groups of people generate a single song thus qualifying it as a "folk" song does not need discussion here, but it is true that succeeding generations of singers and players can preserve songs. Anonymity of authorship is sometimes considered a partial definition of folk music, but this is increasingly undermined by improved methods of information retention, and would rule out those composers who deliberately chose to write in the folk idiom.

Since it is performers who have the greatest impact in popular music so far as audiences are concerned, classification in category P should be governed by the style and performance reputation of the performer, rather than the definitions of musicologists. Bob Dylan, Joan Baez, and Buffy Ste. Marie may sing contemporary songs, but their style of expression and performance draws on the American folk tradition, so they are considered folk singers by the public as much as Burl Ives, Pete Seeger or Theodore Bikel.

Category M is designed for all forms of popular music not

included in categories K, L, P, Q, and R. In view of the vast amount of material this covers, category M has been divided into three sub-categories.

As has been pointed out, any number of styles of popular music exist, but to isolate them into numerous separate categories would make recordings less, rather than more accessible to the general public. For this reason, only two styles of contemporary popular music have been given separate categories: country and western, category MC, and jazz, category MJ. These two are selected because each has a long history of continuous development and creativity, and each has a well defined and loyal following. In addition, they are distinctive styles of music which retain their special personalities even when borrowed or adapted in the area of general pop music.

Category MA is for recordings of contemporary pop music other than jazz or country and western. If well maintained, the contents of this category will change rather rapidly and a certain percentage of the material will be ephemeral, just like a current fiction collection. It will also have its share of "classic" recordings by durable artists such as Sinatra, Williams, the Beatles, Presley, and so forth. The type of performer and type of patron interest represented in category MA is broad in scope but not unwieldy. Nevertheless, the principle of expansion of categories through subdivision which exists in the ANSCR scheme provides a tool for future expansion within category M, should developments within the pop music field make it advisable.

One category which has not been discussed is the first category in the scheme, category A, MUSIC APPRECIATION. This category is first because its contents relate to all the categories for music recordings, from B to R. Recordings in category A deal with the subject of music and musicians, whether in the form of documentaries, lectures, biographies, or special types of anthologies. Since the subject is music and the objective is appreciation, all types and styles of music may be represented, but only certain types of recordings qualify to be classed in this category. Recordings intended to be included in category A are those in which the orientation, preparation, and presentation of the recorded material are best brought out by placement in category

A, rather than in any of the other music categories. An anthology of Beethoven symphonies, for example, is accessible and appropriate in category ES; whereas, because of its unique presentation, a discussion on Beethoven's symphonies accompanied by musical examples is more apt to reach its intended user in category A.

Both the content of the recording and its intended audience must be kept in mind when selecting recordings for category A. All recordings of music contribute in some fashion to the appreciation of music, but recordings in category A must have some specific instructional or informational function beyond that of simply hearing the music. It may be that this special function is not a part of the recording itself, but is in the form of accompanying material, such as a textbook or scholarly booklet. (Those accompanying materials should not be confused with the normal amount of information included on most record jackets, or the separate librettos which are provided in opera albums.) At all costs, category A should not be used as dumping ground for the miscellaneous, unusual, or hard-to-classify recording. Because of this, the placement of any recording within category A should be done only within the context of the rules and examples given in Part Two, category A.

SPOKEN RECORDINGS CATEGORIES

Categories A through R are for recordings of music or for recordings which pertain to music. The next six categories are for recordings of the speaking human voice, and encompass a wide spectrum of subjects. Within the ANSCR System the arrangement of spoken recordings is by type of recorded work, and not by subject, unlike other classification systems such as the Dewey System. The reasons for this arrangement are based upon the realities of record production as evidenced in the types of spoken recordings generally available to the public. Although anything which can be read aloud could be recorded, spoken recordings are generally confined to reproducing those types of written works which are enhanced by their being spoken aloud. Since reading aloud is very time-consuming, oral recordings of written works such as novels, text-books, newspapers, or certain picture books cannot compete with printed texts and except for the benefit of the sightless or very young, are not usually produced. The most satisfactory spoken recordings are those of works which were written to be spoken, such as lectures, speeches, monologs, plays and poetry. Recordings of this nature dominate the field of spoken recordings. Consequently, the ANSCR categories divide recordings by form of presentation or type of work. Subject matter is indicated in the catalog.

Category S is for recordings of comic theatrical acts and monologs, categories T and U for readings of plays and poetry. Recordings of prose works are classed in category V, including speeches, lectures and sermons, as well as readings of essays, novels, biographies, and all other types of non-fiction. Wide as the scope of category V appears, the amount of recorded material of this type is slight when compared to many other categories, and subject arrangement would be unnecessarily detailed and cumbersome.

Categories S, T, U, and V are intended for recordings which are basically oral presentations of works that appeared originally in printed form. Category W differs substantially from this definition because the documentary is an art form of the audio and visual media. In recorded documentaries, voices, sounds and music blend to convey the passage of time, underscore the drama, or emphasize the message. Many documentaries are produced specifically for recordings and use original music, actors, sound effects, scripts, etc., to heighten the storyline and produce dramatic effects. These documentaries usually portray the lives of famous men or events of current or historical interest and are better suited to these than to the portrayal of ideas or concepts. Other types of documentary, however, may simply record actual events, such as discussions or interviews, so that the impact is not the use of special effects but hearing the actual voices of participants.

The sixth in this series of categories for spoken recordings is category X which is entitled "Instructional," a word chosen with intention to avoid confusion with "educational recordings." Within the recording industry, the educational recording is one produced to support a specific school curriculum or teaching program. Since the type of audience, objective and use of the educational record are all predetermined, the appeal beyond the specified market is slight or non-existent. Schools may enrich their collections with recordings of general market appeal, but other institutions and individuals, in contrast, have a lesser interest in purely educational recordings. The function of the ANSCR System is to serve collections of general public interest, not to be a tool for organizing teaching aids by curriculum subject, grade level, etc.

Instructional recordings are aimed at the general public, without reference to set curriculum or age level. They are usually engineered to replace the teacher, rather than to act as a supplement to the teacher's work. Consequently, they deal with very specific skills, of a technical nature rather than abstract, and the approach is practical as opposed to academic. In simplest terms, instructional recordings could be described as "how to..." records: "How to Type," "How to Dance," "How to Speak French," "How to Play the Clarinet," and so forth.

The specific reason for using a sound recording instead of a book to acquire skill is if sound is a significant tool in the learning process. Understandably then, most instructional recordings concern skills in which sound is a necessary part, such as foreign language pronunciation, dictation, Morse code, playing musical instruments or doing certain dance steps in time to music. Other types of recordings may be classed as instructional, even though sound is not significant except for the use of a voice instead of printed words. A practical description of divorce laws, or advice on making a will would fit within this category, but a discussion of American history would not. In the same way, a lecture on the appreciation of literature could be included.

RECORDINGS OF SOUNDS AND SPECIAL EFFECTS

Category Y deals with material which can be retrieved only on a sound recording. Category Z is for recordings produced for a special age group. Little need be said about category Y, since the type of recording for which it is designed is easily recognized. Recordings of nature sounds, car motors, train whistles, applause, and other varieties of sounds and sound effects have a steady appeal. A separate category is mandatory since these recordings are unique, and bear no relationship to other music or spoken recordings.

CHILDREN'S RECORDINGS CATEGORY

Since many libraries prefer to maintain collections of children's recordings in a separate location, the letter "Z" was assigned to children's recordings so that, if the category's contents were transferred elsewhere, the internal order of the scheme would not be interrupted. Category Z is actually divided into three sub-categories, so that the letter "Z" is never used alone. This category is unique because it may be used as an integral part of the entire ANSCR System, or operate as a separate entity.

For example, if the Z category is retained in the same physical location as the rest of the ANSCR categories, it will contain only those recordings which have been specifically produced by manufacturers to be used by and with children. On the other hand, if a separate collection is maintained for use by children, the librarian will want to enrich the collection with many fine recordings, such as ballet music, symphonies, etc., which are not produced specifically for children. These additional recordings may be fitted easily into the three Z sub-categories, and will carry a Z class number. Certain of those recordings may exist in the adult collection as well, and in that collection they will be assigned to whichever of the thirty-six categories is appropriate. This means that the same title (but not the same copy) will have two different class numbers, but since the adult and children's collections are separate, with separate shelflists, no problems arise. (The same situation frequently occurs in adult and children's book collections.)

The three sub-categories of Z provide a rudimentary organization for children's recordings, or for recording collections for children. There are two reasons for avoiding a more detailed arrangement than this. First, it is assumed that children will have direct access to their recordings, which makes the simplest form of organization the easiest to maintain. Second, the increasing skill and knowledge of young people in handling electronic equipment, and the gradual lowering of the age level in defining "children," indicates that separate children's collections may be geared increasingly only to the very young, and adult collections opened to a wider age group.

CHAPTER THREE

THE CLASS NUMBER

The thirty-six subject categories represent only one aspect of the ANSCR classification system. Implementation of the ANSCR scheme involves the use of a unique class number for each and every recording. The unique class number serves two functions. First, it indicates the exact shelving location of the recording, and, second, it identifies the individual recording.

Identification of the individual recording is of paramount importance because of certain problems peculiar to sound recording. Recordings are performances, and, in most cases, performances of works which exist in another form. A play is performed from a script, a novel read from a book, and music played from a score. In their original form these works are easily identified by author and title, and despite occasional variations in editions, almost any standardized version is satisfactory to the user. Once these works are recorded, other variables enter in. Twenty-five recordings of Beethoven's Fifth Symphony may be currently available, but each will be different because of the conductor, the orchestra, the time and place of the recording, the tempo, phrasing and interpretation, and the additional works which may accompany the symphony in order to fill the remaining space on the disc or tape. Therefore, these recordings are not twenty-five editions of the same work, but twenty-five separate, artistic entities. If this were not the case, there would be no reason for purchasing more than one recorded version of a musical work, and no incentive for artists to record new versions.

The unique class number differentiates between the several recorded versions of the same work, and makes it possible for the catalog user to locate a specific recording quickly and accurately. He has only to make a note of the class number given on the catalog card, and then seek the recording with the corresponding class number. This eliminates any need to examine each jacket cover for content, performers' names, or commercial record number. Record librarians can see immediately the practical advantages of the unique class number both as a shelving device and as a circulation tool.*

The ANSCR class number for a recording is composed of four parts, and each part has a specific function. The combination of the four parts results in a unique class number which applies to one recording and one recording only. The four parts of the class number are called "terms," and are referred to as Term One, Term Two, Term Three, and Term Four. The various terms are easily identified because they are written one under another in vertical fashion, as seen in the following example:

A complete class number	**B**	(Term One)
	VERD	(Term Two)
	RIG	(Term Three)
	B 21	(Term Four)

Since each of these four terms performs a separate function, the rules for using and forming each term differ. Learning to use the different rules for each term may appear confusing or difficult unless the classifier knows why each term is used and what it is supposed to do. A thorough understanding of the logic underlying the terms will make it easy to comprehend and apply the specific rules, so each of the terms will be discussed in detail in this section. The specific rules of use and formation will be found in Part Two.

TERM ONE

As with all class numbers, the ANSCR class number is read from the top, which in this case is Term One. Term One indicates in which subject area the recording is to be shelved, and is composed of the letter or letters which represent one of the thirty-six subject categories of the ANSCR scheme, such as B for Operas, or MJ for Jazz Music. Selection of the appropriate category is the fundamental step in determining the complete class number for a recording. For this information the reader is referred to chapter two, the Categories.

(*A major headache in the circulation of record albums is ascertaining that the right disc is in the right album. When the unique ANSCR class number appears on both the record jacket and the disc, clerical personnel can catch such errors without difficulty.)

TERM TWO

Once the category for the recording has been determined, the next step is to decide how to file the recording within its particular category. While there are only two ways — by author and by title — of arranging books within a subject category, more flexibility is needed for arranging recordings, since recordings are performances as well as works, and therefore have an extra dimension of interest. The philosophy of the ANSCR System is to arrange recordings by the feature which is of primary importance to the record user.

The feature of a recording which is of primary importance depends to a large extent on the type of category in which the recording is classed. For example, in the category for recordings of symphonies (category ES), the name of the composer is the most important feature. If recordings of symphonies are arranged according to the surnames of composers, all of one composer's symphonies will be grouped together.

In categories K and L, which are for recordings of musical shows and motion pictures, it is more convenient for the record user if the contents are arranged by title. The many names associated with productions of shows and films, tend to obscure the composers' names, so identification by title is easiest and most obvious for most people.

It can be seen in these examples that the arrangement of recordings within a category should be geared to the browser who approaches the shelves directly without having first consulted the catalog or library staff. If the browser is to find what he wants, the arrangement with which he is confronted must anticipate his primary interest or objective.

An example of anticipation of interest is demonstrated in the arrangement of recordings of popular music. Rarely is a composer or a title a matter of primary interest in this field, because popular music depends so heavily on performance for its flavor and personality. This means that the performer's name is the center of interest. To enable people to locate all the recordings by their favorite performers, the recordings in categories such as Jazz Music, Folk and Ethnic Music, Pop Music., etc., must be arranged alphabetically by the surnames of performers.

Applying the principle of primary user interest to category Q (INTERNATIONAL FOLK AND ETHNIC MUSIC), it becomes apparent that this category requires an entirely different approach. Titles and names of composers and performers may be of varying degrees of interest, but the most significant factor of interest is country of origin. If the recordings in this category are arranged in alphabetical order by name of country of origin, the record user can immediately locate the music of those countries which particularly interest him.

Therefore the arrangement of recordings will vary with each category, and the tool for implementing the arrangement is Term Two. Term Two is composed of the first four consecutive letters of a word which may be a surname, a part of a title, the name of a country, etc. Since recordings in category ES are to be arranged by composer, the first four letters of a composer's surname will be used to form Term Two. For instance, in the class numbers on recordings of Beethoven symphonies, the abbreviation BEET will appear in Term Two, so that all recordings of his symphonies will be grouped together in shelf or bin arrangement. In category MJ, performers' surnames will be used in Term Two, and in category Q the abbreviation in Term Two will represent the name of a specific country. Without deciphering the class number, the record user will quickly understand the arrangement of the recordings in each category as he flips through the albums, especially since the arrangement is in each case suited to the contents of the category.

More often than not, a single form of arrangement within a category is not sufficient. Category D is a good example. This category is designated for recordings of solo vocal music. Some of the recordings in this category will be arranged by the composer's surname, just like recordings of symphonies in category ES. For instance, a collection of songs by Mozart, or two song cycles by Brahms, or oratorio arias by Handel — recordings of this type should obviously be arranged by surname of the composers. On the other hand, there are many recordings of vocal music which are produced solely to feature the talents of individual singers. These recordings contain a variety of selections by many different composers, and very often the album itself

TERM TWO—PRINCIPAL FORM OF ARRANGEMENT

Category Letter and Name	Feature of Primary Interest	Example of Term Two Entry	
A Music Appreciation	Title of the album	"Minnesong and Prosody" Telefunken (S) 9487	A MINN
B Operas	Name of the composer	Berg: *Lulu*	B BERG
C Choral Music	Name of the composer	Handel: *Messiah*	C HAND
D Vocal Music	Name of the composer	Brahms: *Ernste Gesange*	D BRAH
EA General Orchestral	Name of the composer	Offenbach: *Gaite Parisienne*	EA OFFE
EB Concert Music	Name of the composer	Tchaikovsky: *Sleeping Beauty*	EB TCHA
EC Concertos	Name of the composer	Mozart: *Piano concerto no. 21*	EC MOZA
F Chamber Music	Name of the composer	Telemann: *Quartets*	EF TELE
GG through GX Solo Instrumental Music	Name of the composer	Diabelli: *Sonata in A for Guitar*	GG DIAB
H Band Music	Name of the composer	Grainger: *Lincolnshire Posy*	H GRAI
J Electronic Music	Name of the composer	Stockhausen: *Zyklus*	J STOC
K Musical Shows	Title of the work	*Brigadoon*	K BRIG
L Soundtrack Music	Title of the film	*Mondo Cane*	L MOND

Code	Category	Example	Type of heading	Short code
MA	Popular Music	Frank Sinatra	Name of the performer	MA SINA
MC	Country and Western Music	Chet Atkins	Name of the performer	MC ATKI
MJ	Jazz Music	Louis Armstrong	Name of the performer	MJ ARMS
P	Folk and Ethnic Music	Pete Seeger	Name of the performer	P SEEG
Q	International Folk and Ethnic Music	"Songs of Norwegian Fjords"	Name of the country	Q NORW
R	Holiday Music	"Christmas with the Trapp Family Singers" Decca 9553	Name of the performer	R TRAP
S	Varieties and Humor	"Best of Frickert and Suggins" (Jonathan Winters)	Name of the performer	S WINT
T	Plays	Shakespeare: *Hamlet*	Name of the author	T SHAK
U	Poetry	"Poems and Tales of Edgar Poe"	Name of the author	U POE
V	Prose	Joyce: *Ulysses*	Name of the author	V JOYC
W	Documentaries	"America's Men in Space"	Title of the album	W AMER
X	Instructional	"How to Dance the Mambo"	Subject of instruction	X DANCE
Y	Sounds	"Sports Car Races"	Name of the sound	Y CARS
Z	Children's Recordings	*Robin Hood*	Title of the album	ZS ROBIN

Z1 through ZS

has a nondescript title such as "World of Song." If the recording "World of Song" were to be filed by title or by the name
of one of the numerous composers represented on the recording, the most significant aspect of the recording would be lost;
i.e., the fact that it was designed to feature soprano Victoria
de los Angeles. Therefore, a performer's name must sometimes
be used in Term Two on recordings in category D, rather than
a composer's name. It makes no difference if composers' surnames are used in some of the class numbers and performers'
surnames in others, since the filing is still by straight alphabetical order, and the record user will find the name which
interests him by alphabetical progression, whether it is Schubert or Sutherland.

Two, three or more types of arrangement may be needed
within a single category, but the filing order always remains
alphabetical. Although multiple forms of arrangement within
one category are possible, they should only be used when they
are useful to the browser; otherwise, the result is pure confusion.

The ANSCR system actually provides thirteen different types
of arrangement, but all thirteen are never used in a single
category. Of these thirteen, six are so specialized that each is
designed solely for one particular category. One of these has
already been mentioned, *i.e.*, the use of the name of a country
in Term Two. This type of arrangement by country may only
be used in category Q.

The thirteen forms of arrangement (or entries, as they are
called in the rules) are as follows:

1. Name of a composer
2. Name of an author
3. Name of a performer
4. Title of a work
5. Bible entry
6. Ethnic entry
7. Geographic entry (*i.e.*, name of a country)
8. Gregorian entry
9. Name of a skill
10. Name of a language

11. Name of a person
12. Name of a sound
13. Collections

Chapter II in Part Two of this book defines each form of entry in detail and provides the rules on their formation in Term Two. However, the use of each form of entry depends entirely on the category in which a recording is being classed. Chapter I of Part Two defines each of the thirty-six subject categories, and, at the same time, indicates exactly which forms of entry or arrangement are to be used within a specific category.

The following diagram shows the principal form of arrangement by Term Two in each category, and is meant to give the classifier an overall view of each category's feature of primary interest so far as the browser is concerned. Other forms of arrangement may be possible, but the classifier must consult the individual category in Part Two, chapter I, for detailed information.

TERM THREE

Term Three of the ANSCR class number is used to indicate a title. Book titles and recording titles present different classification problems and cannot be approached in the same way. A book has only one title, and the correct form of this title is determined from the title page. With recordings, two types of titles must be considered, the work title and the album title.

A work title is the title of a work of literature or music which is on the recording, such as the *String Quartet no. 14*, by Beethoven, or *Moby Dick*, by Herman Melville. The album title is a corporate title given to the recording as a whole to characterize the contents of the recording without identifying specific works. Such titles as *Melodies of the Masters*, *The Golden Trumpet of Harry James*, and *Music from the Court and Chapel of Henry VIII* are representative album titles. Sometimes the album title and the work title are identical if the entire recording is devoted to one work, such as an opera or a novel.

Both album titles and work titles are used to form Term Three. The decision as to which is to be used depends on the structure of the recording, the category in which it is classed, the basic

27

rule of classification, and to a large extent, the form of entry in Term Two.

The basic rule of classification states that if the first work on side one of the recording occupies one-third or more of the space on side one, the recording is classed according to the type and nature of this work, regardless of the other selections on the recording. It is this work which determines the category, and therefore determines the full class number. For example, if the first work on the recording is a symphony by Haydn, the recording is classed in category ES. In category ES the principal arrangement is by composer's surname, therefore an abbreviation of Haydn will be used in Term Two. It follows that if Haydn's name is used in Term Two, then the entry in Term Three must describe the title of the work by Haydn, which will be the name or number of the particular symphony. Should this recording happen to have an album title, such as "The Philadelphia Orchestra Plays Haydn," this title is ignored in the classification. Such a title is not a work by Haydn, but the specific symphony is.

Another hypothetical example might be an album entitled "John Doe Performs the Emperor." Upon examination, this is actually a recording of Beethoven's *Piano Concerto no. 5*. Therefore, the recording is classed in category EC, in which arrangement is by composer's surname. An abbreviation of Beethoven is used in Term Two, and Term Three will identify the specific piano concerto. This will draw together in category EC all recordings of this concerto, since they will have identical abbreviations in Terms Two and Three. The album title is ignored because its use would serve to separate this recording from other versions of the same piano concerto.

The Basic Rule of classification also states that if the first work on side one does *not* occupy one-third or more of the space on side one, then the entire recording must be examined to determine its general content. If the recording were entitled "Piano Music by Mozart," and contained twelve short works for solo piano by Mozart, the general content would class it in category GP. In that category the rules state that if the first half or more of the recording is devoted to the works of one

28

composer, regardless of the length of the individual pieces, the surname of the composer is used to form Term Two. By definition then, an abbreviation of Mozart will appear in Term Two. In this case, since the first work on the recording was too short and could not be used to determine the classification of the recording, a work title cannot be used in Term Three, so the album title "Piano Music by Mozart" must be used for Term Three. Therefore, the use of a composer's name in Term Two does not always mean that a work title is to be used to form Term Three.

In practice, the decisions regarding album title and work title are easy and clearcut. There are thirteen forms of entry which may be used in Term Two. Album title is used in Term Three following all those forms of Term Two entry except for Author Entry and Composer Entry. If the names of composers or of authors are used in Term Two, then the form of title used in Term Three depends on the length of the first work on side one of the recording. If the work occupies one-third or more of side one, the work title is used; if the first work does not occupy one-third of side one, then the album title is used.

A title is indicated in Term Three by the use of capital letters, numbers or a combination of both. The basic rule regarding letters is to use the first letter of each key word in the title, up to a total of three letters. Therefore, A *N*ight on *B*ald *M*ountain would be indicated in Term Three as *NBM*, and *H*ello, *D*olly! would be *HD*. One-word titles are indicated by using the first three consecutive letters, such as *RIG* for Rigoletto.

Numbers are sometimes used, either alone or in combination with letters, and always to indicate work titles of music. Many of the work titles used for musical compositions are repetitive and non-distinctive, since they simply indicate the form of musical structure or arrangement. There are hundreds of symphonies, concertos, sonatas, quartets, etc., and a single composer can write dozens of works in the same musical form. Haydn, for example, wrote over one hundred symphonies, many of which have been recorded, and of the more popular ones there are least ten or more different recorded versions available. If the only indication in Term Three were "symphony" or an abbreviation thereof, the result would be a mass of unorganized material, and would require endless searching to locate a particular symphony even in collections of modest size.

There are tools for identifying specific works of music with non-distinctive titles and these are the music numbers. Various types of music numbers are in use. Some are called opus numbers, some form or serial numbers, and others are referred to as thematic catalog numbers. The function of these numbers is to provide accurate identification of musical works with non-distinctive titles, and for this reason they are often used in Term Three. The rules in Part Two, chapter III, define music numbers and indicate precisely when and how they are to be used in Term Three.

TERM FOUR

The three terms discussed so far indicate where the recording is to be placed (*i.e.*, the category), how it is to be arranged in the category, and which title to associate with the recording. To this point there is nothing unique about the ANSCR class number, especially in the many instances where a work title is used in Term Three. At least twenty-five recordings could carry the terms **BEET** $^{ES}_{5}$ which represent Beethoven's *Symphony no. 5*, and there would be no way to differentiate the Bernstein version from the one by Furtwangler. Yet each recording is a separate entity, as has been pointed out, rather than a different edition of the same work. On the Ormandy version, for example, there also appears Mozart's *Symphony no. 40*, and on the flip side of the Steinberg version there is a recording of Beethoven's *Symphony no. 8*. The problem of several major works on one recording is one which can never be resolved in classification, because it is impossible to place one thing in two places. However, the classification number can serve as a tool for the retrieval of "lost" works if it can be made unique.

For example, if the Ormandy recording is properly cataloged, there will be a main entry under Beethoven, and added entry for Mozart. Assuming the user's interest is in Mozart, he will go directly to Mozart in the catalog and find the added entry. By noting the unique class number he can locate the recording, without being obliged to remember the other composer or symphony on the recording. The more diverse the types of music on the recording, the more helpful the unique class number becomes.

The role of Term Four, therefore, is to provide information which, combined with the preceding three terms, will produce a unique class number. This is achieved by the use of a LETTER followed by two DIGITS. The letter, or alpha symbol as it is referred to, represents the name of an individual associated with the performance on the recording, and the digits are the last two numbers of the commercial record number. For example, on the Ormandy recording referred to previously, the full class number will read $\begin{smallmatrix} ES \\ BEET \\ 5 \\ O\ 98 \end{smallmatrix}$. The alpha symbol "O" refers to conductor Eugene Ormandy, and the digits "98" come from the record number, Columbia ML 5098.

The advantage of Term Four is that it provides an alphabetical arrangement for the recordings of Beethoven's Fifth Symphony by order of the conductor's surname, and the conductor of course is the person of primary interest in such recordings, after composer. Secondly, Term Four is tied to a number which is integral to the recording. The possibility of duplication of this complete four-term class number is exceedingly slight. But in the very rare event that two different recordings have class numbers in which all four terms are exactly identical, the addition of a third digit from the commercial record number will immediately differentiate between them.

The surname used to determine the alpha symbol in Term Four will vary with the nature of the recording, but the rule is that it will be the surname of someone featured in the performance. Some recordings do not feature individuals, such as recordings of sounds. Wherever an individual's name cannot be used, the initial of the record company's name is substituted.

In Part Two of this book there are four chapters, each of which corresponds to one of the terms of the ANSCR class num-

31

STRUCTURE OF THE ANSCR CLASS NUMBER

Terms	Formation	Function
Term One (**B**—Opera Category)	Alphabetical letter or letters representing an ANSCR category.	To group related recordings.
Term Two (**PUCC**—Puccini)	First four consecutive letters of a name or word.	To arrange the recordings within a category.
Term Three (**ML**—Manon Lescaut)	First letters of first three key words of a title, or first three consecutive letters of a one word title.	To identify a work title or an album title.
Term Four (**T**—Tebaldi, soprano) (**17**—London 1317)	First letter of a performer's surname, followed by last two digits of commercial record number.	To make the class number unique.

class number

B

PUCC

ML

T 17

ber. In these four chapters, the classifier will find all necessary definitions and rules for the use and formation of Terms One, Two, Three and Four. Although the physical structure of each term may be different, the content of the four terms is inter-related, so that each is dependent on the one which precedes.

The following diagram summarizes for easy reference the basic structure and function of each term of the ANSCR class number. The charts which follow the diagram show examples of actual recordings as they would be classified by the ANSCR System.

EXAMPLES OF ANSCR CLASS NUMBERS

CATEGORY A Music Appreciation

"Unashamed Accompanist."	**A**	History of Music Series	**A**
Gerald Moore, piano.	**MOOR**	"Ars Nova and Renaissance."	**HIST**
Seraphim 60017	**UA**	RCA Victor LM 6016	**ANR**
	M 17		**R 16**

"Gregorian Chants."	**A**	"How a Great Symphony	**A**
Benedictine Monks	**GREG**	Was Written."	**BERN**
Everest 3159	**GC**	Leonard Bernstein.	**HGS**
	B 59	(A record accompanying	**B 68**
		the performance of	
		Beethoven's Symphony	
		No. 5. Columbia MS 6468)	

CATEGORY B Operas: Complete and Highlights

Bizet: "Carmen."	**B**	Ginastera: "Bomarzo."	**B**
Callas, Gedda, Massard,	**BIZE**	Turner, Simon, Novoa;	**GINA**
Guiot; Georges Pretre	**CAR**	Rudel conducting the	**BOM**
conducting the Paris Opera	**C 50**	Washington Opera Society	**T 06**
Orchestra. Angel SC 3650		Orchestra. CBS 32310006	

"Arias From French Opera."	**B**	"Opera Arias."	**B**
Marilyn Horne	**HORN**	Elisabeth Schwarzkopf	**SCHW**
London 26064	**AFO**	Angel S36434	**OA**
	H 64		**S 34**

CATEGORY C Choral Music

Verdi: "Requiem Mass,	**C**	Handel: "Messiah."	**C**
in Memory of Manzoni."	**VERD**	Harper, Watts, Wakefield,	**HAND**
Sutherland, Horne, Pavarotti,	**REQ**	Shirley-Quirk; Colin Davis	**MES**
Talvela; Solti conducting the	**S 75**	conducting the London	**H 92**
Vienna Philharmonic		Symphony Orchestra and	
Orchestra. London 1275		Chorus. Phillips PHS 3-992	

Monteverdi: "Madrigals."	**C**	"The Lord's Prayer."	**C**
Antonellini conducting	**MONT**	Mormon Tabernacle	**MORM**
the Rome Polyphonic	**MAD**	Choir, Richard Condie	**LP**
Ensemble.	**R 35**	conducting.	**M 68**
RCA Victor LSC 7035		Columbia MS 6068	

CATEGORY D Vocal Music

Tchaikovsky: "Songs."	**D**	Schubert: "Schwanengesang."	**D**
Arkhipova	**TCHA**	Dietrich Fischer-Dieskau.	**SCHUB**
Melodia/Angel S40047	**SON**	Angel S3628	**SCHW**
	A 47		**F 28**

Mahler: "Das Lied Von	**C**	"Cantos de España."	**D**
der Erde." Chookasian,	**MAHL**	Victoria de los	**DELO**
Lewis; Eugene Ormandy	**LE**	Angeles.	**CE**
conducting the	**C 46**	Angel S36351	**D 51**
Philadelphia Orchestra.			
Columbia MS6946			

CATEGORY EA   General Orchestral Music

Respighi: "Pines of Rome."	**EA**	"Opera Without Singing."	**EA**
Karajan conducting the	**RESP**	Boston Pops Orchestra,	**BOST**
Philharmonia Orchestra.	**PR**	Arthur Fiedler conducting.	**OWS**
Angel S3710	**K 10**	RCA Victor LM 1906	**F 06**

CATEGORY EB   Ballet Music

Stravinsky: "Le Sacre du	**EB**	Sullivan: "Pineapple Poll."	**EB**
Printemps." Monteux	**STRAV**	(Arranged by Charles	**SULL**
conducting the Paris	**SP**	McKerras.) McKerras	**PP**
Conservatoire Orchestra.	**M 26**	conducting the	**M 63**
RCA Victor LSC-3026		Royal Philharmonic	
		Orchestra. Capitol SP-8663	

CATEGORY EC   Concertos

Mozart: "Concerto No. 20,	**EC**	Gershwin: "Rhapsody in	**EC**
D Minor." Serkin; Szell	**MOZA**	Blue." Wild; Fiedler	**GERS**
conducting the Columbia	**P-20**	conducting the Boston	**RB**
Symphony Orchestra.	**S 34**	Pops Orchestra.	**W 67**
Columbia MS 6534		RCA Victor LSC-2367	

CATEGORY ES   Symphonies

Beethoven: "Symphony	**ES**	Prokofiev: "Classical	**ES**
No. 9." Ormandy conducting	**BEET**	Symphony in D." Sargent	**PROK**
the Philadelphia Orchestra.	**9**	conducting the London	**CS**
Columbia MS 7016	**O 16**	Symphony Orchestra.	**S 83**
		RCA Victor LSC-2783	

CATEGORY F   Chamber Music

Beethoven: "Piano Trio	**F**	Prokofiev: "Quintet for	**F**
No. 6, Archduke." Stern,	**BEET**	Winds and Strings."	**PROK**
Rose, Istomin.	**TRI**	Rozhdestvensky, Chamber	**QUI**
Columbia MS 6819	**S 19**	Ensemble.	**R 05**
		Melodia/Angel S 40005	
Kabelac: "Eight Inventions."	**F**	Schubert: "Quintet in A	**F**
(For percussion ensemble.)	**KABA**	Major, Op. 114." Hebzibah	**SCHUB**
Op. 45. Percussions of	**EI**	Menuhin and the Amadeus	**QUI**
Strasbourg. Limelight 86051	**P 51**	Quartet. Angel S 35777	**M 77**

CATEGORY GG   Music for Solo Guitar

"Evening with Segovia."	**GG**	Bach: "Suites for Lute."	**GG**
Andres Segovia.	**SEGO**	Julian Bream (Guitar).	**BACH**
Decca 9733	**ES**	RCA Victor LSC 2896	**SUI**
	S 33		**B 96**

CATEGORY GO   Music for Solo Organ

Bach: "Toccata and Fugue	**GO**	"Vale of Dreams."	**GO**
in D Minor." E. Power Biggs,	**BACH**	Virgil Fox.	**FOX**
Organ. Columbia MS 6261	**TOC**	Capitol SP8557	**VD**
	B 61		**F 57**

35

CATEGORY GP   Music for Solo Piano

Brahms: "Sonata No. 1 for
Piano." Katchen, Piano.
London 6410.

**GP
BRAH
SON-1
K 10**

Chopin: "Nocturnes."
Artur Rubinstein, Piano.
Victor LSC 7050

**GP
CHOP
NOC
R 50**

CATEGORY GS   Music for Solo Stringed Instruments

Philips: "Sonata for String
Bass." Turetsky.
Medea S-1001

**GS
PHIL
SON
T 01**

"Harp Music of France."
Robles, Harpist.
Argo 5458

**GS
HARP
HMF
R 58**

CATEGORY GV   Music for Solo Violin

Debussy: "Sonata No. 3
for Violin and Piano."
Stern. Columbia MS 6139

**GV
DEBU
SON-3
S 39**

"Immortal Performances."
Fritz Kreisler.
RCA Victor LM 6099

**GV
KREI
IP
K 99**

CATEGORY GW   Music for Solo Wind Instruments

Poulenc: "Sonata for
Clarinet and Piano."
Boutard, Fevrier.
Nonesuch 71033

**GW
POUL
SON
B 33**

Kraus: "Duo in D for
Flute and Viola."
Monteux, Trampler.
Music Guild S 0147

**GW
KRAU
DUO
M 47**

CATEGORY GX   Percussion and Unusual Instruments

Mozart: "Adagio in C for
Glass Harmonica, K.617a."
Hoffmann. Vox 501110

**GX
MOZA
ADA
H 10**

"Music of Foster."
Albright playing the
carillon.
Decca 78923

**GX
FOST
MF
A 23**

CATEGORY H   Band Music

Gould: "Symphony No. 4 for
Band, West Point." Fennell,
Eastman Wind Ensemble.
Mercury 90220

**H
GOUL
SYM
F 20**

"Massed Bands."
Scots Guards.
London 99462

**H
SCOT
MB
S 62**

CATEGORY J   Electronic and Mechanical Music

Babbitt: "Ensembles for
Synthesizer."
Columbia MS 7051

**J
BABB
ES
B 51**

"Switched-On Bach."
Carlos, Moog Synthesizer.
Columbia MS 7194

**J
BACH
SB
C 94**

CATEGORY K   Musical Shows and Operettas

"Oklahoma." By Rodgers
and Hammerstein. Jones,
McRae. Capitol SWAO 595

**K
OKLA
OKL
J 95**

"Golden Age of Operetta."
Joan Sutherland.
London 1268

**K
SUTH
GAO
S 68**

36

CATEGORY L   Soundtrack Music

"Pink Panther."	**L**	"The Graduate."	**L**
Soundtrack. Composed and	**PINK**	Soundtrack.	**GRAD**
conducted by Henry Mancini.	**PP**	Simon and Garfunkel.	**GRA**
RCA Victor LSP 2095	**M 05**	Columbia OS 3180	**S 80**

CATEGORY MA   Pop Music

"Beggar's Banquet."	**MA**	"Ella Sings Cole Porter."	**MA**
Rolling Stones.	**ROLL**	Ella Fitzgerald.	**FITZ**
London 539	**BB**	Verve 64049	**ESC**
	R 39		**F 49**

CATEGORY MC   Country and Western Music

"I've Got You On My Mind."	**MC**	"Nashville Airplane."	**MC**
Buck Owens and His	**OWEN**	Flatt and Scruggs.	**FLAT**
Buckaroos. Capitol ST-131	**IGY**	Columbia CS 9741	**NA**
	O 31		**F 41**

CATEGORY MJ   Jazz Music

"Day in the Life."	**MJ**	"Live at the Lighthouse."	**MJ**
Wes Montgomery.	**MONT**	Modern Jazz Quartet.	**MODE**
A & M 3001	**DL**	Atlantic S 1486	**LL**
	M 01		**M 86**

CATEGORY P   Folk and Ethnic Music: National

"Any Day Now."	**P**	"Dust Bowl Ballads."	**P**
Joan Baez.	**BAEZ**	Woody Guthrie.	**GUTH**
Vanguard VSD 79306/7	**ADN**	RCA Victor LPV-502	**DBB**
	B 06		**G 02**

CATEGORY Q   International Folk and Ethnic Music

"Somali Freedom Songs."	**Q**	"Calypso Through the	**Q**
Folkways 5443	**SOMA**	Looking Glass."	**CALY**
	SFS	Lord Melody.	**CTL**
	F 43	Cook S 927	**M 27**
"Greek Mountain Dances."	**Q**	"African Music."	**Q**
Peters KT 1001	**GREE**	Folkways 4361	**AFRICA**
	GMD		**AM**
	P 01		**F 61**

CATEGORY R   Holiday Music

"That Christmas Feeling."	**R**	"Christmas Music of France."	**R**
Glen Campbell.	**CAMP**	Capitol DT 10484	**CHRI**
Capitol ST 2978	**TCF**		**CMF**
	C 78		**C 84**

CATEGORY S   Varieties and Humor

"P.D.Q. Bach."	**S**	"Why Is There Air?"	**S**
Peter Schickele.	**SCHI**	Bill Cosby.	**COSB**
Vanguard 79195	**PDQ**	Warner Bros. S 1606	**WIT**
	S 95		**C 06**

CATEGORY T   Plays

Albee: "Who's Afraid   **T**
of Virginia Woolf?"   **ALBE**
Read by Hagen and Hill.   **WAV**
Columbia DOS 687   **H 87**

Shakespeare: "Midsummer   **T**
Night's Dream."   **SHAK**
Marlowe Society.   **MND**
Argo 250/2   **M 50**

CATEGORY U   Poetry

"Love Poems of John Donne." **U**
Read by Richard Burton.   **DONN**
Caedmon 1141   **LPJ**
                   B 41

"Voices of Eight   **U**
Canadian Poets."   **CANA**
Folkways 9905   **VEC**
                   F 05

CATEGORY V   Prose

Poe: "The Pit and   **V**
the Pendulum."   **POE**
Alexander Scourby.   **PP**
Spoken Arts 830   **S 30**

"Five Books of Moses."   **V**
Read by Charlton Heston. **BIBLE**
Vanguard 9060/61   **FBM**
                   H 60

CATEGORY W   Documentary

Churchill: "Wartime   **W**
Speeches."   **CHUR**
Capitol TBO-2192   **WS**
                   C 92

"A Reporter Remembers." **W**
Edward R. Murrow.   **MURR**
Columbia 02L-332   **ARR**
                   M 32

CATEGORY X   Instructional Recordings

"Conversation Course   **X**
in French."   **LANG**
Conversaphone 130   **FRE**
                   C 30

"Steno-Disc Business   **X**
Letters." 60-70 wpm.   **DICT**
Steno-disc 501   **SHO**
                   S 01

CATEGORY Y   Sounds and Special Effects

"Assorted Sound Effects." **Y**
Folkways 6181   **COLL**
                   ASE
                   F 81

"New York Central   **Y**
Steam Locomotives."   **TRAINS**
Folkways 6155   **NYC**
                   F 55

"Bird Songs of Dooryard, **Y**
Field, and Forest."   **BIRDS**
Ficker 107   **BSD**
                   F 07

"Stereo Frequency   **Y**
Test Record."   **TESTS**
Columbia STR-100   **SFT**
                   C 00

CATEGORY ZI   Instructional Recordings for Children

"Nature Guide About Birds, **ZI**
Bees, Beavers and Bears." **NATURE**
Disneyland 1300   **D 00**

"Musical Multiplication." **ZI**
Key 664   **MUSICAL**
                   K 64

"Napoleon and the Battle **ZI**
of Waterloo."   **NAPOLEO**
Enrichment 306   **E 06**

"Great Stories from   **ZI**
the Bible."   **GREAT**
Word 3029   **W 29**

CATEGORY ZM   Music Recordings for Children

"Folk Songs for Young Folk." Folkways 7021/2	**ZM** **FOLK** **F 21**	"Mary Poppins and Other Favorites." Do-Re-Mi Singalong. Kapp 3419	**ZM** **MARY** **K 19**
"Child's Introduction to the Orchestra." Golden 1.	**ZM** **CHILDS** **G 1**	"Liszt: Story in Words and Music." Desto 301	**ZM** **LISZT** **D 01**

CATEGORY ZS   Spoken Recordings for Children

"The Prince and the Pauper." Disneyland 1311	**ZS** **PRINCE** **D 11**	"Johnny Appleseed." Camden S 1054	**ZS** **JOHNNY** **C 54**
Grimm: "Fairy Tales." Danny Kaye. Golden 92	**ZS** **GRIMM** **G 92**	"Golden Treasury of Poetry." Golden 84	**ZS** **GOLDEN** **G 84**

PART TWO

Part Two is made up of four chapters. Each chapter provides rules and definitions pertaining to one of the four parts, or TERMS, of the ANSCR class number. These chapters are:

CHAPTER   I — Rules on Use and Formation of Term One; Definition of Categories A through Z.

CHAPTER II — Rules on Use and Formation of Term Two.

CHAPTER III — Rules on Use and Formation of Term Three.

CHAPTER IV — Rules on Use and Formation of Term Four.

The section to which the classifier will refer most often is CHAPTER I. It is considered the key to successful use of the ANSCR System because it is CHAPTER I which clearly defines the content of each of the thirty-six ANSCR categories, illustrates the steps necessary in forming the complete class number, and indicates by rule and example the matching of recording to class category. In CHAPTERS II, III, and IV the classifier will find more detailed rules and tables for the use and formation of Terms Two, Three, and Four of the class number.

CHAPTER
I

CHAPTER I

---

100. BASIC RULE FOR CLASSIFICATION OF RECORDINGS

The principle of classification in the ANSCR System is based on *physical measurement of the recording*. Two forms of this basic rule are given: one for disc recordings and one for tape recordings.

BASIC RULE FOR DISC RECORDINGS

If the first work on side one of the disc occupies one-third or more of the space on side one, the recording is classed according to the type or form of this first work. If the first work on side one *does not* occupy one-third or more of the space on side one, the entire recording is examined for general content to determine its classification.

BASIC RULE FOR TAPE RECORDINGS

If the first work on side one of the tape occupies one-third or more of the time of side one, the recording is classed according to the type or form of this first work. If the first work on side one *does not* occupy one-third or more of the time of side one, the entire recording is examined for general content to determine its classification.

WHEN A FEATURED WORK IS NOT IN BAND ONE

The preceding rules apply to most situations that the classifier will encounter in classifying sound recordings. In some exceptional cases, however, the classifier may have a recording in which the obvious intent of the album cover design and title is to feature a work which does *not* happen to be on band one of side one. If this featured work occupies at least one-third of a side of the recording, it should be used to classify the recording. In rare cases such as these, it would be misleading or confusing for the classifier to use the work in band one, side one.

CATEGORY A — MUSIC APPRECIATION

A 1. TYPES OF RECORDINGS TO BE CLASSED IN CATEGORY A

Class in category A recordings produced specifically to increase the listener's knowledge and enjoyment of music: include those recordings which approach music of all types from an historical, critical or comparative point of view, such as documentaries on the development of music and the lives of musicians, discussions and lectures on the subject of music, and specialized anthologies.

> "Unashamed Accompanist." Seraphim 60017
> (a demonstrated lecture on the art of accompaniment by pianist Gerald Moore.)

> "Art of Ornamentation and Embellishment."
> Bach 70697/8
> (comparative examples of the different styles of ornamentation and embellishment in the Renaissance and Baroque periods of music.)

> "History of Music: Ars Nova and Renaissance."
> RCA Victor LM6016
> (an historical anthology of music of a specific style and period.)

> "Plainsong to Polyphony." Everest 3174
> (a selected anthology demonstrating the development of vocal music.)

> "Invitation to Music." Folkways 3603
> (introduction to music appreciation and understanding by composer Elie Siegmeister.)

A. Anthologies

Class in category A recordings of specialized anthologies; that is, collections which have been compiled from a specified historical, comparative or critical viewpoint and which involve a variety of musical forms and composers, selected and arranged for purposes of demonstration. The subject of the anthology must outweigh all other considerations, such as the musical forms, the individual works, or the composers in order to be considered a "specialized anthology." (Anthologies or collections of works of one musical form, or by one composer are classed in the appropriate music categories according to the content of the recording.)

> "Two Thousand Years of Music."
> Folkways 3700   **class in category A**

> "English Madrigals from the Reigns of Queen Elizabeth and Her Successor James I."
> Purcell Consort of Voices.
> Turnabout 34202   **class in category C**

"Heart of the Ballet."
Mercury SR2 9127   **class in category EB**

Schumann: "Songs."
Fischer-Dieskau.
DGG 139326   **class in category D**

B. Anthologies of Popular Music

Anthologies of popular music are classed in the appropriate categories (K through R). (Anthologies on the general topic of popular music, and encompassing in one album several areas of popular music, such as folk, jazz and pop, are classed in category A.)

"Rare Bands of the 20's."
Historical ASC 6   **class in category MJ**

"Ballads of the American Revolution 1767-81."
Folkways 5001   **class in category P**

"Those Wonderful Girls of Stage, Screen and Radio."
Epic BSN 159   **class in category MA**

C. Gregorian Chants

Class in category A recordings of Gregorian and other chants developed for use in religious services of the early Christian Church.

"Gregorian Chants." (Edmunite Novices.) Folkways 9485
"Chants of the Church." (Mt. Angel Choir.) WLSM 7

D. Music Instruction

Recordings devoted solely to music theory and the techniques of playing musical instruments are classed in category X.

"Banjo Instruction." (Pete Seeger.) Folkways 8303
"Modal Counterpoint." (Nelhybel.) Folkways 3606
"Music Minus One." (complete series)

A 2. FORMATION OF THE CLASS NUMBER IN CATEGORY A

A. Term One

Term One is composed of the letter "A."

B. Term Two

Four types of entry may be used to form Term Two in this category: Author Entry, Gregorian Entry, Persons-As-Subjects Entry, and Title Entry.

1. *Author Entry*

Use the surname of the author of the narration or lecture on the recording if the author also acts as performer and delivers the lecture or narration himself.

"Invitation to Music."   **A**
(Lecture by Elie   ● **SIEG**
Siegmeister.)   **IM**
Folkways 3603   **S 03**

2. *Gregorian Entry*

Use the letters GREG representing Gregorian Entry in Term Two for recordings of collections of Gregorian and other religious chants of the early Christian Church.

"Forty Hours Adoration."	A
St. Mary's Seminary Schola.	☉ GREG
Gregorian E1-8	FHA
	M 8

3. *Person-As-Subject Entry*

If the topic of the recording is an individual, use the appropriate abbreviation of the surname of that individual to form Term Two.

"J. S. **Bach** — His Story and His Music."	A
Vox 3500	☉ BACH
	HSH
	V 00

4. *Title Entry*

Use the ALBUM TITLE of the recording to form Term Two if the rules for Author Entry, Performer Entry, Gregorian Entry, and Person-As-Subject Entry given above do not apply.

"**Minnesong** and Prosody."	A
Telefunken S9487	☉ MINN
	MP
	T 87

C. Term Three

Always use the ALBUM TITLE to form Term Three. (section III-303.)

D. Term Four

Use the surname of the featured performer or name of the performing group to form the alpha symbol in Term Four. If there is more than one featured performer or performing group, and no unifying individual, such as a conductor or narrator, use the initial of the record company's name to form the alpha symbol in Term Four. (See section IV for Term Four rules.)

CATEGORY B — OPERAS: COMPLETE AND HIGHLIGHTS

B 1. TYPES OF RECORDINGS TO BE CLASSED IN THIS CATEGORY

As its title indicates, this category is for recordings of opera performances, and not for recordings which may contain orchestral music arranged from operas; this concept underlies the following rules for classification in category B.

A. Complete and Abbreviated Versions of an Opera

Class in category B a complete recording of an opera, or a partial recording of an opera (that is, selected excerpts from one opera).

Bizet: "Carmen." Angel S 3650	(The complete version on three discs.)
Bizet: "Carmen." Angel S 36312	(Selected highlights from the complete version cited above.)
Bizet: "Carmen." Capitol SP 8605	(A collection of excerpts from the opera.)

B. Excerpts from Different Operas

If the recording contains excerpts from more than one opera, or if it contains only *orchestral* excerpts from one or more operas, the recording is classed according to one of the following types of music.

1. *Arias*

Collections of songs for solo voice of which the major portion are opera arias are classed in category B.

"Arias from French Opera." (Marilyn Horne) London 26064

2. *Ballet Music*

Recordings of ballet music from operas are classed in category EB (BALLET MUSIC).

Gounod: "Ballet Music from Faust." Angel S35607

3. *Choruses*

Collections of choruses of which the major portion is from opera are classed in category B (OPERAS).

"Opera Choruses." (Hamburg State Opera) Audio Spectrum S1003

4. *Orchestral Excerpts and Arrangements*

Recordings of opera overtures, interludes and incidental music, as well as orchestral arrangements of operatic arias and choruses are classed in category EA (GENERAL ORCHESTRAL MUSIC). (Do not include ballet music; see B1-B-2.)

Verdi: "Overtures." Angel S35676
"Puccini for Orchestra." Westminster 14026
Wagner: "Gotterdammerung: Funeral Music." London 6386

5. *Vocal Combinations*

Recordings of works for combinations of solo voices, such as vocal duets, trios, quartets, etc., from one or more operas are classed in category B (OPERAS).

"Famous Duets." Angel S 36293

B 2. FORMATION OF THE CLASS NUMBER IN CATEGORY B

A. Term One

Term One is composed of the letter "B."

B. Term Two

Three types of entry may be used to form Term Two in this category:

1. *Composer Entry*

Use the surname of the composer of the opera to form Term Two. (See section II-204 for Term Two rules.)

Verdi: "Ernani."	**B**
With Price, Bergonzi, Sereni,	● **VERD**
Flagello, the RCA Italian Opera	**ERN**
Orchestra, Schippers conducting.	**P 81**
RCA Victor LSC 6183	

2. *Performer Entry*

Use the surname of the featured singer or the name of the choral group to form Term Two when the rules for Composer Entry do not apply. (See section II-206 for Term Two rules.)

"Arias from French Operas."	**B**
Marilyn **Horne.**	● **HORN**
London 26064	**AFO**
	H 64

3. *Collections Entry*

Use the abbreviation COLL indicating "collection" to form Term Two if the rules for Composer Entry do not apply and more than one singer or choral group is featured on the recording.

C. Term Three

Use the name of the opera to form Term Three if the recording is of one opera (disregarding any introductory words such as "complete," "highlights," "selections from," etc.). Use the album title to form Term Three if the recording has selections from more than one opera. (See section III-304 for Term Three rules.)

D. Term Four

Use the name of the featured singer of the highest register to form the alpha symbol of Term Four. (See section IV-407 for Term Four rules.)

CATEGORY C — CHORAL MUSIC

C 1. TYPES OF RECORDINGS TO BE CLASSED IN CATEGORY C

Class in category C recordings of secular and sacred music written or arranged to be performed, with or without instrumental accompaniment, by a group of singers, and in which the number of singers per vocal line may vary with the size of the performing group.

> Britten: "Ceremony of Carols."
> "Lord's Prayer." (Mormon Tabernacle Choir.) Columbia 6068
> "Madrigals." (Vienna Choir Boys.) Philips 900011
> Verdi: "Requiem Mass."
> Lassus: "Madrigals."
> Handel: "Messiah."
> Stravinsky: "Symphony of Psalms."

A. Arrangements

Class in category C recordings of choral arrangements of works originally written for orchestra, solo voices or solo instruments.

> Brahms: "Liebeslieder Waltzes." (Written for piano and vocal quartet, but frequently performed by a chorus and orchestra.)

B. Folk Songs

Recordings of folk songs arranged for choral groups are classed in category P (FOLK AND ETHNIC MUSIC, NATIONAL), or in category Q (INTERNATIONAL FOLK AND ETHNIC MUSIC).

> "Folk Songs of the New World."
> Roger Wagner Chorale.
> Capitol S 8324   **class in category P**

> "Red Army Ensemble."
> Angel S36206   **class in category Q**

> "Irish Folk Songs."
> Robert Shaw Chorale.
> RCA Victor LSC 2992   **class in category Q**

C. Holiday Songs

Recordings of collections of songs and carols written or arranged for choral groups and intended for use on Christian, Jewish, or national holidays, as indicated by the album cover and title, are classed in category R (HOLIDAY MUSIC).

> "Joy to the World."
> Columbus Boychoir
> Decca 78920

> "Wonderful Songs of Christmas."
> Harry Simeone Chorale
> Mercury 60820

D. Hymns

Recordings of hymns performed by choral groups are classed in category C. [Exceptions: (1) If the featured choral group is known for a particular style of popular singing, then class the recording in the appropriate popular music category. (2) If the hymns on the recording are representative of the language and style of a particular country, class the recording in category Q (INTERNATIONAL FOLK AND ETHNIC MUSIC).]

"Holy, Holy, Holy."
Roger Wagner Chorale
Capitol S 8498   **class in category C**

"Coptic Music."
Coptic Cathedral, Cairo
Folkways 8960   **class in category Q**

"Songs of Faith"
Chuck Wagon Gang
Harmony 11221   **class in category MC**

E. Musical Shows and Operettas

Recordings of collections of songs from musical shows and operettas written or arranged for choral groups are classed in category K (MUSICAL SHOWS AND OPERETTAS).

"On Broadway." (Robert Shaw Chorale)
RCA Victor LSC 2799

F. Opera

Class in category B recordings of opera excerpts sung by a choral group.

"Operatic Choruses." (Robert Shaw Chorale)
RCA Victor LSC 2416

G. Orchestral Works with Chorus

The use of a chorus does not automatically categorize a composition as a choral work. If a chorus is used in only part of a work, and is treated essentially as an extension of the orchestra, class the recording in the appropriate orchestral category.

Beethoven: "Symphony No. 9."   **class in category ES**

H. Popular Songs

Recordings of collections of popular songs arranged for choral groups are classed in categories MA (POP MUSIC) and MC (COUNTRY AND WESTERN MUSIC).

"Love Is Blue."
Johnnie Mann Singers
Liberty 7553   **class in category MA**

"Music of the West."
Winchester Chorale
Audio Fidelity 6164   **class in category MC**

C 2. FORMATION OF THE CLASS NUMBER IN CATEGORY C

A. Term One

Term One is composed of the letter "C."

B. Term Two

Three types of entry may be used to form Term Two in this category: Composer Entry, Performer Entry, and Collections Entry.

1. *Composer Entry*

Use the surname of the composer to form Term Two if the rules for Composer Entry apply. (See section II-204 for Term Two rules.)

Britten: "Ceremony of Carols."	C
With Endich, Kopleff, and the	● **BRIT**
Robert Shaw Chorale	CC
RCA Victor LSC 2759	E 59

2. *Performer Entry*

Use the name of the featured choral group to form Term Two when the rules for Composer Entry do not apply. (See section II-206 for Term Two Performer Entry rules.)

"The Lord's Prayer."	C
Mormon Tabernacle Choir	● **MORM**
Columbia MS 6068	LP
	M 68

3. *Collections Entry*

Use the abbreviation COLL indicating "collection" in Term Two if the rules for Composer Entry do not apply, and more than one choral group is featured on the recording.

"First International University Choral Festival."	C
RCA Victor LSC 7043	● **COLL**
	FIU
	R 43

C. Term Three

Use the *album title* to form Term Three when a Performer Entry or a Collections Entry has been used in Term Two. When a Composer Entry is used in Term Two, consult the rules in section III-303, 304 to determine whether to use an *album title* or a *work title* in Term Three.

D. Term Four

The name of the choral group is usually used to form the alpha symbol in Term Four unless solo singers are also featured on the recording; then the rule indicates that the surname of the soloist takes precedence. (See sections IV-405, 407 for Term Four rules.) If Collections Entry is used in Term Two, use the initial of the record company's name to form the alpha symbol in Term Four. (See section IV-403.)

CATEGORY D — VOCAL MUSIC

D 1. TYPES OF RECORDINGS TO BE CLASSED IN CATEGORY D

Class in category D recordings of secular and sacred music written or arranged for the human voice, and performed, with or without accompaniment, by solo voices trained for the concert or operatic stage.

> Schubert: "Schwanengesang, D. 957."
> "Art of the Cantor." (Jan Peerce) Vanguard 79237
> "Sacred Songs." (Kirsten Flagstad) London 25038
> Glière: "Concerto for Coloratura Soprano."

A. Arias — Collections

Recordings of collections of arias, of which the major portion are opera arias, are classed in category B.

Recordings of collections of arias excerpted from oratorios, cantatas, masses, requiems, etc., are classed in category D.

> "Aria Recital."
> Renata Tebaldi
> London 25912   **class in category B**

> "Bach Arias."
> (Bach Aria Group)
> Decca 79405   **class in category D**

B. Duets, Trios, Quartets, etc.

Class in this category recordings of vocal works written or arranged for combinations of solo voices: that is, compositions containing two or more vocal lines, with only one singer allowed per vocal line, such as duets, trios, quartets, etc. (Do not include in category D vocal works in which the number of singers per vocal line may be doubled or tripled, such as madrigals and part songs.)

> Schubert: "Three Quartets for Male Voices, Op. 11."
> Mahler: "Das Lied von der Erde." (tenor and contralto)

Collections of songs from operas for combinations of solo voices are classed in category B.

> "Famous Duets."
> Angel S 36293

C. Folk Songs

Recordings of folk songs arranged for solo voice are classed in category P (FOLK AND ETHNIC MUSIC, NATIONAL), or in category Q (INTERNATIONAL FOLK AND ETHNIC MUSIC).

> "Yiddish Folk Songs."
> Jan Peerce.
> Vanguard 2135   **class in category Q**

> "Spirituals."
> Paul Robeson.
> Columbia MI 4105   **class in category P**

D. Holiday Music

Recordings of collections of songs and carols written or arranged for solo voice and intended for use on Christian, Jewish or national holidays, as indicated by the album cover and title, are classed in category R (HOLIDAY MUSIC).

"A Christmas Offering." (Leontyne Price) London 25280

E. Hymns, Spirituals, and Gospel Songs

Recordings of hymns, spirituals, and gospel songs performed by a solo voice or combinations of solo voices are classed (1) in category D when the performer is known best as a concert or operatic performer, or (2) in the appropriate poular music category when the performer is associated with a particular style of popular music.

"My Favorite Hymns."
Leontyne Price.
RCA Victor LSC 2918   **class in category D**

"Sing for Joy."
Blackwood Brothers.
RCA Victor LSP 3851   **class in category MC**

Class recordings of hymns performed by a solo voice in category Q (INTERNATIONAL FOLK AND ETHNIC MUSIC) when the selections are representative of the language and style of a particular country.

F. Musical Shows and Operettas

Recordings of collections of songs from musical shows and operettas are classed in category K (MUSICAL SHOWS AND OPERETTAS).

"Golden Age of Operetta." (Joan Sutherland)
London 1268

G. Popular Songs

Recordings of collections of popular songs for solo voice are classed in the appropriate "M" categories.

"What Now My Love?"
Richard Tucker
Columbia MS 6895   **class in category MA**

"Where or When."
Eileen Farrell
Harmony 11235   **class in category MA**

D 2. FORMATION OF THE CLASS NUMBER IN CATEGORY D

A. Term One

Term One is composed of the letter "D."

B. Term Two

Three types of entry may be used to form Term Two in this category: Composer Entry, Performer Entry, and Collections Entry.

1. *Composer Entry*

Use the name of the composer in Term Two if all the selections on the recording are by one composer, or if the first work on side one is a song cycle (a related series of songs with a corporate title), and occupies one-third or more of the space on side one.

Liszt: "Songs."	**D**
Fischer-Dieskau	● **LISZ**
DGG 138793	**SON**
	F 93
Mahler: "Das Lied von der Erde."	**D**
Kathleen Ferrier and Murray Dickie	● **MAHL**
London 4212	**LE**
	F 12

2. *Performer Entry*

Use the name of the featured singer in Term Two if the rule above for Composer Entry (D2-B1) does not apply.

"My Favorite Hymns."	**D**
John Charles **Thomas**	● **THOM**
Word 8320	**MFH**
	T 20
"Lotte Lehman — Brahms/Wolf."	**D**
Lotte **Lehman**	● **LEHM**
RCA Victor VICS 1320	**BW**
	L 20

3. *Collections Entry*

If the rules for Composer Entry (D2-B1) do not apply, and more than one singer is featured, use the abbreviation COLL to indicate "collection" in Term Two.

C. Term Three

Use the album title in Term Three when Performer Entry or Collections Entry has been used in Term Two. When a Composer Entry is used in Term Two, consult the rules in section III-303, 304, to determine whether to use an *album title* or a *work title* in Term Three.

D. Term Four

The surname of the singer is used to form the alpha symbol in Term Four when the Composer Entry or the Performer Entry has been used in Term Two. If Collections Entry is used in Term Two, use the initial of the record company's name as the alpha symbol. (See section IV-403 for Term Four rules.)

CATEGORY E — ORCHESTRAL MUSIC

E 1. STRUCTURE OF CATEGORY E

Category E is intended for recordings of music written or arranged for and performed by an orchestra, chamber orchestra, or string ensemble with more than nine players. This category is divided into four sub-categories so that symphonies, concertos, and ballet music can be grouped separately, and thereby be more accessible to the user. The four sub-categories are:

EA — General Orchestral Music
EB — Ballet Music
EC — Concertos
ES — Symphonies

E 2. GUIDE TO CLASSIFICATION IN THE E CATEGORIES

Guidelines are provided under the four sub-categories indicating the types of recordings to be classed in each. There are instances in which several types of orchestral music are included on one recording, and the final decision regarding its classification is determined by the first work on side one.

CATEGORY EA — GENERAL ORCHESTRAL MUSIC

EA 1. TYPES OF RECORDINGS TO BE CLASSED IN CATEGORY EA

Class in category EA recordings of music written or arranged for and performed by an orchestra, chamber orchestra, or string ensemble with more than nine players, such as serenades, suites, and tone poems, and excluding concertos, symphonies and ballet music.

Respighi: "Pines of Rome."
Tchaikovsky: "Manfred." (Symphonic poem)
"Light Classics." (Boston Pops) RCA Victor LSC 2547
Ravel: "Mother Goose Suite."
Debussy: "La Mer."
"Famous Overtures and Preludes." Parliament 108

A. Ballet Suites and Arrangements

Arrangements of ballet music, and orchestral suites derived from ballets are classed in category EB (BALLET MUSIC).

Stravinsky: "Petrouchka Suite."
"Evening at the Ballets Russes." Mercury 18095

B. Opera Overtures and Arrangements

Class in category EA recordings of opera overtures, interludes and incidental music, as well as orchestral arrangements of operatic arias and choruses.

"Opera Without Singing." (Boston Pops.) RCA Victor LM 1906
"German Opera Overtures." Mace S 9037

C. Sinfonias, Sinfoniettas, Sinfonia Concertantes

Class recordings of sinfonias, sinfoniettas and sinfonia concertantes in category EA if performed by more than nine instruments. (Works performed by nine instruments or less are classed in category F [CHAMBER MUSIC].)

Mozart: "Sinfonia Concertante in E Flat, K. Anh. 9."

EA 2. FORMATION OF THE CLASS NUMBER IN CATEGORY EA

A. Term One

Term One is composed of the letters "EA."

B. Term Two

Three types of entry may be used to form Term Two in this category: Composer Entry, Collections Entry, and one type of Performer Entry.

1. *Composer Entry*

Use the the surname of the composer to form Term Two if the rules for Composer Entry apply. (See section II-204 for Term Two Composer Entry rules.)

Strauss: "Also Sprach Zarathustra."	**E**
Fritz Reiner conducting the	● **STRAU-R**
Chicago Symphony.	**ASZ**
RCA Victor LSC 2609	**R 09**

2. *Collections Entry*

Use the abbreviation COLL indicating "collection" in Term Two when the rules for Composer Entry or Performer Entry (Boston Pops) do not apply.

"Greatest Hits."	**EA**
Eugene Ormandy conducting	● **COLL**
the Philadelphia Orchestra.	**GH**
Columbia MS 6934	**O 34**

3. *Performer Entry (Boston Pops)*

Use of the Performer Entry in category EA is not allowed with one exception: The Boston Pops Orchestra is treated as a performer, if the rule for Composer Entry does not apply to the recording. The Boston Pops as performer is entered as BOST in Term Two. (See section II-206 for Performer Entry [Boston Pops].)

"America's Favorites."	**EA**
Boston Pops Orchestra,	● **BOST**
Arthur Fiedler conductor.	**AF**
RCA Victor LSC 2991	**F 91**

C. Term Three

Use the *album title* to form Term Three when Collections Entry or Performer Entry (Boston Pops) has been used in Term Two. When a Composer Entry is used in Term Two, consult the rules in section III-303, 304 to determine whether to use an *album title* or a *work title* in Term Three.

D. Term Four

The surname of the orchestra conductor is used to form the alpha symbol in Term Four. (If there is more than one conductor, or if there is a featured performer, such as a narrator, see section IV-409 for detailed rules.)

CATEGORY EB — BALLET MUSIC

EB 1. TYPES OF RECORDINGS TO BE CLASSED IN CATEGORY EB

Class in category EB recordings of music written or arranged for classic and modern ballet.

> Bernstein: "Fancy Free."
> Stravinsky: "Le Sacre du Printemps."
> Delibes: "Coppélia."
> "Evening at the Ballets Russes." Mercury 18095

A. Music Adapted to the Ballet

Music which was not written originally for ballet performance, but which has been borrowed for ballet use is treated in two ways:

1. *Unaltered Works*

Recordings or works in which no alterations have been made in the original score are classed according to their original form.

> Bizet: "Symphony in C"   **class in category ES**

2. *Adapted Works*

Recordings of works which have been altered from their original form and adapted to fit the needs of choreography and story line are considered ballet music, and are classed in category EB.

> Sullivan: "Pineapple Poll." (An arrangement of the music of Arthur Sullivan by Charles McKerras.)
> Bizet: "Carmen Ballet." (An arrangement of the music of Georges Bizet by Rodion Shchedrin.)

B. Ballets from Operas

Class in category EB recordings of ballet music written for ballet performance within an opera.

> Gounod: "Ballet Music from Faust."

C. Ballets from Musical Shows and Operettas

Class in category EB recordings of ballet music written for ballet performance within a musical show or operetta.

> Bernstein: "Ballet Music from West Side Story."

EB 2. FORMATION OF THE CLASS NUMBER IN CATEGORY EB

A. Term One

Term One is composed of the letters "EB."

B. Term Two

Three types of entry may be used in Term Two in this category: Composer Entry, Collections Entry, and one type of Performer Entry.

1. *Composer Entry*

Use the surname of the composer to form Term Two if the rules for Composer Entry apply. (See section II-204 for Term Two Composer Entry rules.)

Tchaikovsky: "Sleeping Beauty."	**EB**
Minneapolis Symphony Orchestra,	● **TCHA**
Antal Dorati, conductor.	**SB**
Mercury 18012	**D 12**

2. *Collections Entry*

Use the abbreviation COLL indicating "collection" in Term Two when the rules for Composer Entry or Performer Entry (Boston Pops) do not apply.

"Pas de Deux."	**EB**
London Symphony, Richard	● **COLL**
Bonynge, conductor.	**PD**
London 6418	**B 18**

3. *Performer Entry (Boston Pops)*

Use of the Performer Entry in category EB is not allowed, with one exception: The Boston Pops Orchestra is treated as a performer, if the rule for Composer Entry does not apply to the recording. The Boston Pops as performer is entered as BOST in Term Two. (See section II-206 for Performer Entry [Boston Pops].)

"Slaughter on 10th Avenue."	**EB**
Boston Pops, Arthur Fiedler,	● **BOST**
conductor.	**STA**
RCA Victor LSC 2747	**F 47**

C. Term Three

Use the *album title* to form Term Three when Collections Entry or Performer Entry (Boston Pops) has been used in Term Two. When a Composer Entry is used in Term Two, consult the rules in section III-303, 304 to determine whether to use an *album title* or a *work title* in Term Three.

D. Term Four

The surname of the orchestra conductor is used to form the alpha symbol in Term Four. (If more than one conductor is featured on the recording, see section IV-409 for detailed rules.)

CATEGORY EC — CONCERTOS

EC 1. TYPES OF RECORDINGS TO BE CLASSED IN CATEGORY EC

Class in category EC recordings of music for one or several solo instruments teamed with an orchestra, whether or not the word "concerto" is used in the title of the work.

> Mozart: "Concerto for Piano, No. 20, D Minor, K.466."
> Gershwin: "Rhapsody in Blue."
> Fauré: "Elégie for Cello and Orchestra."
> Tchaikovsky: "Variations on a Rococo Theme for Cello and Orchestra, Op. 33."
> Berlioz: "Harold in Italy."
> Mozart: "Concerto No. 10 in E Flat for Two Pianos."
> "Heart of the Piano Concerto." Mercury SR2-9129

A. Concertino

Titles which use the term "concertino" or other variants of the word "concerto" are classed in category EC if they describe works for solo instrument or instruments teamed with an orchestra.

> Weber: "Concertino for Clarinet and Orchestra, Op. 26."

B. Concerto Grosso

Recordings of concerti grossi are classed in category EC.

> Handel: "Concerti Grossi, Op. 3."
> Bach, J. S.: "Brandenburg Concerti, S.1046/51."

EC 2. FORMATION OF THE CLASS NUMBER IN CATEGORY EC

A. Term One

Term One is composed of the letters EC.

B. Term Two

Two types of entry may be used to form Term Two in this category: Composer Entry, and Collections Entry.

1. Composer Entry

Use the surname of the composer to form Term Two if the rules for Composer Entry apply. (See section II-204 for Term Two Composer Entry rules.)

> Beethoven: "Piano Concerto No. 3."   EC
> Rudolf Serkin, pianist, and the   ● BEET
>   New York Philharmonic, Leonard   P-3
>   Bernstein, conductor.   S 16
> Columbia MS 6616

59

2. *Collections Entry*

Use the abbreviation COLL indicating "collection" in Term Two when the rules for Composer Entry do not apply.

"The Heart of the Piano Concerto."	**EC**
Various artists performing excerpts	● **COLL**
of different works.	**HPC**
Mercury SR2-9129	**M 29**

C. Term Three

Use the *work title* to form Term Three when a Composer Entry has been used in Term Two, or an *album title* when a Collections Entry has been used.

Gershwin: "Rhapsody in Blue."	**EC**
	GERS
	● **RB** (work title)
"The Heart of the Piano Concerto."	**EC**
	COLL
	● **HPC** (album title)

1. *Non-Distinctive Work Titles*

Many concertos do not have distinctive titles, and are identified by means of the featured instrument and a form number. (For a complete discussion on non-distinctive titles, consult section III-306-B.)

> Mozart: **"Piano** Concerto No. **26."**
> Mendelssohn: Concerto for **Violin**, Op. **64."**
> Beethoven: "Concerto for **Violin, Cello,**
>   and **Piano**, Op. **56."**

In the case of concertos with non-distinctive titles, indicate in Term Three by the proper abbreviation the name of the featured instrument and the form number.

Mozart: **"Piano** Concerto No. **26."**	**EC**
	MOZA
	● **P-26**

Consult the following rules (C2, C3) on the proper abbreviations for instruments and the use of music numbers.

NOTE: *It is not necessary to use the word "concerto" in Term Three since the letters "EC" in Term One represent "concertos."*

2. *Abbreviations for Musical Instruments*

To indicate the instrument featured in the concerto, select the appropriate abbreviation from the following table.

BA	bassoon	**L**	lute
C	cello (violoncello)	**O**	oboe
CL	clarinet	**OR**	organ
G	guitar	**P**	piano
F	flute	**VA**	viola
H	harp	**VN**	violin
HD	harpsichord	**TM**	trombone
HO	horn	**TR**	trumpet

a. Works with More Than One Featured Instrument

If a concerto is written for more than one featured instrument, indicate only one instrument in Term Three. If the instruments are of different types, indicate the instrument named first in the title of the work.

Mozart: "Concerto for Three **Pianos,** **K. 242."** ("P" is used to indicate single or multiple pianos.)	EC MOZA ● P-242
Brahms: "Concerto for **Violin** and Cello, **Op. 102."**	EC BRAH ● VN-102

b. Concerti Grossi

Individual instruments are not indicated in Term Three for concerti grossi. Treat these works like distinctive titles (see III-306A) but with the addition of a music number. The order of preference in selecting the music number is form number, opus number, thematic catalog number; never use the sub-opus number. (See section III-307 for detailed explanation of music numbers.)

Handel: "Concerto **Grosso, Op. 6,** No. 2."	EC HAND ● CG-6
Bach: "**B**randenburg Concerto, **No. 4."**	EC BACH ● BC-4

c. Concertos for Orchestra

Concertos for orchestra are treated like distinctive titles. Instrument abbrevation is not used in Term Three, nor is a music number used.

Vivaldi: "**C**oncerto for **O**rchestra, P. 143."	EC VIVA ● CO

3. *Use of Music Numbers in Term Three*

Concertos which are without distinctive titles may have several identifying numbers. The order of preference in selecting the music number is form number, opus number, thematic catalog number; never use the sub-opus number in Term Three. (See section III-307 for detailed explanation of music numbers.)

Beethoven: "**Piano** Concerto **No. 2** in B Flat, Op. 19."	EC BEET ● P-2
Mendelssohn: "**Violin** Concerto in E Minor, **Op. 64."**	EC MEND ● VN-64
Mozart: "**Clarinet** Concerto in A Major, **K. 622."**	EC MOZA ● CL-622

a. Concertos without Music Numbers

If a concerto does not have any type of music number as identification, simply indicate the featured instrument.

> Stravinsky: "Concerto for **Piano** and   **EC**
> Wind Orchestra."   **STRAV**
>   ● **P**

4. *Other Types of Non-distinctive Titles*

The preceding rules pertain to non-distinctive work titles in which the word "concerto" is used. There are, however, many works for solo instrument or instruments teamed with an orchestra which do not have a distinctive title, and do not have the word "concerto" in their titles; instead, there is another musical form word followed by identification of the featured instrument and a music number.

> "Rhapsody for Piano and Orchestra, No. 3."
> "Variations for Viola and Orchestra, Op. 2."

For titles of this type, do not use any instrument or number identification in Term Three; use only the first three consecutive letters of the musical form word.

> Mozart: **"Ron**do in C Major for Violin   **EC**
> and Orchestra, K. 373."   **MOZA**
>   ● **RON**

D. Term Four

The surname of the solo instrumentalist is used to form the alpha symbol in Term Four when the Composer Entry is used in Term Two. (If more than one instrumentalist is featured, see section IV-406.) If Collections Entry is used in Term Two, use the initial of the record company's name as the alpha symbol in Term Four.

CATEGORY ES — SYMPHONIES

ES 1. TYPES OF RECORDINGS TO BE CLASSED IN CATEGORY ES

Class in category ES recordings of works for orchestra described as "symphonies" by their composers.

> Beethoven: "Symphony No. 9."
> Berlioz: "Symphonie Fantastique."
> Prokofiev: "Classical Symphony."
> Dukas: "Symphony in C."
> Dello Joio: "Triumph of St. Joan Symphony."

A. Symphonic Works

Recordings of works for orchestra described as "symphonic," such as variations, suites, etc., are classed in category EA.

> Dvorak: "Symphonic Variations, Op. 78."
> Rachmaninoff: "Symphonic Dances."

B. "Symphonies" Which Are Not Symphonies

When a composer has used the word "symphony" in the title of a work, but the musical form of the work is not that of a symphony, class the work according to the appropriate musical form.

> D'Indy: "Symphony on a French Mountain Air."
> (This is a work for solo piano and orchestra,
>   and, therefore, fits the definition of category **EC.**)
>
> Stravinsky: "Symphony of Psalms."
> (This is a work for chorus and orchestra,
>   and is classed in category **C.**)

C. Sinfonias, Sinfoniettas and Sinfonia Concertantes

Class recordings of sinfonias, sinfoniettas and sinfonia concertantes in category EA if performed by more than nine instruments. (Works performed by nine instruments or less are classed in category F [CHAMBER MUSIC].)

> Mozart: "Sinfonia Concertante in E Flat"   **class in category EA**
> Surinach: "Sinfonietta Flamenca"   **class in category EA**

ES 2. FORMATION OF THE CLASS NUMBER IN CATEGORY ES

A. Term One

Term One is composed of the letters "ES."

B. Term Two

Two types of entry may be used to form Term Two in this category: Composer Entry, and Collections Entry.

1. *Composer Entry*

Use the surname of the composer to form Term Two if the rules for Composer Entry apply. (See section II-204 for Term Two Composer Entry rules.)

> **Brahms:** "Symphony No. 4."   **ES**
> Berlin Philharmonic Orchestra,   ● **BRAH**
>   Karajan, conductor.   **4**
> DGG 138927   **K 27**

2. *Collections Entry*

Use the abbreviation COLL for "collection" for recordings which contain excerpts from symphonies by different composers.

> "Treasury of Music: Symphony."   **ES**
> RCA Victor LE 6005   ● **COLL**
>   **TMS**
>   **R 05**

C. Term Three

Use the *work title* to form Term Three when a Composer Entry has
been used in Term Two, and the *album title* where a Collections Entry
has been used.

Prokofiev: "Classical Symphony."   ES
                                          PROK
                                        ● CS (work title)

"Treasury of Music: Symphony."   ES
                                          COLL
                                        ● TMS (album title)

1. *Non-distinctive Work Titles*
Many symphonies do not have distinctive names, and are identified
by a number. (For a complete discussion on non-distinctive titles,
consult section III-306 B.)

Mozart: "Symphony **No. 41.**"

In the case of symphonies with non-distinctive titles, use the number
of the symphony to form Term Three. (Note that it is not necessary
to use the word "symphony" in Term Three when a number is used
since the letters "ES" represent "symphonies.")

Beethoven: "Symphony No. **8.**"   ES
                                          BEET
                                        ● 8

2. *Use of Music Numbers in Term Three*
Symphonies without distinctive titles may have several identifying
numbers. The order of preference in selecting the musical number for
use in Term Three is form number, opus number, thematic catalog
number; never use the sub-opus number. (See section III-307 for detailed explanation of music numbers.)

Shostakovich: "Symphony No. **3,** Op. 20."   ES
                                          SHOS
                                        ● 3

Goldmark: "Symphony, Op. **26.**"   ES
                                          GOLD
                                        ● 26

3. *Symphonies Without Music Numbers*
If a symphony has neither a number nor a distinctive name, it is
treated like a one word title: use the first three letters of the word to
form Term Three.

Kodaly: "**Sym**phony."   ES
                                          KODA
                                        ● SYM

4. *Popular Titles*

Distinctive titles and popular titles should not be confused. A distinctive title is a descriptive name which the composer himself has assigned to his work. A popular title is one which someone other than the composer has given to the work (such as a publisher, critic or musicologist). Popular titles are never used in Term Three.

> Mozart: "Symphony No. 41. **Jupiter.**"
> Haydn: "Symphony No. 92. **Oxford.**"

D. Term Four

The surname of the orchestra conductor is used to form the alpha symbol in Term Four. (If more than one conductor is featured on the recording, see section IV-409.)

CATEGORY F — CHAMBER MUSIC

F 1. TYPES OF RECORDINGS TO BE CLASSED IN CATEGORY F

Class in category F recordings of music written for, or performed by, instrumental groups of not less than three nor more than nine instruments, and in which only one player is assigned to each part. These instrumental groups may be comprised of instruments from one, several, or all of the instrumental choirs: that is, strings, woodwinds, brass, keyboard or percussion.

> Prokofiev: "Quintet for Winds and Strings, Op. 39."
> Handel: "Sonata for Two Violins and Piano, Op. 2, No. 1."
> Bloch: "Three Nocturnes for Piano Trio (1924)."
> Kabelac: "Eight Inventions (for percussion ensemble), Op. 45."

A. Chamber Orchestras and String Ensembles

Chamber orchestras (small orchestras of about twenty-five players), and string ensembles of more than nine players, are treated like orchestras and classed according to the type of music performed on the recording.

> Hindemith: "Trauermusik for Viola and Strings"
> (string ensemble)   **class in category EC**
>
> Lully: "Le Triomphe de l'Amour."
> (chamber orchestra)   **class in category EB**
>
> Poulenc: "Aubade for Piano and
> 18 Instruments."   **class in category EA**

B. Wind Ensembles

Recordings of music for wind ensembles of more than nine instruments are classed in category H (BAND MUSIC).

> Mozart: "Serenade No. 10 for 13 Wind Instruments."

F 2. FORMATION OF THE CLASS NUMBER IN CATEGORY F

A. Term One

Term One is composed of the letter "F."

B. Term Two

Two types of entry may be used to form Term Two in this category: Composer Entry, and Collections Entry.

1. *Composer Entry*

Use the surname of the composer to form Term Two if the rules for Composer Entry apply. (See section II-204 for Term Two Composer Entry rules.)

Schubert: "Quintet in A Major, Op. 114."	**F**
Hepzibah Menuhin and the Amadeus Quartet.	● **SCHUB**
Angel S 35777	**QUI**
	M 77

2. *Collections Entry*

Use the abbreviation COLL indicating "collection" in Term Two when the rules for Composer Entry do not apply.

"Pastorales."	**F**
Philadelphia Woodwind Quintet	● **COLL**
Columbia MS 6584	**PAS**
	P 84

C. Term Three

Use the *album title* to form Term Three when the Collections Entry has been used in Term Two. When a Composer Entry is used in Term Two, consult the rules in section III-303, 304 to determine whether to use an *album title* or a *work title* in Term Three. Many of the *work titles* in this category are Non-Distinctive Work Titles; consult the rules carefully on their formation for Term Three. (See section III-306.)

D. Term Four

The name of the featured instrumental group, or the surname of a featured instrumentalist is used to form the alpha symbol when the Composer Entry has been used in Term Two. (See section IV-406, 408 for Term Four rules.) If the Collections Entry has been used in Term Two, and more than one instrumental group is featured, use the initial of the record company's name as the alpha symbol.

CATEGORY G — SOLO INSTRUMENTAL MUSIC

G 1. STRUCTURE OF CATEGORY G

A. Scope

Category G is intended for recordings of music written or arranged for and performed on a solo instrument, with or without the accompaniment of another instrument. This category is divided into seven sub-categories in order to group together recordings of the same or similar instruments. The seven sub-categories are:

GG — GUITAR (includes lute and mandolin)
GO — ORGAN
GP — PIANO (includes clavichord and harpischord)
GS — STRINGED INSTRUMENTS (excluding violin)
GV — VIOLIN
GW — WIND INSTRUMENTS (brass and woodwind)
GX — PERCUSSION AND UNUSUAL INSTRUMENTS

B. The Sub-categories

These categories are of two types: broad and specific. Specific categories are designated for recordings of the guitar, piano, violin and organ. These instruments are both versatile and popular, and a major proportion of solo instrumental music is written for them.

Guitar, lute and mandolin are categorized together, however, as are piano, harpischord and clavichord, because these two sets of instruments are interrelated historically and physically, and are often used interchangeably to perform the same music.

The three broad categories—string, percussion, and wind—group all other instruments by instrumental choir. This broader grouping eliminates the necessity for a separate sub-category corresponding to every known musical instrument, and organizes the recordings by type of instrument as an aid to the record user.

G 2. GUIDE TO CLASSIFICATION IN THE G CATEGORIES

In classifying recordings, it is important to keep in mind that it is what is actually *heard on the recording* that is being classed. The class system is not a bibliographical tool nor a catalog, but a direct reflection of the record content. Many works originally written for one type of instrument may be played on another; the classification is interested solely in the instrument which is heard on the recording, regardless of the original form or medium of the work of music itself. The rules and definitions under the sub-categories indicate the types of recordings to be classed in each.

CATEGORY GG — MUSIC FOR SOLO GUITAR

GG 1. TYPES OF RECORDINGS TO BE CLASSED IN CATEGORY GG

Class in category GG recordings of music written or arranged for and performed on the guitar, the lute or the mandolin, with or without the accompaniment of another instrument.

> Villa-Lobos: "Choros No. 1 for Guitar."
> Cimarosa: "Harpsichord Sonata in A" (arranged for guitar).
> Bach: "Suites for Lute."
> "Evening with Segovia." (Segovia) Decca 9733
> Beethoven: "Sonatina in C for Mandolin."

A. Concertos

Class in category EC recordings of works for solo guitar (lute, or mandolin), and orchestra.

> Vivaldi: "Concerto in D for Guitar and Orchestra."
> Hasse: "Concerto in G for Mandolin."

B. Duos

Class in category GG recordings of duos: that is, works written or arranged with equal parts for two players. If two different instruments are used, class the recording by the instrument named first in the title of the work. [Works for three or more instruments are classed in category F (CHAMBER MUSIC).]

> Fauré: "Pavane, Op. 50" (arranged for two guitars).

> Paganini: "Sonata for Violin and Guitar." (Class
> in category GV because the violin is
> the first instrument named in the title.)

GG 2. FORMATION OF THE CLASS NUMBER IN CATEGORY GG

A. Term One

Term One is composed of the letters "GG."

B. Term Two

Three types of entry may be used to form Term Two in this category: Composer Entry, Performer Entry, and Collections Entry.

1. *Composer Entry*

Use the surname of the composer to form Term Two if the rules for Composer Entry apply. (See section II-204 for Term Two Composer Entry rules.)

> Visée: "Guitar Pieces."   **GG**
> Julian Bream.   ● **VISE**
> RCA Victor LSC 2878   **GP**
>   **B 78**

2. *Performer Entry*

Use the surname of the featured performer to form Term Two if the
rules for Composer Entry do not apply. (See section II-206 for Term
Two Performer Entry rules.)

> "Evening of Flamenco Music."   **GG**
> Pepe **Romero.**   ● **ROME**
> Mercury 90434   **EFM**
>   **R 34**

3. *Collections Entry*

If the rules for Composer Entry (II-204.), and Performer Entry (II-
206) do not apply, use the abbreviation COLL to indicate "collection"
in Term Two. (II-208)

> "Masters of Guitar."   **GG**
> RCA Victor LSC 2717   ● **COLL**
>   **MG**
>   **R 17**

C. Term Three

Use the *album title* to form Term Three when Performer Entry or
Collections Entry has been used in Term Two. When a Composer Entry
is used in Term Two, consult the rules in section III-303, 304 to determine whether to use an *album title* or a *work title* in Term Three.

D. Term Four

The surname of the featured instrumentalist is used to form the alpha
symbol in Term Four when the Composer Entry or Performer Entry
is used in Term Two. (section IV-406.) The initial of the record company's name is used as the alpha symbol when Collections Entry appears in Term Two. (section IV-406D.)

CATEGORY GO — MUSIC FOR SOLO ORGAN

GO 1. TYPES OF RECORDINGS TO BE CLASSED IN CATEGORY GO.

Class in category GO recordings of music written or arranged for and
performed on the organ, with or without the accompaniment of another instrument.

> Bach: "Toccata and Fugue in D Minor for Organ."
> Soler: "Concerti for Two Organs."
> "Voluntaries and Processions." (Biggs) Columbia CML 4603

A. Concertos

Class in category EC recordings of works for solo organ and orchestra.

> Sowerby: "Classic Concerto for Organ and Orchestra."
> Haydn: "Concerti in C for Organ."

B. Duos

Class in category GO recordings of duos: that is, works written or arranged with equal parts for two players. If two different instruments are used, class the recording by the instrument named first in the title of the work. [Works for three or more instruments are classed in category F (CHAMBER MUSIC).]

> Pasquini: "Sonatas for Two Organs." **class in category GO**

GO 2. FORMATION OF THE CLASS NUMBER IN CATEGORY GO

A. Term One

Term One is composed of the letters "GO."

B. Term Two

Three types of entry may be used to form Term Two in this category: Composer Entry, Performer Entry, and Collections Entry.

1. *Composer Entry*

Use the surname of the composer to form Term Two if the rules for Composer Entry apply. (See section II-204 for Term Two Composer Entry rules.)

> **Hindemith:** "Sonatas for Organ."
> E. Power Biggs.
> Columbia CMS 6234

GO
● HIND
SON
B 34

2. *Performer Entry*

Use the surname of the featured performer to form Term Two if the rules for Composer Entry do not apply. (See section II-206 for Term Two Performer Entry rules.)

> "Vale of Dreams."
> Virgil **Fox.**
> Capitol SP 8557

GO
● FOX
VD
F 57

3. *Collections Entry*

If the rules for Composer Entry (II-204), and Performer Entry (II-206) do not apply, use the abbreviation COLL to indicate "collections" in Term Two. (II-208.)

C. Term Three

Use the *album title* to form Term Three when Performer Entry or Collections Entry has been used in Term Two. When a Composer Entry is used in Term Two, consult the rules in section III-303, 304 to determine whether to use an *album title* or a *work title* in Term Three.

D. Term Four

The surname of the featured organist is used to form the alpha symbol in Term Four when the Composer Entry or Performer Entry has been used in Term Two (section IV-406). The initial of the record company's name is used as the alpha symbol when Collections Entry appears in Term Two (section IV-406D).

CATEGORY GP — MUSIC FOR SOLO PIANO

GP 1. TYPES OF RECORDINGS TO BE CLASSED IN CATEGORY GP

Class in category GP recordings of music written or arranged for and performed on the piano, the clavichord, or the harpsichord, with or without the accompaniment of another instrument.

> Brahms: "Sonata No. 1 for Piano."
> Pinkham: "Partita for Harpsichord."
> Arensky: "Suite for Two Pianos."
> Haydn: "Sonatas for Clavier and Violin."
> Beethoven: "Symphony No. 5" (piano arrangement
>   by Liszt).
> "Keyboard Fantasies." (Pennario) Capitol P 8391

A. Concertos

Class in category EC recordings of works for solo piano (clavichord or harpsichord) and orchestra.

> Khachaturian: "Concerto for Piano and Orchestra."
> Franck: "Symphonic Variations for Piano and
>   Orchestra."

B. Duos

Class in category GP recordings of duos: that is, works written or arranged with equal parts for two players. If two different instruments are used, class the recording by the instrument named first in the title of the work. [Works for three or more instruments are classed in category F (CHAMBER MUSIC).]

> Mendelssohn: "Lied ohne Worte, Op. 109 for
> Cello and Piano." **class in category GS**
> Haydn: "Sonatas for Clavier and Violin." **class in
> category GP**
> Poulenc: "Sonata for Piano, Four Hands." **class in
> category GP**

GP 2. FORMATION OF THE CLASS NUMBER IN CATEGORY GP

A. Term One

Term One is composed of the letters "GP."

B. Term Two

Three types of entry may be used to form Term Two in this category: Composer Entry, Performer Entry, and Collections Entry.

1. *Composer Entry*

Use the surname of the composer to form Term Two if the rules for Composer Entry apply. (See section II-204 for Term Two Composer Entry rules.)

    Chopin: "Nocturnes."   **GP**
    Rubinstein.   ● **CHOP**
    RCA Victor LSC 7050   **NOC**
                                    R 50

2. *Performer Entry*

Use the surname of the featured performer to form Term Two if the rules for Composer Entry do not apply. (See section II-206 for Term Two Performer Entry rules.)

    "Horowitz on TV."   **GP**
    Vladimir **Horowitz.**   ● **HORO**
    Columbia MS 7106   **HTV**
                                   H 06

3. *Collections Entry*

If the rules for Composer Entry (II-204), and Performer Entry (II-206) do not apply, use the abbreviation COLL to indicate "collections" in Term Two. (II-208.)

    "Famous Pianists at the Turn of the Century." **GP**
    Telefunken 37   ● **COLL**
                                    FPT
                                    T 37

C. Term Three

Use the *album title* to form Term Three when Performer Entry or Collections Entry has been used in Term Two. When a Composer Entry is used in Term Two, consult the rules in section III-303, 304, to determine whether to use an *album title* or a *work title* in Term Three.

D. Term Four

The surname of the featured instrumentalist is used to form the alpha symbol in Term Four when the Composer Entry or the Performer Entry has been used in Term Two (section IV-406). The initial of the record company's name is used as the alpha symbol when the Collections Entry appears in Term Two. (See section IV-406D for Term Four rules.)

CATEGORY GS — MUSIC FOR SOLO STRINGED INSTRUMENTS

GS 1. TYPES OF RECORDINGS TO BE CLASSED IN CATEGORY GS

Class in category GS recordings of music written or arranged for and performed on a solo stringed instrument, such as the cello, the harp, the viola, etc., with or without the accompaniment of another instrument. (Do not include in this category works for solo violin, guitar, lute or mandolin, since separate categories exist for these instruments.)

> Fauré: "Impromptu, Op. 86, for Harp."
> Bach: "Suites for Cello Unaccompanied."
> Philips: "Sonata for String Bass."
> Stamitz: "Divertissement for Viola d'Amore and
>   Harpsichord."
> "Harp Music of France." (Robles) Argo 5 458

A. Concertos

Class in category EC recordings of works for solo stringed instrument and orchestra.

> Boccherini: "Concerto in B Flat for Cello and
>   Orchestra."
> Bloch: "Suite Hebraique for Viola and Orchestra."
> Vanhal: "Concerto in E for Bass and Orchestra."

B. Duos

Class in category GS recordings of duos: that is, works written or arranged for two players. If two different instruments are used, class the recording by the instrument named first in the title of the work. [Works for three or more instruments are classed in category F (CHAMBER MUSIC).]

> Martinu: "Duo for Violin and Cello."   **class in
>   category GV**
> Saint-Saens: "Fantasie for Harp and Violin, Op. 124."
>   **class in category GS**

GS 2. FORMATION OF THE CLASS NUMBER IN CATEGORY GS

A. Term One

Term One is composed of the letters "GS."

B. Term Two

Three types of entry may be used to form Term Two in this category: Composer Entry, Performer Entry, and Collections Entry.

1. *Composer Entry*

Use the surname of the composer to form Term Two if the rules for Composer Entry apply. (See section II-204 for Term Two Composer Entry rules.)

Bach: "Sonatas for Viola da Gamba and	**GS**
Harpsichord."	● **BACH**
Starker, cello, and Sebok, piano.	**SON**
Mercury 90480	**S 80**

2. *Performer Entry*

Use the surname of the featured performer to form Term Two if the rules for Composer Entry do not apply. (See section II-206 for Term Two Performer Entry rules.)

"Harp Music of France."	**GS**
Marisa **Robles.**	● **ROBL**
Argo 5453	**HMF**
	R 53

3. *Collections Entry*

If the rules for Composer Entry (II-204) and Performer Entry (II-206) do not apply, use the abbreviation COLL to indicate "collections" in Term Two. (II-208.)

C. Term Three

Use the *album title* to form Term Three when Performer Entry or Collections Entry has been used in Term Two. When a Composer Entry is used in Term Two, consult the rules in section III-303, 304, to determine whether to use an *album title* or a *work title* in Term Three. (Note that formation of Term Three differs in this category from the practice in category EC since the solo instrument is not indicated; only the *work title* or *album title* is used.)

D. Term Four

The surname of the featured instrumentalist is used to form the alpha symbol in Term Four when the Composer Entry or Performer Entry has been used in Term Two (section IV-406). The initial of the record company's name is used as the alpha symbol when Collections Entry appears in Term Two. (See section IV-406D for Term Four rules.)

CATEGORY GV — MUSIC FOR SOLO VIOLIN

GV 1. TYPES OF RECORDINGS TO BE CLASSED IN CATEGORY GV

Class in category GV recordings of music written or arranged for and
performed on the violin, with or without the accompaniment of another instrument.

> Paganini: "Caprices (24), Op. 1."
> Sessions: "Sonata for Violin Solo."
> Prokofiev: "Sonata for Two Violins, Op. 56."
> Debussy: "Sonata No. 3 in G Minor for Violin
>   and Piano."
> "Immortal Performances." (Kreisler)
> RCA Victor LM 6099

A. Concertos

Class in category EC recordings of works for solo violin and orchestra.

> Beethoven: "Concerto in D Major for Violin."
> Saint-Saens: "Havanaise for Violin and Orchestra."

B. Duos

Class in category GV recordings of duos: that is, works written or arranged for two players. If two different instruments are used, class
the recording by the instrument named first in the title of the work.
[Works for three or more instruments are classed in category F (CHAM-
BER MUSIC).]

> Bartok: "Duos for Two Violins."
> Scarlatti: "Sonatas for Violin and Harpsichord."

GV 2. FORMATION OF THE CLASS NUMBER IN CATEGORY GV

A. Term One

Term One is composed of the letters GV.

B. Term Two

Three types of entry may be used to form Term Two in this category:
Composer Entry, Performer Entry, and Collections Entry.

1. *Composer Entry*

Use the surname of the composer to form Term Two if the rules for
Composer Entry apply. (See section II-204 for Term Two Composer
Entry rules.)

> **Scarlatti:** "Sonatas for Violin and Harpsichord."   GV
> Olevsky, violin, and Valenti, harpsichord.   ● SCAR
> Westminster 9046   SON
>   O 46

2. *Performer Entry*

Use the surname of the featured performer to form Term Two if the rules for Composer Entry do not apply. (See section II-206 for Term Two Performer Entry rules.)

"Heifetz Encores."	**GV**
Jascha **Heifetz.**	● **HEIF**
RCA Victor LM 2382	**HE**
	H 82

3. *Collections Entry*

If the rules for Composer Entry (II-204) and Performer Entry (II-206) do not apply, use the abbreviation COLL to indicate "collection" in Term Two. (II-208.)

C. Term Three

Use the *album title* to form Term Three when Performer Entry or Collections Entry has been used in Term Two. When a Composer Entry is used in Term Two, consult the rules in section III-303, 304, to determine whether to use an *album title* or a *work title* in Term Three.

D. Term Four

The surname of the violinist is used to form the alpha symbol in Term Four when the Composer Entry or Performer Entry has been used in Term Two (section IV-406). The initial of the record company's name is used as the alpha symbol when Collections Entry appears in Term Two. (See section IV-406D for Term Four rules.)

CATEGORY GW — MUSIC FOR SOLO WIND INSTRUMENTS

GW 1. TYPES OF RECORDINGS TO BE CLASSED IN CATEGORY GW

Class in category GW recordings of music written or arranged for and performed by a solo wind instrument, either woodwind or brass, such as the recorder, flute, clarinet, oboe, trumpet, horn, tuba, etc., with or without the accompaniment of another instrument.

> Poulenc: "Sonata for Clarinet and Piano."
> Handel: "Sonata for Oboe."
> Wolff: "Duet for Horn and Piano."
> Mamlok: "Variations for Solo Flute."
> Kuhlau: "Duos for Two Flutes."
> "Flutists' Showcase." Golden Crest 4020

A. Concertos

Class in category EC recordings of works for solo wind instrument and orchestra.

> Reinecke: "Concerto for Flute and Orchestra,
>   Op. 283."
> Chaikin: "Concerto for Accordion and Orchestra."

B. Duos

Class in category GW recordings of duos: that is, works written or arranged for two players. If two different instruments are used, class the recording by the instrument named first in the title of the work. [Works for three or more instruments are classed in category F (CHAMBER MUSIC).]

> Kuhlau: "Duos for Two Flutes."
> Kraus: "Duo in D for Flute and Viola."
> Telemann: "Duo Sonatas for Recorders Alone."

GW 2. FORMATION OF THE CLASS NUMBER IN CATEGORY GW

A. Term One

Term One is composed of the letters "GW."

B. Term Two

Three types of entry may be used to form Term Two in this category: Composer Entry, Performer Entry, and Collections Entry.

1. *Composer Entry*

Use the surname of the composer to form Term Two if the rules for Composer Entry apply. (See section II-204 for Term Two Composer Entry rules.)

> **Handel:** "Sonatas, Op. 1, for Flute."　　　　　GW
> Rampal, flute, and Veyron-Lacroix, harpsichord.　● **HAND**
> Epic BSC-153　　　　　　　　　　　　　　　SON
> 　　　　　　　　　　　　　　　　　　　　R 53

2. *Performer Entry*

Use the surname of the featured performer to form Term Two if the rules for Composer Entry do not apply. (See section II-206 for Term Two Performer Entry rules.)

> "Richard Fote: Trombone Virtuoso."　　　　　GW
> Richard **Fote.**　　　　　　　　　　　　　● **FOTE**
> Mark 28250　　　　　　　　　　　　　　　TV
> 　　　　　　　　　　　　　　　　　　　　F 50

3. *Collections Entry*

If the rules for Composer Entry (II-204) and Performer Entry (II-206) do not apply, use the abbreviation COLL to indicate "collection" in Term Two. (II-208.)

> "Flutists' Showcase."　　　　　　　　　　　GW
> Golden Crest 4020　　　　　　　　　　　● **COLL**
> 　　　　　　　　　　　　　　　　　　　　FS
> 　　　　　　　　　　　　　　　　　　　　G 20

C. Term Three

Use the *album title* to form Term Three when Performer Entry or Collections Entry has been used in Term Two. When a Composer Entry is used in Term Two, consult the rules in section III-303, 304, to determine whether to use an *album title* or a *work title* in Term Three. (Note that formation of Term Three differs in this category from the practice in category EC since the solo instrument is not indicated; only the *work title* or *album title* is used.)

D. Term Four

The surname of the featured instrumentalist is used to form the alpha symbol in Term Four when the Composer Entry or Performer Entry has been used in Term Two (section IV-406). The initial of the record company's name is used as the alpha symbol when the Collections Entry appears in Term Two. (See section IV-406D for Term Four rules.)

CATEGORY GX — PERCUSSION AND UNUSUAL INSTRUMENTS

GX 1. TYPES OF RECORDINGS TO BE CLASSED IN CATEGORY GX

Class in category GX recordings of music written or arranged for and performed on a solo percussion instrument, such as the drum, xylophone, glockenspiel and carillon, with or without the accompaniment of another instrument. Include in this category recordings of music written or arranged for and performed on unusual instruments which cannot be described as stringed, wind, or percussive, such as the glass harmonica.

> "Music of Foster" (Albright at the carillon).
> Decca 78923
> Mozart: "Adagio in C for Glass Harmonica, K.617a."

A. Concertos

Class in category EC recordings of works for solo percussion (or unusual) instrument and orchestra.

> Milhaud: "Concerto for Percussion and Small Orchestra."

B. Duos

Class in category GX recordings of duos: that is, works written or arranged for two players. If two different instruments are used, class the recording by the instrument named first in the title of the work. The body of written and recorded music for solo percussion instruments is relatively slight, and most works featuring percussion instruments call for the use of more than two percussion instruments.

Therefore, most recordings of "percussion music" will be classed in category F (CHAMBER MUSIC), or in category EC (CONCERTOS).

> Colgrass: Variations for Four Drums and Viola."
> **class in category F**
> Hovhaness: "Suite for Violin, Piano, and
> Percussion." **class in category F**

GX 2. FORMATION OF THE CLASS NUMBER IN CATEGORY GX

A. Term One

Term One is composed of the letters "GX."

B. Term Two

Three types of entry may be used to form Term Two in this category: Composer Entry, Performer Entry, and Collections Entry.

1. *Composer Entry*

Use the surname of the composer to form Term Two if the rules for Composer Entry apply. (See section II-204 for Term Two Composer Entry rules.)

> Naumann: "Duet in G for Glass Harmonica and
> Lute."
> Hoffman, glass harmonica, and Gerwig, lute.
> DGG ARC 3111

> GX
> • NAUM
> DUE
> H 11

2. *Performer Entry*

Use the surname of the featured performer to form Term Two if the rules for Composer Entry do not apply. (See section II-206 for Term Two Performer Entry rules.)

> "Percussion-Clinician Series."
> Saul **Feldstein.**
> Golden Crest 1005

> GX
> • FELD
> PCS
> F 05

3. *Collections Entry*

If the rule for Composer Entry (II-204) and Performer Entry (II-206) do not apply, use the abbreviation COLL to indicate "collections" in Term Two. (II-208.)

C. Term Three

Use the *album title* to form Term Three when Performer Entry or Collections Entry has been used in Term Two. When a Composer Entry is used in Term Two, consult the rules in section III-303,304, to determine whether to use an *album title* or a *work title* in Term Three. (Note that formation of Term Three differs in this category from the practice in category EC since the solo instrument is not indicated; only the *work title* or *album title* is used.)

D. Term Four

The surname of the featured instrumentalist is used to form the alpha symbol in Term Four when the Composer Entry or Performer Entry has been used in Term Two (section IV-406). The initial of the record company's name is used as the alpha symbol when Collections Entry appears in Term Two. (See section IV-406D for Term Four rules.)

CATEGORY H — BAND MUSIC

H 1. TYPES OF RECORDINGS TO BE CLASSED IN CATEGORY H

Class in category H recordings of music written or arranged for and performed by marching and concert bands, including brass bands, wind ensembles, fife and drum corps, and bagpipe bands.

> Bennett: "Symphonic Songs for Band."
> Hindemith: "Symphony in B Flat for Band."
> Grainger: "Lincolnshire Posy."
> Sousa: "Sousa on Review." Mercury 90284
> "Trooping the Colors." (Black Watch Regiment)
>   RCA Victor LPM 1527

A. Popular Bands

Recordings by instrumental ensembles which play various types of popular music, and use the designation "band," such as balalaika, marimba, calypso, jug, jazz or dance bands, are not included in category H, but are classed in other categories according to the style of music and performance.

> "What Now, My Love?"
> Herb Alpert and the Tijuana Brass.
> A&M 4114   **class in category MA**

> "Adventures in Jazz."
> Stan Kenton's Band.
> Capitol ST 1796   **class in category MJ**

> "Back to Erin."
> Acqua String Band.
> Sure S 16   **class in category Q**

B. Wind Ensembles

Recordings by wind ensembles of more than nine instruments are classed in category H. [Works performed by nine instruments or less are classed in category F (CHAMBER MUSIC).]

> "Sousa Favorites." (Eastman Wind Ensemble)
>   Mercury 90291
> Mozart: "Serenade No. 10 in B Flat for 13 Wind
>   Instruments, K.361."

H 2. FORMATION OF THE CLASS NUMBER IN CATEGORY H

A. Term One

Term One is composed of the letter "H."

B. Term Two

Three types of entry may be used to form Term Two in this category: Composer Entry, Performer Entry, and Collections Entry.

1. *Composer Entry*

Use the surname of the composer to form Term Two if the rules for Composer Entry apply. (See section II-204 for Term Two Composer Entry rules.)

Holst: "Suite No. 1 for Band."	**H**
Eastman Wind Ensemble,	● **HOLS**
Frederick Fennell, conductor.	**SUI**
Mercury 90388	**E 88**

2. *Performer Entry*

Use the name of the featured band to form Term Two if the rules for Composer Entry do not apply. (See section II-206 for Term Two Performer Entry rules.)

"Marching On."	**H**
The **Goldman** Band, Goldman, conducting.	● **GOLD**
Vocalion 73838	**MO**
	G 38

3. *Collections Entry*

If the rule for Composer Entry does not apply, and more than one band is featured on the recording, use the abbreviation COLL to indicate Collections Entry in Term Two.

"Pass in Review."	**H**
London 44001	● **COLL**
	PR
	L 01

C. Term Three

Use the *album title* in Term Three when Performer Entry or Collections Entry has been used in Term Two. When a Composer Entry is used in Term Two, consult the rules in section III-303, 304, to determine whether to use an *album title* or a *work title* in Term Three.

D. Term Four

The name of the band is used to form the alpha symbol in Term Four when the Composer Entry or Performer Entry is used in Term Two. If the Collections Entry is used in Term Two, then use the initial of the record company's name to form the alpha symbol. (See section IV-408.)

CATEGORY J — ELECTRONIC AND MECHANICAL MUSIC

J 1. TYPES OF RECORDINGS TO BE CLASSED IN CATEGORY J

Class in category J recordings of music written for and produced on electronic and mechanical devices, alone or in combination with conventional musical instruments or voice.

> Babbitt: "Ensembles for Synthesizer."
> Stockhausen: "Mikrophonie I for Tamtam, Two
>   Microphones, Two Filters and Potentiometer."
> Cage: "Variations II."
> "Switched-on Bach." Columbia MS 7194

NOTE: *The term "electronic devices" does not refer to standard instruments with electronic amplification, such as electronic guitar or organ, nor to the engineering techniques employed by sound engineers in standard record production.*

J 2. FORMATION OF THE CLASS NUMBER IN CATEGORY J

A. Term One

Term One is composed of the letter "J."

B. Term Two

Two types of entry may be used to form Term Two in this category: Composer Entry and Collections Entry.

1. *Composer Entry*

Use the surname of the composer to form Term Two if the rules for Composer Entry apply. (See section II-204 for Term Two Composer Entry rules.)

Varese: "Poeme Electronique."	**J**
Direct magnetic tape creation.	● **VARE**
Craft Ensemble performing.	**PE**
Columbia MS 6146	**C 46**

2. *Collections Entry*

Use the abbreviation COLL for "collection" in Term Two when the rules for Composer Entry do not apply.

"Nonesuch Guide to Electronic Music."	**J**
Nonesuch HC 73018	● **COLL**
	NGE
	N 18

C. Term Three

Use the *album title* to form Term Three when Collections Entry is used in Term Two. Use either *album title* or *work title* after Composer Entry has been used. (See section III-303, 304, for Term Three rules.)

D. Term Four

The surname of the conductor, a featured performer, or the name of the performing group is used to form the alpha symbol in Term Four. If the Collections Entry is used in Term Two and more than one performer or performing group is featured, use the initial of the name of the record company to form the alpha symbol.

CATEGORY K — MUSICAL SHOWS AND OPERETTAS: COMPLETE AND EXCERPTS

K 1. TYPES OF RECORDINGS TO BE CLASSED IN CATEGORY K

Class in category K recordings of complete versions of musical shows and operettas as well as collections of vocal excerpts from those shows.

> "The Merry Widow."
> "Hello, Dolly!"
> "H.M.S. Pinafore."
> "Golden Age of Operetta." (Joan Sutherland)
>   London 1268

A. Vocal Collections

Recordings of collections of songs taken exclusively from musical shows and operettas, and featuring that fact prominently in the title of the album, are classed in this category. (If the album title does not indicate that the collection is taken from musical shows or operettas, class the recording by the style of performance.)

> "Cavalcade of Show Tunes."
> Mario Lanza.
> RCA Victor LSC 2090   **class in category K**

> "Shall We Dance?"
> Jack Jones
> Kapp 1228   **class in category MA**

B. Orchestral Collections

Recordings of orchestral excerpts (such as ballet music and overtures) and orchestral arrangements of songs from musical shows and operettas are classed by type of music or performance.

> Bernstein: "Ballet Music from West Side Story."
> New York Philharmonic, Bernstein, conductor.
> Columbia MS 6251   **class in category EB**

> "Music from Shows."
> Boston Pops.
> RCA Victor LSC 2965   **class in category EA**

> "Decade on Broadway."
> Guy Lombardo and his orchestra.
> Capitol DT 788   **class in category MA**

K 2. FORMATION OF THE CLASS NUMBER IN CATEGORY K

A. Term One

Term One is composed of the letter "K."

B. Term Two

Four types of entry may be used to form Term Two in this category:
Title Entry, Composer Entry, Performer Entry, and Collections Entry.

1. *Title Entry*

Use the title of the musical show or operetta to form Term Two if all
the selections on the recording are from one show or operetta.

"**Kiss** Me, Kate."	K
Morison and Drake.	● KISS
Capitol TAO 1267	KMK
	M 67

2. *Performer Entry*

Use the surname of the featured singer to form Term Two if the rule
above (K2-B1) for Title Entry does not apply.

"Golden Age of Operetta."	K
Joan **Sutherland.**	● SUTH
London 1268	GAO
	S 68

3. *Composer Entry*

Use the surname of the composer to form Term Two if the recording
contains a collection of excerpts from two or more shows or operettas
by one composer, and an individual singer is not featured.

Sullivan: "Choruses." (From	K
Gilbert and Sullivan Operettas.)	● SULL
D'Oyly Carte Opera Company	CHO
Richmond 23060	D 60

4. *Collections Entry*

Use the abbreviation COLL to indicate "collection" when the preceding three rules of entry do not apply.

"Songs from Viennese Operettas."	K
Wunderlich, Sailer, etc.	● COLL
Vox STPL 512980	SVO
	S 80

C. Term Three

If all the selections on the recording are from one show, use the name
of the show to form Term Three, disregarding introductory words
such as "highlights," "selections from" and so forth. If the selections
on the recording are from more than one show, use the *album title*
to form Term Three.

D. Term Four

Use the surname of the featured singer of the highest register to form the alpha symbol in Term Four (section IV-405). When the recording features a performing vocal group, use the initial of the corporate group name as the alpha symbol rather than using the names of individual singers. (See section IV-407 for Term Four rules.)

CATEGORY L — SOUNDTRACK MUSIC: MOTION PICTURES AND TELEVISION

L 1. TYPES OF RECORDINGS TO BE CLASSED IN CATEGORY L

It should be clearly understood that this category is not designed for all soundtrack recordings, but only for recordings of soundtrack music; that is, music written or arranged for the soundtracks of motion pictures and television programs.

A. Original Soundtrack Music

Class in category L recordings of music written originally for the soundtrack of a motion picture or television program.

> "Mondo Cane." (soundtrack) United Artists 5105
> "The Wizard of Oz." (soundtrack) MGM S 3996 ST
> "The Graduate." (soundtrack) Columbia OS 3180
> "Peter Gunn." RCA Victor LSP 1956
> "Music from the Films." (Mantovani) London 112

B. Original Soundtrack Music — Collections

Class in category L recordings of collections of songs or mood music written for the soundtracks of motion pictures or television programs, provided the album title indicates clearly and specifically that the collection is drawn from films or television.

> "Academy Award Winners." (Frank Sinatra) Reprise S1011
> "Music from the Films." (Mantovani) London 112
> "Detectives, Agents, and Great Motion Picture Themes."
> Mainstream 6079

C. Music Adapted to Soundtracks

Class in category L recordings of motion picture or television soundtracks on which the music used was not written originally for the motion picture or television program, but was borrowed and altered to fit the visual action or dialogue. Alteration may be in tempo, scoring, or by combining several unrelated works of music.

> "Interlude." (soundtrack) Colgems S 5007
> (Excerpts from Beethoven, Brahms, Tchaikovsky,
> Dvorak and Rachmaninoff.)

Do not class in category L the original recordings which were borrowed to be used on a soundtrack.

> Mozart: "Piano Concerto No. 21." DGG 138783
> (This recording was used for the music soundtrack
> of the film "Elvira Madigan"; class this recording
> in category **EC.**)

> Strauss: "Also Sprach Zarathustra, Op. 30." DGG 136001
> (Parts of this recording were used on the music
> soundtrack of the film "2001: A Space Odyssey." Class
> the complete Strauss recording in category **EA.** The
> actual soundtrack of "2001: A Space Odyssey" is classed
> in category **L.**)

D. Musical Works Produced on Television or in Motion Pictures

Soundtrack recordings of complete musical works, or musical performances which have been produced on television or in motion pictures, such as operas, oratorios, musical shows and concerts, are classed in appropriate musical categories other than category L.

> Menotti: "Amahl and the Night Visitors."
> King, Yaghjian, etc.
> RCA Victor LSC 2762   **class in category B**

> "Horowitz on Television"
> Vladimir Horowitz.
> Columbia MS 7106   **class in category GP**

> "Finian's Rainbow."
> Soundtrack from film
> Warner Bros. SB 2550   **class in category K**

E. Musical Specials on Television

Class in category L soundtrack recordings of musical variety shows produced specifically for television.

> "Movin' with Nancy." (Nancy Sinatra) Reprise 6277

F. Spoken Works Produced on Television or in Motion Pictures

Soundtrack recordings of spoken works which have been written for or adapted to television and motion pictures are classed according to the form of the work.

> "Mark Twain Tonight"
> Hal Holbrook.
> Columbia OS 3080   **class in category S**

> "Years of Lightning, Day of
>   Drums."
> Capitol ST 2486   **class in category W**

> "Romeo and Juliet."
> Zeffirelli film version
> Capitol ST 2993   **class in category T**

L 2. FORMATION OF THE CLASS NUMBER IN CATEGORY L

A. Term One

Term One is composed of the letter L.

B. Term Two

Three types of entry may be used to form Term Two in this category:
Title Entry, Performer Entry, and Collections Entry.

1. *Title Entry*

Use the title of the motion picture or television program to form Term
Two if all the selections on the recording are from one film or program.

> "**Movin'** with Nancy."   L
> Nancy Sinatra.   ● MOVI
> Reprise 6277   MN
>   S 77

2. *Performer Entry*

Use the surname of the featured performer to form Term Two if the
rule above for Title Entry does not apply, and the recording features
a particular performer.

> "Music from the Films."   L
> **Mantovani** and his orchestra.   ● MANT
> London 112   MF
>   M 12

3. *Collections Entry*

Use the abbreviation COLL to indicate "collection" in Term Two when
the rule for Title Entry does not apply, and there is more than one
featured performer or performing group, or no featured performer.

> "New Themes from Motion   L
> Pictures."   ● COLL
> Time 2065   NTM
>   T 65

C. Term Three

If all the selections on the recording are from one motion picture or
television program, use the name of the film or program to form Term
Three, disregarding introductory words such as "Highlights," "selections from," and so forth. If the selections on the recording are from
more than one motion picture or television program, use the album
title to form Term Three.

D. Term Four

Use the surname of the featured performer to form the alpha symbol
in Term Four; in the case of vocal performances, select the surname
of the featured singer of the highest register; in the case of orchestral
performances, use the initial of the conductor's surname. When Col-

lections Entry is used in Term Two, use the initial of the record company's name as the alpha symbol in Term Four. (See section IV for specific Term Four rules.)

CATEGORY M — POPULAR MUSIC

M 1. STRUCTURE OF CATEGORY M

A. Scope

Category M is intended for all forms of contemporary popular music, and for popular music of the past which has not been absorbed into the folk tradition. This category is divided into three sub-categories in order to group together recordings of the same basic styles. The three sub-categories are:

> **MA — Pop Music**
> **MC — Country and Western Music**
> **MJ — Jazz Music**

B. The Sub-categories

Country and Western Music, and Jazz Music are separated into distinct categories because each is a form of pop music which has a history of creative activity and has sustained public interest for over half a century. No attempt has been made to create sub-categories for every trend and style in popular music because the field is too volatile. The rapidity of change and the eclecticism of pop music make narrow classification too confining and quickly obsolete.

C. Adaptation of Sub-categories

The sub-categories in category M are designed for record classification in the United States. Classifiers in other countries who adopt this classification scheme will want to change or add to these sub-categories in order to reflect popular music interests unique to their own countries. They may, therefore, establish sub-categories which they feel to be necessary or more appropriate. Their selections must be governed by the following concepts: sub-categories should be created only for distinctive areas of popular music in which there has been continued, creative activity and public interest over a substantial period of time, and only if the separate grouping of such music would be an advantage to the record user.

M 2. GUIDE TO CLASSIFICATION IN THE M CATEGORIES

A. Use of the Schwann Long Playing Record Catalog

The recordings in the M sub-categories are usually arranged by performer. The *Schwann Long Playing Record Catalog* also lists popular recordings by performer and divides popular recordings into separate subject listings: that is, Popular, Country and Western, Jazz, and Folk, with a supplementary catalog of international pop, folk and jazz recordings.

Because of its arrangement, the *Schwann* catalog can be a valuable tool to the classifier in selecting the appropriate category for a recording. It should be taken into account, however, that the Schwann catalog tends to categorize performers rather than recordings. Once a performer's name has been placed in a particular subject listing, such as in Country and Western music, all the recordings by that performer will be listed in that section, whether or not all the individual recordings actually contain country and western music.

This policy should be avoided in library classification and style of performance on the recording be used as the sole criteria in determining how to class the recording. It is the function of the book or card catalog, and not of the classification number, to draw together all works by a performer. For this reason, the Schwann catalog may be used as an aid, but is not to be considered the final authority.

B. Foreign Pop Music

Popular music of all countries and in all languages is classed in the "M" categories. A problem may arise, however, when the classifier must determine whether certain foreign music is actually popular or traditional (i.e., ethnic). This problem usually occurs when dealing with the music of less familiar cultures and languages. When in doubt, the recording may be classed in category Q by country. It can be assumed that most persons seeking recordings of foreign pop music are as interested in the cultural and linguistic aspects of the recording as they are in the music; therefore, placement by country will be both logical and helpful.

"La Vie en Rose." (Edith Piaf)   **class in category MA**
"Twinkling Star." (Umm Kulthumm)   **class in category MA
or in category Q
under "Egypt."**

C. Anthologies and Documentaries

Anthologies and documentaries dealing with popular music and musicians are classed in the appropriate categories, K through R. If more than one style of music is discussed or contained on recordings of this type, class the recording in category A (MUSIC APPRECIATION).

CATEGORY MA — POP MUSIC

MA 1. TYPES OF RECORDINGS TO BE CLASSED IN CATEGORY MA

Class in category MA recordings of all types of contemporary pop music, and popular music of the past which has not been absorbed into the folk tradition; include vocal and instrumental recordings from all countries and in all languages.

> "Sgt. Pepper's Lonely Hearts Club Band." (Beatles)
> Capitol MAS 2653
> "Mon Amour." (Gilbert Becaud) Liberty 7495
> "Ire Grossen Erfolge." (Caterina Valente) Polydor 46766
> "Sweet and Lovely." (Lawrence Welk) Dot 25296
> "Concert by Candlelight." (Liberace) Harmony 11161
> "MacArthur Park." (Ray Charles) Command S 936
> "Underground" (Electric Prunes) Reprise S 6262

MA 2. FORMATION OF THE CLASS NUMBER IN CATEGORY MA

A. Term One

Term One is composed of the letters "MA."

B. Term Two

Three types of entry may be used to form Term Two in this category: Performer Entry, Composer Entry, and Collections Entry.

1. *Performer Entry*

Use the surname of the featured performer or the name of the performing group to form Term Two when classifying recordings which feature one performer or one performing group.

"Magical Mystery Tour." The **Beatles.** Capitol S MAL 2835	MA ● BEAT MMT B 35
"Ella Sings Cole Porter." Ella **Fitzgerald.** Verve 64049	MA ● FITZ ESC F 49

2. *Composer Entry*

Use the surname of the composer to form Term Two in only one instance: if all the selections on the recording are by one composer, and a performer or performing group is *not* featured.

"All the Things You Are."	MA
Album of tunes by Jerome **Kern**.	● KERN
Monmouth-Evergreen 6808	ATY
	M 08

3. *Collections Entry*

Use the abbreviation COLL indicating "collection" in Term Two when the rules for Performer Entry and Composer Entry above do not apply.

"Fifteen Golden Hits."	MA
United Artists 6192	● COLL
	FGH
	U 92

C. Term Three

Always use the album title to form Term Three. (See section III-303 for Term Three rules.)

D. Term Four

The same name used for the Performer Entry in Term Two is used to form the alpha symbol in Term Four. Use the initial of the record company's name as the alpha symbol when Collections Entry or Composer Entry has been used in Term Two. (See section IV for specific Term Four rules.)

CATEGORY MC — COUNTRY AND WESTERN MUSIC

MC 1. TYPES OF RECORDINGS TO BE CLASSED IN CATEGORY MC

Class in category MC recordings of vocal and instrumental country and western music. (See also category P [FOLK AND ETHNIC MUSIC—NATIONAL].)

"Our Man in Nashville." (Chet Atkins) RCA Victor LSP 2616
"Country Hits." (Ernie Ford) Capitol ST 2097
"Gentle on My Mind." (Glen Campbell) Capitol ST 2809
"Square Dances." (Tommy Jackson) Dot 25580
"Harper Valley PTA." (Jeannie C. Riley) Plantation PLP 1
"Gospel Songs." (Hylo Brown) Rural 187

MC 2. FORMATION OF THE CLASS NUMBER IN CATEGORY MC

A. Term One

Term One is composed of the letters "MC."

91

B. Term Two

Three types of entry may be used for Term Two in this category: Performer Entry, Composer Entry, and Collection Entry.

1. *Performer Entry*

Use the surname of the performer to form Term Two when classifying recordings which feature one performer or one performing group.

"Soul of a Convict."	MC
Porter **Wagoner.**	● WAGO
RCA Victor LSP 3683	SC
	W 83

"Roger Miller Songbook."	MC
Bobby **Bond.**	● BOND
Somerset St. Fi. 24400	RMS
	B 00

2. *Composer Entry*

Use the surname of the composer to form Term Two in only one instance: if all the selections on the recording are by one composer, and a performer or performing group is *not* featured.

3. *Collections Entry*

Use the abbreviation COLL indicating "collection" in Term Two when the rules for Performer Entry and Composer Entry above do not apply.

"Early Rural String Bands."	MC
RCA Victor LPV 552	● COLL
	ERS
	R 52

C. Term Three

Always use the *album title* to form Term Three. (See section III-303 for Term Three rules.)

D. Term Four

The same name used for the Performer Entry in Term Two is used to form the alpha symbol in Term Four. Use the initial of the record company's name as the alpha symbol when Collections Entry or Composer Entry has been used in Term Two. (See chapter IV for specific Term Four rules.)

CATEGORY MJ — JAZZ MUSIC

MJ 1. TYPES OF RECORDINGS TO BE CLASSED IN CATEGORY MJ

Class in category MJ recordings of vocal and instrumental jazz music.

"Greatest Hits." (Louis Armstrong) Columbia CS 9438
"Blue Bechet." (Sydney Bechet) RCA Victor LPV 535
"Ugetsu." (Art Blakey) Riverside S 3022
"At Duke's Place." (Ella Fitzgerald) Verve 64070
"Live at the Lighthouse." (Modern Jazz Quartet) Atco S 1486

MJ 2. FORMATION OF THE CLASS NUMBER IN CATEGORY MJ

A. Term One

Term One is composed of the letters "MJ."

B. Term Two

Three types of entry may be used for Term Two in this category: Performer Entry, Composer Entry, and Collection Entry.

1. *Performer Entry*

Use the surname of the featured performer or the name of the performing group to form Term Two when classifying recordings which feature one performer or one performing group.

"Day in the Life."   MJ
Wes **Montgomery.**   ● MONT
A&M SP 3001   DL
                                                              M 01

"Shades of Blue."   MJ
Billie **Holiday.**   ● HOLI
Sunset 5147   SB
                                                            H 47

2. *Composer Entry*

Use the name of the composer to form Term Two in only one instance: if all the selections on the recording are by one composer, and a performer or performing group is *not* featured.

3. *Collections Entry*

Use the abbreviation COLL indicating "collection" in Term Two when the rules for Performer Entry and Composer Entry above do not apply.

"Dixieland All-Stars."   MJ
Stereo Fidelity 16700   ● COLL
                                                            DAS
                                                            S 00

93

C. Term Three

Always use the *album title* to form Term Three. (See section III-303 for Term Three rules.)

D. Term Four

The same name used for the Performer Entry in Term Two is used to form the alpha symbol in Term Four. Use the initial of the record company's name as the alpha symbol when Collections Entry or Composer Entry is used in Term Two. (See chapter IV for specific Term Four rules.)

CATEGORY P — FOLK AND ETHNIC MUSIC: NATIONAL

P 1. TYPES OF RECORDINGS TO BE CLASSED IN CATEGORY P

Class in category P recordings of vocal and instrumental music described or treated as American folk or ethnic music, regardless of origin.

> "All Time Hootenanny Favorites." Decca 74469
> "Blue Ridge Mountain Music." Atco S1347
> "Farewell, Angelina." (Joan Baez) Vanguard 79200
> "Cajun Songs from Louisiana." Folkways 4438
> "Spanish and Mexican Music of New Mexico." Folkways 4426
> "Eskimo Songs from Alaska." Folkways 4069
> "Flathead Indian Music." Folkways 4445
> "Negro Folk Music of Alabama." Folkways 4418
> "Hawaiian Chant, Hula and Music." Folkways 8750

A. Afro-American Music

Class in category P recordings of spirituals, work songs, blues, and other traditional music attributed to the early Negro-American. (Contemporary music which draws heavily on Afro-American influence, such as jazz, rock and roll, rhythm and blues, etc., is classed in the appropriate M categories.)

> "Goodnight, Irene." (Leadbelly) Allegro 9025
> "Fisk Jubilee Singers." Folkways 2372

B. Contemporary "Folk" Music

Class in category P recordings of music written by contemporary composers in deliberate imitation of traditional folk styles, and played or sung by "folk style" performers, such as Joan Baez, Bob Dylan, Peter, Paul and Mary, Buffy Ste. Marie, etc.

C. Cowboy Music

Class in category P recordings of authentic cowboy songs and songs of the frontier.

> "'Frontier Ballads, 1791-1814." Folkways 2175
> "The Cowboy: His Songs, Ballads and Brag Talk."
>   Folkways 5723
> "Songs of The West." (Norman Luboff Choir)
>   Columbia 8329

D. Gospel Music

Gospel music—rural, religious music—is classed usually in categories MC and MA. However, classification is determined largely by the style and reputation of the performer; for this reason, some recordings of gospel music may be classed in category P.

> "Faith and Joy." (Burl Ives) Word 8140

E. Indigenous Ethnic Music

Class in category P recordings of music identified with ethnic groups (*i.e.:* Indians, Eskimos and Polynesians-Hawaii) which were within the current boundaries of the fifty United States prior to the arrival of Europeans or Americans.

> "Music of the Sioux and the Navajo." Folkways 4401
> "Eskimo Songs from Alaska." Folkways 4069
> "Hawaiian Chant, Hula and Music." Folkways 8750

(Do not include in the term "current boundaries" those territories administered by treaty or mutual agreements such as the Virgin Islands, Guam, Okinawa, Puerto Rico, etc. These areas are treated as independent entities in category Q.)

P 2. FORMATION OF THE CLASS NUMBER IN CATEGORY P

A. Term One

Term One is composed of the letter "P."

B. Term Two

Three types of entry may be used for Term Two in this category: Performer Entry, Ethnic Entry, and Collection Entry.

1. *Performer Entry*

Use the surname of the featured performer to form Term Two for recordings which feature a performer or performing group. (See section II-208 for Term Two rules.)

> "Times Are A-changin'."   **P**
> Bob **Dylan.**   **● DYLA**
> Columbia CS 8905   **TAA**
>   **D 05**

2. *Ethnic Entry*

a. Definition

Ethnic Entry refers to the use of an abbreviation for the name of an ethnic group to form Term Two so that certain recordings are grouped together. (Ethnic Entry is used only in category P.)

b. When To Use the Ethnic Entry

Use the Ethnic Entry to form Term Two when classifying recordings of authentic Cajun, Indian, Hawaiian and Eskimo music. The proper abbreviations for these are:

```
Cajun    = CAJUN
Hawaiian = HAWA
Indian   = INDI
Eskimo   = ESKI
```

> "War Whoops and Medicine Songs."   **P**
> Folkways 4381   ● **INDI**
>   **WHM**
>   **F 81**

3. *Collections Entry*

Use the abbreviation COLL to indicate "collection" if the rules for Performer Entry or Ethnic Entry do not apply.

> "Southern Appalachians Instrumental Music."   **P**
> Tradition 1007   ● **COLL**
>   **SAI**
>   **T 07**

C. Term Three

Always use the *album title* to form Term Three. (See section III-303.)

D. Term Four

The same name used for the Performer Entry in Term Two is used to form the alpha symbol in Term Four. When an Ethnic Entry or a Collections Entry appears in Term Two, use the initial of the record company's name as the alpha symbol. (See Chapter IV for Term Four rules.)

CATEGORY Q — INTERNATIONAL FOLK AND ETHNIC MUSIC

Q 1. TYPES OF RECORDINGS TO BE CLASSED IN CATEGORY Q

Class in category Q recordings of vocal and instrumental music which reflect the culture, language and traditions of foreign countries.

> "Les Chansons du Bearn, Pays Basque." RCA Fr 430.186
> "Bantu Choral Folk Songs." Folkways 6912
> "Greek Mountain Dances." Peters KT 1001
> "Hungarian Folk Songs." (Sari Barabas) Odeon S 80811
> "Ragas Prabhakali and Bhairavi." (Ali Akbar Khan)
>   Odeon MOAE 145
> "Bedouin Sahda." (Naif Agby) Audio Fidelity 6122
> "Fado." (Amalia Rodriguez) Kapp 1120

A. Popular Music

Popular music of all countries and in all languages is classed in the M categories. A problem may arise, however, when the classifier must determine whether certain music is actually popular or traditional (*i.e.:* ethnic). This problem usually occurs when dealing with the music of less familiar cultures and languages. When in doubt, the recording may be classed in category Q by country. It can be assumed that most persons seeking recordings of international folk and ethnic music are as interested in the cultural and linguistic aspects of the recording as they are in the music; therefore, placement by country will be both logical and helpful.

> "The Bracelet." (Feirouz)   **class in category MA, or in category Q under Lebanon**

Q 2. FORMATION OF THE CLASS NUMBER IN CATEGORY Q

A. Term One

Term One is composed of the letter "Q."

B. Term Two

Two types of entry may be used for Term Two in this category: Geographic Entry and Collections Entry. This is the only category in which the Geographic Entry is used, so the rules on use and formation are given here rather than in section II.

1. *Geographic Entry*

a. Definition

Geographic Entry refers to the use of the first four (or more) consecutive letters of the name of a country, or of a broad geographic area, or of a specific style of music, to form Term Two so that the recordings are grouped geographically.

b. How To Form the Geographic Entry

A Table of Abbreviations is provided at the end of section Q in which are listed the names and abbreviations to be used in Term Two. The list of countries is drawn from the 1968 edition of the *World Almanac*, and the names of some colonies and territorial dependencies are included. Instructions are given in the table for the addition of new names.

c. When To Use the Name of a Country in Term Two

Use the name of a country to form Term Two if the entire recording is devoted to the folk or ethnic music of one country.

"Greek Mountain Dances."	Q
Peters KT 1001	● GREE
	GMD
	P 01

d. When To Use the Name of a Geographic Area

Use the name of a geographic area in Term Two if the recording features the folk or ethnic music of two or more countries, all of which are located in the same geographic area. These areas are: AFRICA, ASIA, EUROPE, LATIN AMERICA, and NEAR AND MIDDLE EAST. (See Table of Abbreviations, page 101.)

"Africa South of the Sahara."	Q
Folkways 4503	● AFRICA
	AS
	F 03

e. When To Use the Name of a Specific Style

Use the name of a specific style to form Term Two if the recording features only music of that style. The specific styles of music are: CALYPSO, GYPSY, and YIDDISH. (See Table of Abbreviations, page 101.)

"Yiddish Folk Songs."	Q
Jan Peerce.	● YIDD
Vanguard 2135	PEER
	P 35

2. *Collections Entry*

Use the abbreviation COLL indicating "collection" to form Term Two if the rules for Geographic Entry do not apply.

"Folk Dances 'Round the World."	Q
Rhythms A 106	● COLL
	FDR
	R 06

C. Term Three

Use the *album title* to form Term Three when Collections Entry has been used in Term Two. If a Geographic Entry is used to form Term Two, use either the *album title* or the *name of the featured performer* to form Term Three.

1. *When to Use the Performer's Name in Term Three*

If the recording features a known performer or performing group, use the performer's surname to form Term Three so that all the recordings by that performer will be grouped together.

2. *How to Use the Performer's Name to Form Term Three*

If the performer's name is to be used in Term Three, it is treated like the Performer Entry in Term Two: use the first four consecutive letters of the artist's surname, or the first four consecutive letters of the corporate group name.

"Fado."	**Q**
Amalia **Rodriguez**.	**PORT**
Kapp 1120	● **RODR**
	R 20

D. Term Four

If the performer's name is used to form Term Three, use the initial of his surname as the alpha symbol in Term Four; otherwise, use the first initial of the record company's name as the alpha symbol. (See section IV for Term Four rules.)

Q 3. TABLE OF ABBREVIATIONS TO BE USED IN TERM TWO

This table provides the abbreviations to be used in Term Two for the names of geographic and political areas.

A. Definition of a Country

A country is treated in this list as the political, geographic unit which exists at the present time, regardless of former status or history. Therefore, there are separate abbreviations for East Germany and West Germany, and for the same reason, such areas as Lithuania, Russia, Georgia, etc., are included under the corporate heading for the Union of Soviet Socialist Republics.

B. Status of Colonies, etc.

Colonies and territorial dependencies are treated as separate entities and entry made under their own names.

Angola   **not Portugal**
Puerto Rico   **not U.S.A.**

C. Rules of Abbreviation

Use the first four consecutive letters of the American English spelling of the country's name.

  Netherlands **NETH**

If the name is composed of five letters, use all five in the entry.

  Spain **SPAIN**

If the first four consecutive letters of two names are identical, add a fifth letter to each in order to differentiate between them.

  Malawi **MALAW**
  Malaysia **MALAY**

If two countries share a name in common, use a hyphen and the initial of the modifying word which identifies each.

  North Korea **KORE-N**
  South Korea **KORE-S**

(Note that although Korea is a five-letter name, all the letters are not used because of the need to add the hyphen and identifying initial.)

TABLE OF ABBREVIATIONS

AREA ENTRIES (Broad Geographic Areas)

The function of the Area Entry is to make it possible to group together recordings of collections of music from several different countries which are related geographically. The areas selected are purposely broad and arbitrary; it is not possible to establish area entries which take into account every possible geographic and cultural relationship, and the creation of too many such areas has been avoided, since it would be unnecessarily cumbersome for both classifier and record user.

AREA	DESCRIPTION	ABBREVIATION
Africa	The continent of Africa and adjacent islands, such as Madagascar, the Canaries, etc.	AFRICA
Asia	Asia ceases at the western boundaries of the U.S.S.R., Turkey, and India; includes all of the South Pacific area.	ASIA
Europe	Europe starts at the western boundaries of the U.S.S.R. and Turkey; includes islands of the Mediterranean and the British Isles.	EUROPE
Latin America	South America, Central America, Mexico, and the islands of the Caribbean.	LATIN
Near and Middle East	Turkey, Syria, Iraq, Iran, Afghanistan, Pakistan, Israel, Jordan, and the Arabian Peninsula.	EAST

STYLE ENTRIES

These styles transcend national boundaries. Two of them in particular have no fixed general geographic area. In the case of calypso music, it is felt that those who use these recordings will find it more satisfactory to have them grouped together, rather than divided by individual country.

STYLE	ABBREVIATION
Calypso	CALY
Gypsy	GYPS
Yiddish	YIDD

NAMES OF COUNTRIES, ISLANDS, COLONIES AND TERRITORIAL DEPENDENCIES

NAME	ABBREVI-ATION	NAME	ABBREVI-ATION
Afghanistan	AFGH	Egypt	EGYPT
Albania	ALBA	El Salvador	ELSA
Algeria	ALGE	England (see British Isles)	
Andorra	ANDO	Estonia (see U.S.S.R.)	
Argentina	ARGE	Ethiopia	ETHI
Armenia (see U.S.S.R.)		Finland	FINL
Australia	AUSTRA	France	FRAN
Austria	AUSTRI	Gabon Republic	GABON
Azerbaijan (see U.S.S.R.)		Gambia	GAMB
Bahama Islands	BAHA	Georgia (see U.S.S.R.)	
Bali	BALI	Germany, East	GERM-E
Barbados	BARB	Germany, West	GERM-W
Belgium	BELG	Ghana	GHANA
Bermuda	BERM	Greece	GREE
Bhutan	BHUT	Guatemala	GUAT
Bolivia	BOLI	Guinea	GUIN
Borneo (see Malaysia or		Guyana	GUYA
Indonesia)		Haiti	HAITI
Botswana	BOTS	Honduras	HOND
Brazil	BRAZ	Hong Kong	HONG
British Isles	BRIT	Hungary	HUNG
(includes England,		Iceland	ICEL
Scotland, Wales and		India	INDIA
Northern Ireland)		Indonesia	INDO
Bulgaria	BULG	Iran	IRAN
Burma	BURMA	Iraq	IRAQ
Burundi	BURU	Ireland	IREL
Byelorussia (see U.S.S.R.)		Ireland, Northern (see	
Cambodia	CAMB	British Isles)	
Cameroon	CAME	Israel	ISRA
Canada	CANA	Italy	ITALY
Central African Republic	CENT	Ivory Coast	IVORY
Ceylon	CEYL	Jamaica	JAMA
Chad	CHAD	Japan	JAPAN
Chile	CHILE	Jordan	JORD
China (People's	CHIN-P	Kenya	KENYA
Republic)		Kirghizia (see U.S.S.R.)	
China (Republic)	CHIN-R	Korea, North	KORE-N
Colombia	COLO	Korea, South	KORE-S
Congo	CONGO	Kuwait	KUWA
Corsica	CORS	Laos	LAOS
Costa Rica	COSTA	Latvia (see U.S.S.R.)	
Cuba	CUBA	Lebanon	LEBE
Cyprus	CYPR	Lesotho	LESO
Czechoslovakia	CZEC	Liberia	LIBE
Dahomey	DAHO	Libya	LIBYA
Denmark	DENM	Liechtenstein	LIEC
Dominican Republic	DOMI	Lithuania (see U.S.S.R.)	
Ecuador	ECUA	Luxembourg	LUXE

NAME	ABBREVI-ATION	NAME	ABBREVIATION
Malagasy	MALAG	Senegal	SENE
Malawi	MALAW	Sierra Leone	SIER
Malaya (see Malaysia)		Singapore	SING
Malaysia	MALAY	Somalia	SOMA
Maldive Islands	MALD	South Africa	SOUT-A
Mali	MALI	South West Africa	SOUT-W
Malta	MALTA	Spain	SPAIN
Mauritania	MAUR	Sudan	SUDAN
Mexico	MEXI	Sweden	SWED
Moldavia (see U.S.S.R.)		Switzerland	SWIT
Monaco	MONO	Syria	SYRIA
Mongolia	MONG	Tahiti	TAHI
Morocco	MORO	Tanzania	TANZ
Mozambique	MOZA	Thailand	THAI
Muscat and Oman	MUSC	Tibet (see China,	
Nepal	NEPAL	People's Republic)	
Netherlands	NETH	Togo	TOGO
New Zealand	NEWZ	Trinidad and Tobago	TRIN
Nicaragua	NICA	Tunisia	TUNI
Niger	NIGER	Turkey	TURK
Nigeria	NIGERI	Uganda	UGAN
Norway	NORW	Ukraine (see U.S.S.R.)	
Oman (see Muscat and		Union of Soviet Socialist	USSR
Oman)		Republics	
Pakistan	PAKI	United Arab Republic	
Panama	PANA	(see Egypt)	
Paraguay	PARA	United Kingdom (see	
Peru	PERU	British Isles and	
Philippines	PHIL	individual colonies	
Poland	POLA	and protectorates)	
Portugal	PORT	Upper Volta	UPPER
Puerto Rico	PUER	Uruguay	URUG
Rhodesia	RHOD	Uzbek (see U.S.S.R.)	
Rumania	RUMA	Wales (see British Isles)	
Russia (see U.S.S.R.)		Venezuela	VENE
Rwanda	RWAN	Vietnam, North	VIET-N
Samoa, American	SAMO-A	Vietnam, South	VIET-S
Samoa, Western	SAMO-W	Yemen	YEMEN
San Marino	SANM	Yugoslavia	YUGO
Saudi Arabia	SAUDI	Zambia	ZAMB
Scotland (see British			
Isles)			

CATEGORY R — HOLIDAY MUSIC

R 1. TYPES OF RECORDINGS TO BE CLASSED IN CATEGORY R

Class in category R recordings of vocal or instrumental music, in any language, which the album titles indicate have been produced specifically for use on Christian, Jewish, and other religious and national holidays commonly observed.

> "Here We Come A-Caroling." (Ray Coniff Singers)
>   Columbia CS 9206
> "German Carols." (Vienna Choir Boys)
>   Capitol DT 10445
> "Christmas Album." (Elvis Presley)
>   RCA Victor LSP 1915
> "Glory of Christmas." (101 Strings) Somerset XM 4
> "Holiday Music for Happy People." (Bobby Roberts)
>   Decca 78818

A. Classical Music

Recordings of vocal and instrumental works, such as operas, oratorios, cantatas, and orchestral suites, which have a religious or patriotic theme and, therefore, are often performed at the time of certain holidays, are not classed in category R, but are classed according to their musical form (regardless of the wording or design of the album cover).

> Bach: "Christmas Oratorio."   **class in category C**
> Handel: "Messiah."   **class in category C**
> Tchaikovsky: "Nutcracker Suite."   **class in category EB**
> Menotti: "Amahl and the Night Visitors."   **class in category B**

B. Classical Music — Holiday Collections

Class in category R recordings of collections of excerpts from classical works and religious songs when the album title indicates the collection was produced specifically for holiday use.

> "Great Instrumental Christmas Music."
> Hollywood Pops Orchestra.
> Capitol ST 2980

> "A Christmas Offering."
> Leontyne Price.
> London 25280

R 2. FORMATION OF THE CLASS NUMBER IN CATEGORY R

A. Term One

Term One is composed of the letter "R."

B. Term Two

Two types of entry may be used for Term Two in this category: Performer Entry and Collections Entry.

1. *Performer Entry*

Use the surname of the featured performer or the name of the performing group to form Term Two.

"English Medieval Christmas Carols."	R
New York Pro Musica Antiqua.	● **NEWY**
Counterpoint 5521	EMC
	N 21

2. *Collections Entry*

Use the abbreviation COLL indicating "collection" in Term Two when there is more than one featured performer or performing group.

"Renaissance Choral Music for Christmas."	R
Hilversum N.C.R.V. Vocal Ensemble, Voorberg;	● **COLL**
Martinsfinken Kaufberger, Hahn; Hannover	RCH
Niedersachsischer Singkreis, Trader.	N 95
Nonesuch 71095	

C. Term Three

Always use the *album title* to form Term Three. (See section III-303 for Term Three rules.)

D. Term Four

The same name used for the Performer Entry in Term Two is used to form the alpha symbol in Term Four. If Collections Entry is used in Term Two, use the initial of the record company's name as the alpha symbol. (See chapter IV for specific Term Four rules.)

CATEGORY S — VARIETIES AND HUMOR

S 1. TYPES OF RECORDINGS TO BE CLASSED IN CATEGORY S

Class in category S recordings of theatrical entertainment and humor, with or without music accompaniment, such as original monologs, vaudeville and nightclub acts, works of musical satire, and stage reviews. (Do not include musical shows, musical reviews, or plays.)

"Mom Always Liked You Best." (Smothers Brothers)
  Mercury 61051

"PDQ Bach." (Peter Schickele) Vanguard 79195

"Anna Russell Sings?" (Anna Russell)
  Columbia ML 4594

"This Is It!" (Bob Newhart) Warner Bros. S 1717

"Super Bloopers." Jubilee 2004

"Mark Twain Tonight." (Hal Holbrook)
  Columbia OS 3080

"The Loves of Charles II." (Cornelia Otis Skinner)
  Spoken Arts 813

S 2. FORMATION OF THE CLASS NUMBER IN CATEGORY S

A. Term One

Term One is composed of the letter "S."

B. Term Two

Two types of entry may be used for Term Two in this category: Performer Entry, and Title Entry.

1. *Performer Entry*

Use the surname of the featured performer to form Term Two when classifying recordings which feature a performer or performing group.

"Two Hundred Miles Per Hour."	S
Bill **Cosby**.	• COSB
Warner Brothers S 1757	THM
	C 57

2 *Title Entry*

Use the Title Entry to form Term Two when neither a performer nor a performing group is featured on the recording.

"**Super** Bloopers."	S
Jubilee 2004	• SUPE
	SB
	J 04

C. Term Three

Always use the *album title* to form Term Three. (See section III-303 for Term Three rules.)

D. Term Four

The same name used for the Performer Entry in Term Two is used to form the alpha symbol in Term Four. If Title Entry is used in Term Two, use the initial of the record company's name as the alpha symbol.

CATEGORY T — PLAYS

T 1. TYPES OF RECORDINGS TO BE CLASSED IN CATEGORY T

Class in category T recordings of complete plays or excerpts from plays, in any language, and recordings which deal with the appreciation, history and criticism of plays and playwrights.

Racine: "Iphigenie."
Aristophanes: "Lysistrata."
Albee: "Who's Afraid of Virginia Woolff?"
"Plays and Memories: William Butler Yeats." Spoken Arts 752
"Golden Treasury of French Drama." Spoken Arts 715

T 2. FORMATION OF THE CLASS NUMBER IN CATEGORY T

A. Term One

Term One is composed of the letter "T."

B. Term Two

Four types of entry may be used for Term Two in this category: Author Entry, Person-As-Subject Entry, Language Entry, and Collections Entry.

1. *Author Entry*

Use the surname of the author to form Term Two if the plays or excerpts of plays on the recording are all by one author, or if the text on the recording is by one author.

Sheridan: "School for Scandal."	**T**
Kirkland Acting Group	● **SHER**
Command S 13002	**SS**
	K 02
Shakespeare: "Soliloquies and	**T**
Scenes from Shakespeare for Actors."	● **SHAK**
Edwards and MacLimmoir.	**SSS**
Spoken Arts 836/7	**E 36**
"Dear Audience."	**T**
Sample scenes and commentary on	● **YURK**
acting by Blanche **Yurka.**	**DA**
Folkways 9841	**Y 41**

2. *Person-As-Subject Entry*

If the recording discusses or documents the life, works, or significance of a playwright, use the surname of the playwright to form Term Two.

"Plays and Memories: William Butler **Yeats.**"	**T**
Excerpts from his plays read by	● **YEAT**
Nolan and Watkinson; Lennox	**PMW**
Robinson discusses his memories of	**N 52**
personal friend Yeats.	
Spoken Arts 752	

3. *Language Entry*

Recordings of anonymous works, and recordings to which the rules for Author Entry and Person-As-Subject Entry do not apply, are entered by Language Entry, formed according to the rules found in section II-214.

"Golden Treasury of French Drama."	**T**
Barrault and Renaud.	● **FREN**
Spoken Arts 715	**GTF**
	B 15
"Noh Plays of Japan."	**T**
Tokyo Noh Players.	● **JAPA**
Caedmon 2019	**NPJ**
	T 19

4. *Collections Entry*

When there are collections of plays or excerpts of plays representing more than one language on the recording, use the abbreviation COLL indicating "collection" for Term Two.

C. Term Three

Use the *album title* in Term Three after using Person-As-Subject Entry, Language Entry or Collections Entry in Term Two. If Author Entry is used in Term Two, and there is only one play on the recording, use the title of the play (*i.e., work title*) to form Term Three. If there is more than one play, use the *album title*.

D. Term Four

Use the surname of a featured performer or the name of the featured performing group to form the alpha symbol. (See section IV-411.)

CATEGORY U — POETRY

U 1. TYPES OF RECORDINGS TO BE CLASSED IN CATEGORY U

Class in category U recordings of poetry in any language, and recordings which deal with the appreciation, history, and criticism of poetry and poets.

> "Ancient Greek Poetry." Folkways 9984
> Chaucer:"Canterbury Tales."
> Robert Frost: "Reads His Own Works." Decca 9127
> "Golden Treasury of Italian Verse." Spoken Arts 771
> Schreiber: "Understanding and Appreciation of Poetry."
> Folkways 9120
> "The Poet Speaks." (series) Argo 451/6
> "Poetas Colombianos." Miami 1252
> "Homage to Dylan Thomas." Argo 29

U 2. FORMATION OF THE CLASS NUMBER IN CATEGORY U

A. Term One

Term One is composed of the letter "U."

B. Term Two

Four types of entry may be used for Term Two in this category: Author Entry, Person-As-Subject Entry, Language Entry, and Collections Entry.

1. *Author Entry*

Use the surname of the author to form Term Two if all the poetry or all the text on the recording is by one author.

Tennyson: "Idylls of the King." Basil Rathbone, reader. Caedmon 2022	U ● TENN IK R 22
"Marianne **Moore** Reads Her Own Poetry." Marianne Moore, reader. Decca 9135	U ● MOOR RHO M 35
Baxter: "The Nature of Poetry." Dr. Frank Baxter, author and reader. Spoken Arts 703	U ● BAXT NP B 03

2. *Person-As-Subject Entry*

If the recording discusses or documents the life, works, or significance of a poet, use the surname of that poet to form Term Two.

"Homage to Dylan **Thomas.**" Burton, Griffith, MacNeice Williams, readers. Argo 29	U ● THOM HDT B 29

3. *Language Entry*

Recordings of works by anonymous poets, and recordings to which the rules for Author Entry and Person-As-Subject Entry do not apply, are entered in Term Two by Language Entry, formed according to the rules found in section II-214.

"Anthology of 19th Century American Poets." Audley and Scourby, readers. Spoken Arts 963	U ● AMER ANC A 63
"Treasury of Oliver Goldsmith, Thomas Gray and William Collins." Casson, reader. Spoken Arts 927	U ● ENGL TOG C 27

"Golden Treasury of Apollinaire,
    Cocteau, Eluard and Aragon."
Barrault, Duby, Mercure, Philipe,
    readers.
Spoken Arts 801
	U
	● FREN
	GTA
	B 01

"Beowulf." Coghill and Davis, readers. Spoken Arts 918	U ● ENGL BEO C 18

4. *Collections Entry*

If the poetry of more than one language is represented on the recording, use the abbreviation COLL indicating "collection" in Term Two.

"American and British Poetry."   **U**
Gryphon 902/4   ● **COLL**
      ABP
      G 02

(According to rule II-214-B5, American poetry is separated from English poetry in record collections used in the United States; therefore, a recording with both English and American poetry must be given a Collections Entry in Term Two.)

C. Term Three

Use the *album title* to form Term Three when Person-As-Subject Entry, Language Entry, or Collections Entry have been used in Term Two. If Author Entry is used in Term Two, and there is only one poem on the recording, use the title of the poem (*i.e., work title*) to form Term Three. If there is more than one poem, use the *album title*.

D. Term Four

Use the surname of the featured performer or the name of the featured performing group to form the alpha symbol in Term Four. (See section IV-411 for Term Four rules.)

CATEGORY V — PROSE

V 1. TYPES OF RECORDINGS TO BE CLASSED IN CATEGORY V

Class in category V recordings containing readings of prose literature in all languages, both fiction and non-fiction, including recordings of informative talks, sermons, and lectures, as well as recordings which deal with the appreciation, history and criticism of prose literature and writers, or with literature as a general subject (that is, covering all forms of literature: prose, drama and poetry).

> Hawthorne: "The Scarlet Letter."
>
> "Literature of Revolutionary America." Lexington 7673/4
>
> Priestly: "Delight." (Essays)
>
> Teller: "The Size and Nature of the Universe." (Lecture) Spoken Arts 735
>
> Slosson: "The Uses of History." Spoken Arts 702
>
> "Inaugural Addresses of Washington, Jefferson, Lincoln and Theodore Roosevelt." (McGovern, reader.) Spoken Arts 966
>
> Behan: "Behan on Joyce." Folkways 9826
>
> "Love Letters of the Irish Patriots." Spoken Arts 821
>
> "Genesis: The Creation and Noah." (Anderson, reader.) Caedmon 1096
>
> Franklin: "Autobiography." (Lemisch, reader.) Folkways 9771

A. Bible Recordings

Class in this category all recordings of Bible readings, both prose and poetry.

> "Poetry and Prophecy of the Old Testament." Bikel, reader. Elektra 7220
>
> "Psalms of David." Moorehead, reader. Lyric-Art 003

B. Poetry and Prose

Class in this category recordings which include works of both prose and poetry.

> Poe: "Poems and Tales." (Rathbone, reader.) Caedmon 1028
>
> Emerson: "Selections from Essays, Poetry and Journals." (Cort, reader.) Folkways 9758

111

C. Speeches

Class in this category readings of speeches. (Speeches relating to an historic event and recorded at the time of delivery, or reread as part of an historical reenactment [documentary], are classed in category W [DOCUMENTARY].)

> "We Shall Overcome."
> Documentary recording of the March   **class in category W**
> on Washington, Aug. 28, 1963
> with the original address:
> "I Have a Dream," by Dr. Martin
> Luther King, Jr.
> Folkways 5592

> "Inaugural Addresses of Washington,
> Jefferson, Lincoln, and Theodore
> Roosevelt," read by Sen. George   **class in category V**
> McGovern.
> Spoken Arts 966

V 2. FORMATION OF THE CLASS NUMBER IN CATEGORY V

A. Term One

Term One is composed of the letter "V."

B. Term Two

Five types of entry may be used for Term Two in this category: Author Entry, Bible Entry, Person-As-Subject Entry, Language Entry, and Collections Entry.

1. *Author Entry*

Use the surname of the author to form Term Two if all the prose works on the recording are by one author.

> **Boswell:** "London Journal"   V
> Quayle, reader.   ● BOSW
> Caedmon 1093   LJ
>   Q 93

> **Robinson:** "Books and the Bad Life."   V
> (A talk on authors of the 1920's   ● ROBI
>   by Kenneth Allan Robinson.)   BBL
> Spoken Arts 834   R 34

2. *Bible Entry*

Use the entry "BIBLE" in Term Two for all recordings of readings from the Bible, as well as for talks and lectures on the Bible as literature. (Recordings of sermons are given an Author Entry.)

> "Pat Boone Reads from the Bible."   V
> Boone, reader.   ● BIBLE
> Dot 3402   PBR
>   B 02

3. *Person-As-Subject Entry*

If the recording discusses or documents the life, works, or significance of an author, use the surname of that author to form Term Two.

Behan: "Brendan Behan on **Joyce**."	**V**
Behan, speaker.	● **JOYC**
Folkways 9826	**BBJ**
	B 26

4. *Language Entry*

Recordings of anonymous works, and recordings to which the rules for Author Entry, Bible Entry and Person-As-Subject Entry do not apply, are entered by Language Entry in Term Two, according to the rules found in section II-214.

"Golden Treasury of French Literature."	**V**
Gaussens, reader.	● **FREN**
Spoken Arts 822	**GTF**
	G 22

"Irish Literary Tradition."	**V**
Frank O'Connor introduces and	● **IRISH**
reads cross section of Irish	**ILT**
literature.	**0 25**
Folkways 9825	

5. *Collections Entry*

If the prose works of more than one language are represented on the recording, use the Collections Entry in Term Two.

C. Term Three

Use the *album title* in Term Three after Bible Entry, Person-As-Subject Entry, Language Entry, and Collections Entry. If Author Entry is used in Term Two and there is only one prose work on the recording, use the *work title;* if there is more than one work, use the *album title.*

D. Term Four

Use the surname of the featured performer or the name of the featured performing group to form the alpha symbol in Term Four. (See section IV-411 for specific Term Four rules.)

CATEGORY W — DOCUMENTARY

W 1. TYPES OF RECORDINGS TO BE CLASSED IN CATEGORY W

Class in category W recordings of documentaries: that is, reenactments or "live" transcriptions of historical events; also, dramatized biography. Include recorded interviews and group discussions.

> "Inaugural Addresses of Franklin D. Roosevelt, Harry S.
>   Truman, Dwight D. Eisenhower and John F. Kennedy."
> (In the original voices.)
> Spoken Arts 825/7

> Eban: "United Nation Speeches."
> Spoken Arts 986/8

> "I Can Hear It Now."
> (Pre-war broadcasts.)
> Columbia D3L 366

> "Mormon Pioneers."
> Columbia LS 1025

> "Years of Lightning—Day of Drums."
> Capitol ST 2486

> "Portrait of Adlai Stevenson."
> (Conversation between Stevenson and Arnold Michaelis.)
> Spoken Arts 770

> "Berkeley Teach-In: Vietnam."
> (14 speeches from first student demonstration,
>   recorded on campus.)
> Folkways 5765

> "The Untypical Politician."
> (Compiled and narrated by Myles Platt.)
> Folkways 5501

> "Diary of the American Revolution."
> Lexington 7712/3

> "Winston S. Churchill: His Memoirs and His Speeches."
> (Recorded by Churchill.)
> London XL1/12

A. Music Documentaries

Recordings of documentaries on music and musicians are classed in category A (MUSIC APPRECIATION), or in the appropriate categories of the popular music section (K through R).

> "The World's Vocal Arts."
> (Vocal styles from around
>   the world, compiled by
>   Henry Cowell.)
> Folkways 4510   **class in category A**

> "The Story of Jazz."
> Langston Hughes, author
>   and narrator.
> Folkways 7312   **class in category MJ**

W 2. FORMATION OF THE CLASS NUMBER IN CATEGORY W

A. Term One

Term One is composed of the letter "W."

B. Term Two

Three types of entry may be used for Term Two in this category:
Author Entry, Person-As-Subject Entry, and Title Entry.

1. *Author Entry*

To form Term Two, use the surname of the author of the speech or
the narration on the recording if the author also acts as performer and
delivers the speech or narration himself.

Kennedy: "Inaugural Address 1961"	W
Spoken Arts 827	● KENN
	IA
	K 27

"The Glory of Negro History."	W
Documentary written and narrated	● HUGH
by Langston **Hughes.**	GNH
Folkways 7752	H 52

2. *Person-As-Subject Entry*

If the topic of the recording is an individual, use the surname of that
individual to form Term Two.

"That Was the Week That Was."	W
(On the assassination of	● KENN
President John F. **Kennedy.**)	TWW
Decca 7 9116	D 16

"Portrait of Adlai **Stevenson.**"	W
Conversation between Stevenson	● STEV
and Michaelis.	PAS
Spoken Arts 770	M 70

"The Original Confession of	W
Nat **Turner** as Given to T.R. Gray."	● TURN
Read by B. Peters; discussion	OCN
with Peters, Aptheker and Clarke.	A 39
CMS 539	

3. *Title Entry*

Use the title of the documentary to form Term Two if the rules for
Author Entry and Person-As-Subject Entry given above do not apply.

"**Born** to Live."	W
(20th anniversary of Hiroshima;	● BORN
compiled and edited by S. Terkel.)	BL
Folkways 5525	T 25

"**America's** Men in Space."	W
Powers and Haney, narrators.	● AMER
CMS 1000	AMS
	H 00

C. Term Three

Always use the *album title* to form Term Three. (See section III-303.)

D. Term Four

The surname of the narrator or principal speaker is usually used to form the alpha symbol in Term Four. (See section IV-411-A5 for complete rules.)

CATEGORY X — INSTRUCTIONAL RECORDINGS

X 1. TYPES OF RECORDINGS TO BE CLASSED IN CATEGORY X

Class in category X recordings which have been produced to teach or improve specific skills such as shorthand, dictation, Morse code, dancing, accounting, etc.

"Instant Care and Training of Dogs."
Instant 3001

"Color-matic Way to Play the Guitar."
Columbia CIS 101

"How to Avoid Probate." (Dacey)
Philips 600229

"Conversation Course in German."
Conversa-phone 133

"Music for Isometrics."
Musicor 2014

"Legal Dictation."
Conversa-phone 205

A. Music Instruction

Class in category X recordings which give instruction in musical theory, singing, and the playing of musical instruments, or which are designed to help musicians in their practicing.

"The Twelve String Guitar." (Pete Seeger.)
Folkways 8371

"Master Class."
Stradivari 101

"Modal Counterpoint." (Nelhybel.)
Folkways 3606

"Music Minus One Series."

"Piano Accompaniment to Song Repertoire:
Anthology of Modern French Song."
Educo 6005

X 2. FORMATION OF THE CLASS NUMBER IN CATEGORY X

A. Term One

Term One is composed of the letter "X."

B. Term Two

Only one type of entry may be used for Term Two in this category: Instructional Subject Entry. Since category X is the only category in which Instructional Subject Entry is used, the rules on its use and formation are given here rather than in chapter II.

1. *Instructional Subject Entry*

a. Definition

Instructional Subject Entry refers to the use in Term Two of the first four (or more) consecutive letters of the name of a skill. There are two types of skill names used in Term Two: Basic Skill Names, and the Individual Key Names formed from the album title.

b. Basic Instructional Skills — Group Names

Since recordings are for listening, they are best suited to the instruction of skills in which the ear must be trained to distinguish various sounds, such as music and foreign languages, or in which the body and mind must react rapidly to spoken or musical commands, such as shorthand and dancing. Seven Basic Groupings have been designated for the skills most effectively taught by recordings. The names for these groups and the appropriate Term Two abbreviations are as follows:

SKILL	TYPE OF RECORDINGS	ABBREVIATION USED IN TERM TWO
Dance	Recordings of instruction in all forms of dancing, such as ballet, folk, and ballroom, as well as recordings of music specifically for the practice of these forms of dancing.	DANCE
Dictation	Recordings of instruction and dictation of material to teach and improve shorthand and typing skills.	DICT
English	Recordings of instruction on all aspects of the English language, such as reading skills, speech improvement, creative writing, grammar, English as a foreign language, etc.	ENGLISH
Exercise	Recordings which deal with physical fitness, such as reducing exercises, gymnastics, etc.	EXER
Language	Recordings which offer instruction and practice in learning all foreign languages.	LANG
Morse Code	Recordings which offer instruction and practice in learning Morse Code.	MORSE
Music	Recordings which offer instruction on musical theory, singing, and the playing of musical instruments, as well as recordings specifically designed for the practice of singing and of musical instruments.	MUSIC

117

c. Key Names of Skills

When a recording does not fit into one of the seven basic groups named in 1B, then use the name of the specific skill being taught, as indicated in the title of the recording. As a rule, use only the first four letters of the name to form Term Two. An exception is made in the case of five-letter words: all five letters may be used.

"Building Balanced **Child**ren."	**X**
(Skousen)	● **CHILD**
Key 770	**BBC**
	S 70
"**Law,** You and Narcotics."	**X**
(Hurst)	● **LAW**
Law 7108	**LYN**
	H 08
"New **Math.**" (Lanahan)	**X**
RCA Victor LPM 8501/8	● **MATH**
	NM
	L 01
"Auscultation of the **Heart.**"	**X**
London 5873	● **HEART**
	AH
	L 73
"Instant Care and Training	**X**
of **Dogs.**"	● **DOGS**
Instant 3001	**ICT**
	I 01
"How to Avoid **Prob**ate."	**X**
(Dacey)	● **PROB**
Philips 600229	**HAP**
	D 29

C. Term Three

When a "key name" is used to form Term Two, always use the *album title* in Term Three. When a "basic group name" is used in Term Two, the formation of Term Three will depend on the particular group name and the specific recording.

1. *Exercise, Dance, English, Morse Code*

Always use the *album title* to form Term Three when the abbreviations for Exercise (EXER), Dance (DANCE), English (ENGLISH) or Morse Code (MORSE) are used in Term Two.

"How to Write."	**X**
(Schreiber)	**ENGLISH**
Folkways 9106	● **HW**
	S 06

2. *Dictation*

When the abbreviation for Dictation (DICT) is used in Term Two, indicate in Term Three whether the topic is shorthand (SHO) or typing (TYP). If both topics are covered in the recording, then use the *album title* to form Term Three.

"Steno-Disc: Business Letters	X
and Legal Dictation."	DICT
Keane 504	● SHO (shorthand)
	K 04
"Typing Course: Living Method."	X
Living Language MT	DICT
	● TYP (typing)
	L

3. *Language*

When the abbreviation for Language (LANG) is used in Term Two, indicate in Term Three which language is being taught by using the first three letters of the name of the language to form Term Three.

"Getting Along in French."	X
(Pei)	LANG
Folkways 8141	● FRE
	P 41

4. *Music*

When the group word for Music (MUSIC) is used in Term Two and the recording deals with instruction on the playing of a musical instrument, indicate which instrument by using the first three letters of the name of the instrument to form Term Three. If instruction is for the voice, use the abbreviation "VOI" in Term Three. For all other recordings on music instruction, use the *album title* to form Term Three.

"Banjo Instruction."	X
(Pete Seeger)	MUSIC
Folkways 8303	● BAN (instrument)
	S 03
"Master Class."	X
(Persinger)	MUSIC
Stradivari 101	● VOI (Voice)
	P 01
"Modal Counterpoint."	X
(Nelhybel)	MUSIC
Folkways 3606	● MC (album title)
	N 06

D. Term Four

If an individual instructor is featured on the recording, use the initial of his surname as the alpha symbol in Term Four. If an individual is not featured, then use the initial of the record company's name as the alpha symbol in Term Four.

CATEGORY Y — SOUNDS AND SPECIAL EFFECTS

Y 1. TYPES OF RECORDINGS TO BE CLASSED IN CATEGORY Y

Class in category Y recordings of transcriptions and reproductions of all types of natural and man-made sounds, such as the sounds of applause, birds, racing cars, calliopes, city traffic, etc.

"Big Sounds of the Drags."
Capitol ST 2001

"Stereo Frequency Test Record."
Columbia STR 100

"N.Y. Central Steam Locomotives."
Folkways 6155

"Silent Movie Music."
Major 1004

"Home Movie Sound Effects."
Audio Fidelity 7018

"Sounds of the Junk Yard."
Folkways 6143

"Sounds of Animals."
Folkways 6124

"Sounds of Jerusalem."
Folkways 8552

"Under the Big Top."
Somerset/Stereo Fidelity 29600

"Bidden Collection of Music Boxes."
Rivoli 10

Y 2. FORMATION OF THE CLASS NUMBER IN CATEGORY Y

A. Term One

Term One is composed of the letter "Y."

B. Term Two

Two types of entry may be used for Term Two in this category: Sounds Subject Entry and Collections Entry. Since this is the only category in which Sounds Subject Entry is used, the rules on the use and formation of that entry are given here rather than in chapter II.

1. *Sounds Subject Entry*

a. Definition

Sounds Subject Entry refers to the use in Term Two of the first four (or more) consecutive letters of the name of a sound. A sample table of "sound" names and their abbreviations is provided; these have been established in the light of recorded material currently available. New entries may be established when necessary. Every entry should try to identify the particular sound or group of sounds on the recording. This identification is usually accomplished by using a key word from the title of the album to form Term Two. The entries are composed of four letters, unless there are only five letters in the word, in which case all five letters may be used.

SOUND		ABBREVIATION IN TERM TWO
Birds	(songs and calls of all types of birds)	**BIRDS**
Calliope		**CALL**
Cars	(sounds of motors, races, etc.)	**CARS**
Circus		**CIRC**
Music	(background music for home movies, music boxes, etc.)	**MUSIC**
Nature	(collections of sounds of field, forest and sea; include bird sounds when combined with other specific sounds of nature)	**NATURE**
Places	(sounds of cities, countries and areas)	**PLACES**
Tests	(testing recordings for electronic equipment)	**TESTS**
Trains		**TRAINS**

2. *Collections Entry*

Use the abbreviation COLL indicating "collection" in Term Two for recordings which contain sounds of more than one major type, and for miscellaneous collections of all types of sounds or sound effects.

"Assorted Sound Effects." Folkways 6181	X ● **COLL** **ASE** **F 81**
"Sound Patterns." Folkways 6130	X ● **COLL** **SP** **F 30**

C. Term Three

Always use the *album title* to form Term Three.

D. Term Four

Use the initial of the record company's name to form the alpha symbol in Term Four, unless the name of the individual who made the recording is prominently featured. (See section IV-411-B for Term Four rules for "Sounds" recordings.)

CATEGORY Z — CHILDREN'S RECORDINGS

Z 1. STRUCTURE OF CATEGORY Z

Category Z is intended for children's recordings; that is, recordings produced specifically to be used by and with children. The category is divided into three sub-categories:

> ZI — Instructional Recordings
> ZM — Music Recordings
> ZS — Spoken Recordings

Z 2. DEFINITION OF "CHILDREN'S RECORDINGS" AND "RECORDINGS COLLECTIONS FOR CHILDREN"

A Children's Recording is defined as one produced specifically for children, with an indication of the intended audience on the album cover. A Recordings Collection for Children is a collection maintained for the use and enjoyment of children which may contain many recordings not produced solely for children.

Z 3. USE AND CONTENT OF CATEGORY Z

If the library maintains a unified collection of recordings, with adult and childrens recordings housed together, then category Z should contain only children's recordings.

If the library maintains a separate recordings collection for children, housed apart from the general recordings collection, category Z may operate as an independent class system, and contain all types of recordings for use and enjoyment by children. Because many recordings not produced specifically for children might be included in this type of collection, the use and content of category Z is dependent upon the administrative decisions of the individual library.*

Unless the individual library's choice of policy is made known, those who use the ANSCR scheme on a commercial basis must assume that category Z will contain only recordings produced specifically for children, and will classify those recordings by the standard category Z rules.

Z 4. GUIDE TO CLASSIFICATION IN THE Z CATEGORIES

The rules and definitions under each sub-category indicate how to class children's recordings, and how to class other recordings to be included in a children's collection.

*In a unified collection, for example, a recording of Tchaikovsky's *Nutcracker Suite* is classed in category EB (BALLET MUSIC). In a separate recordings collection for children, this same recording might be included and classed in category ZM (MUSIC RECORDINGS FOR CHILDREN). This same basic philosophy is followed for children's book collections in the use of simplified Dewey class numbers and special subject headings.

CATEGORY ZI — INSTRUCTIONAL RECORDINGS FOR CHILDREN

ZI 1. TYPES OF RECORDINGS TO BE CLASSED IN CATEGORY ZI

Class in category ZI recordings which are designed to teach or improve specific skills, and recordings which deal with factual subjects, such as biographies, documentaries, history and real adventure, science, etc.

"Learn to Add and Subtract."
Conversa-phone 641

"Nature Guide about Birds, Bees, Beavers and Bears."
Disney 1300

"Napoleon and the Battle of Waterloo."
Enrichment 306

"Great Stories from the Bible."
Word 3029

"Let's Build a House."
Vocalion 3762

"Do It Yourself Puppet Show."
Harmony 9547

ZI 2. FORMATION OF THE CLASS NUMBER IN CATEGORY ZI

The class number is composed of only three terms.

A. Term One

Term One is composed of the letters "ZI."

B. Term Two

Term Two is composed of the first word of the title of the album. Use the entire word up to a maximum of seven letters, and disregard articles.

"Learning to Tell Time Is Fun." Disney 1263	ZI ● LEARNIN D 63
"Let's Play Trains." Harmony 9513	ZI ● LETS H 13

C. Term Three

Term Three is composed of an alpha symbol and the last two digits of the commercial record number. The alpha symbol is the initial of the record company's name.

ZI 3. HOW TO CLASS OTHER RECORDINGS IN A CHILDREN'S COLLECTION

Instructional recordings, recordings of non-fiction material such as history, science, biography, and documentaries which were not produced as children's recordings may be classed in category ZI if a separate record collection is maintained for children.

"Voices of History."
United Artists 6351

"Benjamin Franklin Autobiography."
Folkways 9771

Use the three-term class number that is used for children's recordings to class the above examples.

A. Term One

Term One is composed of the letters "ZI."

B. Term Two

Term Two is composed of the first word of the title of the album. Use the entire word, up to a maximum of seven letters, and disregard articles.

"Benjamin Franklin's Autobiography."
Folkways 9771

ZI
● **BENJAMIN**
F 71

C. Term Three

Term Three is composed of an alpha symbol and the last two digits of the commercial record number. The alpha symbol is the initial of the record company's name.

CATEGORY ZM — MUSIC RECORDINGS FOR CHILDREN

ZM 1. TYPES OF RECORDINGS TO BE CLASSED IN CATEGORY ZM

Class in category ZM recordings of vocal and instrumental music; include biographies of musicians and composers which contain musical examples and excerpts.

"Child's Introduction to the Orchestra."
Golden 1

"Songs from All Around the World."
Disneyland 1226

"Liszt: Story in Words and Music."
Desto 301

"Children Sing the Seder."
Tikva 82

"French Children's Songs."
Folkways 8003

ZM 2. FORMATION OF THE CLASS NUMBER IN CATEGORY ZM

The class number is composed of only three terms.

A. Term One

Term One is composed of the letters "ZM."

B. Term Two

Term Two is composed of the first word of the title of the album. Use the entire word, up to a maximum of seven letters, and disregard articles.

"Little Toot and Other Sea Songs." ZM
United Artists 11063 ● **LITTLE**
U 63

"Disney Favorites." ZM
Mary Martin ● **DISNEY**
Disney 4016 D 16

"Spanish Songs for Children." ZM
Spoken Arts 865 ● **SPANISH**
S 65

C. Term Three

Term Three is composed of an alpha symbol and the last two digits of the commercial record number. The alpha symbol is the initial of the record company's name.

ZM 3. HOW TO CLASS OTHER RECORDINGS IN A CHILDREN'S COLLECTION

Recordings of vocal and instrumental music which were not produced as children's recordings may be classed in category ZM if a separate recordings collection is maintained for children.

Beethoven: "Symphony No. 5."
London Symphony; Dorati, conductor.
Mercury 90317

Tchaikovsky: "Nutcracker Suite."
London Symphony; Hollingsworth, conductor.
Everest 3111

Use the three term class number that is used for children's recordings to class the above examples.

A. Term One

Term One is composed of the letters "ZM."

B. Term Two

The word chosen for Term Two is tied to the title of the first work on side one of the recording; if the work has a Non-Distinctive Title (see section III-306-B1), use the name of the composer to form Term Two. If the work has a Distinctive Title (see section III-306-A1), use the first word of the work title to form Term Two. Whichever word is used in Term Two, use the entire word up to a maximum of seven letters, and disregard articles.

Beethoven: "Symphony No. 5."
Mercury 90317 (Dorati, conductor)
(This is a Non-Distinctive Title,
  so the name of the composer is
  used in Term Two.)
	ZM
	● **BEETHOV**
	M 17

Tchaikovsky: "Nutcracker Suite." Everest 3111 (Hollingsworth) (This is a Distinctive Title and is used in Term Two.)	ZM ● **NUTCRAC** E 11

C. Term Three

Term Three is composed of an alpha symbol and the last two digits of the commercial record number. The alpha symbol is the initial of the record company's name.

CATEGORY ZS — SPOKEN RECORDINGS FOR CHILDREN

ZS 1. TYPES OF RECORDINGS TO BE CLASSED IN CATEGORY ZS

Class in category ZS recordings of plays and poetry, stories, fairy tales, and other works of fiction.

"The Prince and the Pauper."
Disney 1311

"Treasury of Mother Goose."
Disney 4902

"Japanese Folk and Fairy Tales."
CMS 528

"Jack and the Beanstalk."
Leo, The Lion 1010

ZS 2. FORMATION OF THE CLASS NUMBER IN CATEGORY ZS

The class number is composed of only three terms.

A. Term One

Term One is composed of the letters "ZS."

B. Term Two

Term Two is composed of the first word of the title of the album. Use the entire word, up to a maximum of seven letters, and disregard articles.

"Three Little Pigs." Simon Says 3	ZS ● **THREE** S 3
"Golden Treasury of Nursery Rhymes." Golden 82	ZS ● **GOLDEN** G 82

C. Term Three

Term Three is composed of an alpha symbol and the last two digits of the commercial record number. The alpha symbol is the initial of the record company's name.

ZS 3. HOW TO CLASS OTHER RECORDINGS IN A CHILDREN'S COLLECTION

Spoken recordings of prose, poetry and plays which were not produced as children's recordings may be classed in category ZS if a separate record collection is maintained for children.

> Dickens: "A Christmas Carol."
> Caedmon 1135
>
> "Nonsense Verse of Carroll and Lear."
> Caedmon 1078

Use the same type of three-term class number that is used for children's recordings to class the above examples.

A. Term One

Term One is composed of the letters "ZS."

B. Term Two

Term Two is composed of the first word of the title of the album. Use the entire word, up to a maximum of seven letters, and disregard articles.

> Frost: **"Derry** Down Derry"   **ZS**
> Folkways 9733   ⊕ **DERRY**
>   **F 33**

C. Term Three

Term Three is composed of an alpha symbol and the last two digits of the commercial record number. The alpha symbol is the initial of the record company's name.

CHAPTER
II

CHAPTER II

BASIC RULES FOR TERM TWO

RULES ON THE USE AND FORMATION OF TERM TWO

200. DEFINITION

Term Two is the second part of the class number. Its function is to provide a shelving arrangement within each category which enables the record user to quickly locate a desired recording.

The shelving arrangement of recordings according to Term Two varies with each category to reflect the type of recording being classified and the major interests of the record user. In category ES (SYMPHONIES), for example, the major interest is in the composer. Term Two, consequently, is an abbreviation of the composer's name and serves to bring together all symphonies written by a composer. In category MJ (JAZZ), the users' major interests are their favorite musicians and singers, so Term Two is a reflection of the performer's name. Category L (SOUND-TRACK MUSIC) uses titles of motion pictures to form Term Two.

Since each category varies in scope and content, a variety of Term Two entries are provided to meet the special needs of each category.

201. TYPES OF ENTRY

There are thirteen ways of arranging recordings by use of Term Two. The type of Term Two entry used in a specific category depends upon the content of each recording classed in that category. In Term Two it is possible, therefore, to arrange recordings by:

the name of the Composer	(COMPOSER ENTRY)
the name of the Author	(AUTHOR ENTRY)
the name of the Performer	(PERFORMER ENTRY)
the title of the record album	(TITLE ENTRY)

Sometimes the subject of the recording is of most importance to the user. So, instead of using the name of an individual or an album title to form Term Two, a recording is classified by:

the Bible	(BIBLE ENTRY)
Ethnic origin	(ETHNIC ENTRY)
Geographic location	(GEOGRAPHIC ENTRY)
Gregorian music	(GREGORIAN ENTRY)
the name of a skill	(INSTRUCTIONAL SUBJECT ENTRY)
the name of a language	(LANGUAGE ENTRY)
the name of a person	(PERSON-AS-SUBJECT ENTRY)
the name of a sound	(SOUNDS ENTRY)

If a recording is broad in scope and subject content, all of the above entries may be too specific. If so, the abbreviation COLL is used in Term Two to indicate that the recording is a collection (COLLECTION ENTRY).

202. INTRODUCTION TO USE OF TERM TWO RULES OF ENTRY

The general uses of thirteen Term Two entries are described in this chapter (II).

More specific rules for application of entry within an individual category are provided in chapter I. Refer to each category for these rules. All thirteen forms of Term Two entry are not used within any single category, while some forms of entry are used in only one specific category. For some forms of entry which are to be used in only one category, complete rules on the use and formation of that entry have been provided within the category's general rules (chapter I) rather than in this chapter. This prevents the classifier from having to make multiple references to determine formation of an entry.

When referring to any rule in chapter II governing use and formation of Term Two entry, the classifier is cautioned to also consult the rules of use within the specific category in chapter I, since the stated content of each category may limit the use of the entry.

203. PHYSICAL FORMATION OF TERM TWO

Term Two is placed directly under Term One, and is composed of the first four CONSECUTIVE letters of a name or a word. The number of letters may vary if the rules permit, but all the letters must be written as capitals.

> **ES**   (Term One, representing the category SYMPHONIES)
> ● **BEET**   (Term Two, first four letters of Beethoven's surname)

204. COMPOSER ENTRY

A. Definition

Composer Entry refers to the use of the first four (or more) letters of a composer's surname to form Term Two, so that when this entry is used, all recordings within a category will be arranged by composer.

B. When to Use a Composer Entry

When it has been determined into which category a recording is properly classed, refer to the general rules of that category to see if the use of Composer Entry is allowed. If Composer Entry may be used within the category, examine the content of the recording to see if one of the following three rules applies:

1. *Whole Recording*

If the entire recording is devoted to one work, or a collection of works by one composer, then the composer's surname is used to form Term Two.

Beethoven: "Symphony No. 9."	ES
Philadelphia Orchestra, Ormandy conducting.	● BEET
Columbia MS 7016	
Liszt: "Songs" (a collection).	D
Sung by Fischer-Dieskau.	● LISZ
DGG 138793	

2. *One-half of the Recording*

If the first half of the whole recording is devoted to one work or several works by one composer, then use the composer's surname to form Term Two. (The number of sides comprising one half of the recording depends on the number of discs in the album.)

"Overtures."
Gibson conducting the London Festival Orchestra. (Barber of Seville, La Gazza Ladra, and William Tell by Rossini on one side; Verdi overtures on the other.) **EA**
Crossroads 22160228 ● **ROSS**

3. *One-third of Side One*

If the first work on side one of the recording occupies one-third or more of the physical space on side one, then the surname of the composer of that first work is used to form Term Two.

"Festival of Russian Music."
VICS — 1068
(Side One: Tchaikovsky's "Marche Slave," Mussorgsky's "Night on Bald Mountain." Side Two: Glinka's "Russlan and Ludmila Overture," Tchaikovsky's "Marche Miniature," Borodin's "Polovetsian March" and Kabalevsky's "Colas Breugnon Overture.")
Tchaikovsky's "Marche Slave" occupies well over one-third of side one of this recording; therefore, Composer Entry is used in Term **EA**
Two. ● **TCHA**

IMPORTANT NOTE: If the first work on the recording is a short introductory piece which bears no artistic relationship to the rest of the recording, such as a national anthem played at the start of a "live" performance, disregard this piece when determining Composer Entry.

4. *When a Featured Work is Not in Band One*

The preceding rules apply to most situations that the classifier will encounter in classifying sound recordings. In some exceptional cases, however, the classifier may have a recording in which the obvious intent of the album cover design and title is to feature a work which does *not* happen to be on band one of side one. If this featured work occupies at least one-third of a side of the recording, it should be used to classify the recording. In rare cases such as these, it would be misleading or confusing for the classifier to use the work in band one, side one.

C. How to Form Composers' Names in Term Two

A table of abbreviations of composers' names to be used in Term Two is found on page ....The following rules illustrate how to abbreviate composers' names not found in that table. [For rules and explanations regarding transliterated names, spelling of names, and pseudonyms, see sections II-217, 218.]

1. *Basic Rule*

Use the first four consecutive letters of the composer's surname to form Term Two.

> Rachmaninoff **RACH**

2. *Hyphenated Names*

Disregard the second name in hyphenated surnames.

> Rimsky-Korsakov **RIMS**

3. *Three-Letter Surnames*

In the case of three-letter surnames, three letters may be used in Term Two instead of the standard four.

> Leo **LEO**

4. *Prefixes on Surnames*

If the surname has a separately written prefix, such as an article, a preposition, or a combination of these two, treat the name in Term Two according to established usage.

> De Luca **DELU**
> Von Holst **HOLS**
> Van Beethoven **BEET**
> d'Indy **INDY**

5. *Similar Surnames*

To distinguish between surnames in which the first four letters are identical, add one or two extra letters as needed to differentiate between the names.

Sanders	**SAND**
Sandi	**SANDI**

Thomas	**THOM**
Thompson	**THOMP**
Thomson	**THOMS**

Hill	**HILL**
Hiller	**HILLE**

Johnson	**JOHNS**
Johnston	**JOHNST**

6. *Long Similar Names*

When the first six or more letters of similar names are identical, use the first five letters, then omit the following identical letters until letters are reached which are dissimilar

Reichel	**REICHL**
Reichert	**REICHR**

7. *Identical Surnames*

To distinguish between surnames which are identical, use the first four consecutive letters of the surname followed by a hyphen and the initial of the first name.

Bach, Carl Philipp Emanuel	**BACH-C**
Bach, Wilhelm Friedemann	**BACH-W**

Gabrieli, Andrea	**GABR-A**
Gabrieli, Domenico	**GABR-D**

8. *Famous Surnames*

In some cases, several members of the same family, or unrelated individuals with the same surname have followed the same profession, but one artist in particular has achieved exceptional renown. An arbitrary pattern is adopted for the entry of such names, with the simplest abbreviation used for the most preeminent artist, and a more extended entry for others sharing the same surname.

Bach, Johann Sebastian	**BACH**
Bach, Carl Philipp Emanuel	**BACH-C**

Mozart, Wolfgang Amadeus	**MOZA**
Mozart, Leopold	**MOZA-L**

Schumann, Robert	**SCHUM**
Schumann, Clara	**SCHUM-C**

If two artists of equal preeminence possess identical surnames, assign the simpler abbreviation on the basis of chronology.

> Strauss, Johann (1825-1899)   **STRAU**
> Strauss, Richard (1864-1949)   **STRAU-R**

9. *Doubled Final Letters in Surnames*

The doubling of final letters in otherwise identical surnames is ignored in the classification.

> Strauss, Johann   **STRAU**
> Straus, Oscar   **STRAU-O**
>
> Schumann, Clara   **SCHUM-C**
> Schuman, William   **SCHUM-W**

10. *Identical First Name Initials*

If the initials of the first names are identical, and the surnames are identical, use the initials of both first and middle names after the hyphen.

> Fischer, Johann Christian   **FISC-JC**
> Fischer, Johann Kaspar   **FISC-JK**

11. *Identical Middle Initials*

In cases where surnames are identical, and the initials of both first and middle names are identical, an arbitrary order of entry is established so that the shelving may be in alphabetical order.

> Bach, Johann Christian   **BACH-J**
> Bach, Johann Christoph   **BACH-JC**
> Bach, Johann Christoph Freidrich   **BACH-JF**

205. AUTHOR ENTRY

A. Definition

Author Entry refers to the use of the first four (or more) letters of an author's name to form Term Two, so that all recordings using this entry within a category will be arranged by author.

B. When to Use an Author Entry

When it has been determined into which category a recording is properly classed, refer to the general rules of that category to see if the use of Author Entry is allowed. If Author Entry is allowed examine the recording within the content of the three following rules. (The rule for use of Author Entry is considerably more restricted than that for Composer Entry.)

1. *One Author*

If the entire recording is devoted to one work or a collection of works by one author, then the author's name is used to form Term Two.

Cooper: "Last of the Mohicans." Read by James Mason. Caedmon 1239	V ● COOP
"Mark **Van Doren** Reads from His Collected and New Poems." Folkways 9782	U ● VAND

2. *More Than One Author*

If the works of more than one author are represented on the recording, then it is necessary to use another form of entry, such as Language Entry, Collection Entry, Person-As-Subject Entry, or so forth. Guidelines are provided under the individual categories to assist in determining the correct form of entry.

3. *Anonymous Works*

Use the Language Entry for anonymous works of literature. (See Language Entry, section II-214.)

C. How to Form Authors' Names in Term Two

The following rules illustrate how to abbreviate authors' names to form Term Two. For rules and explanations regarding transliterated names, spelling and pseudonyms, see section II-217, 218.

1. *Basic Rule*

Use the first four consecutive letters of the author's surname to form Term Two.

Shakespeare	**SHAK**
Donne	**DONN**

2. *Hyphenated Names*

Disregard the second name in hyphenated surnames.

Saheb-Ettaba	**SAHE**

3. *Three Letter Surnames*

In the case of three letter surnames, three letters may be used in Term Two instead of the standard four.

Poe	**POE**

4. *Prefixes on Surnames*

If the surname has a separately written prefiix such as an article, a preposition, or a combination of these two, treat the name in Term Two according to established usage.

Du Maurier	**DUMA**
de Tocqueville	**TOCQ**
Van Doren	**VAND**

5. *Similar Surnames*

To distinguish between surnames in which the first four letters are identical, apply rule 205-C6 following for identical surnames.

6. *Identical Surnames*

To distinguish between surnames which are identical, or between names in which the first four letters are identical, use the first four consecutive letters of the surname followed by a hyphen and the initial of the first name.

Crane, Hart	**CRAN-H**
Crane, Stephen	**CRAN-S**
Dickens, Charles	**DICK-C**
Dickinson, Emily	**DICK-E**
Miller, Arthur	**MILL-A**
Millay, Edna	**MILL-E**
Miller, Henry	**MILL-H**

7. *Identical First Name Initials*

If the initials of the first names are identical, and the surnames are identical (or their first four letters are identical), use the initials of both first and middle names after the hyphen.

McFarland, Robert Patterson	**MCFA-RP**
McFarland, Roger Burnham	**MCFA-RB**

8. *Identical Middle Initials*

In cases where surnames are identical (or their first four letters are identical), and the initials of both first and middle names are identical, an arbitrary order of entry is established as needed to distinguish between the two entries.

Smith, James Leonard	**SMIT-J**
Smith, James Lewis	**SMIT-JL**

206. PERFORMER ENTRY

A. Definition

Performer Entry refers to the use of the first four (or more) letters of a performer's surname to form Term Two, so that all recordings using this entry within a category will be arranged by performer. The term "performer" may be applied to an individual, or to a group of individuals who perform as a group under a corporate name.

B. When to Use a Performer Entry

When it has been determined into which category a recording is properly classed, refer to the general rules of that category to see if the use of Performer Entry is allowed. If Performer Entry may be used within the category, examine the content of the recording to see if one of the following rules may be used.

1. *One Performer*

If the entire recording is devoted to the work of one performer or performing group, and this fact is featured in the album title or on the album cover, then use the surname of the performer or the name of the performing group to form Term Two.

"Sgt. Pepper's Lonely Hearts Club Band." Featuring the **Beatles.** Capitol MAS 2653	MA ● BEAT
"French Opera Arias." Featuring Maria **Callas.** Angel S 35882	D ● CALL

2. *Two Performers*

If the entire recording features the work of two individual performers working in concert or separately, use the surname of the performer whose surname comes first in alphabetical order to form the Term Two entry.

"Duets: Jussi **Bjoerling** and Robert Merrill." Victor LM 2736	D ● BJOE
"Bobbie Gentry and Glen **Campbell.**" Capitol ST 2928	MC ● CAMP

3. *Performer and Performing Group*

If the entire recording features the work of an individual performer and a performing group working in concert or separately, use the surname of the individual performer to form Term Two, unless it is obvious that the group is given main billing on the album cover and the individual is mentioned only secondarily; in this case the group's name must be used in Term Two.

"Young Girl." Featuring Gary **Puckett** and the Union Gap. Columbia CS 9664	MA ● PUCK
"Beat of the Brass." Herb **Alpert** and the Tijuana Brass. A&M 4146	MA ● ALPE
"Cheap Thrills." **Big Brother** and the Holding Company; Janis Joplin, vocalist. Columbia KCS 9700	MA ● BIGB

4. *Orchestra Conductors as Performers*

Orchestra conductors' names may be used as performer entries in categories K through R, provided the band or orchestra performs under the conductor's name and is the featured performer on the recording. (Orchestra conductors are never used as performer entries in categories A through J.)

"American Scene."   **MA**
Mantovani and his orchestra   ◉ **MANT**
London 182

5. *Orchestras as Performers*

Orchestras' names may be used as performer entries in categories K through R, provided the orchestra is the featured performer. (Orchestras are never used as performer entries in categories A through J with the single exception of the Boston Pops. See section II-206-B6 for Boston Pops Entry rules.)

"Nat King Cole Songbook."   **MA**
Featuring the **Hollyridge** Strings   ◉ **HOLL**
Capitol ST 2310

6. *Boston Pops as Performer*

The Boston Pops may be used as a Performer Entry in all categories if the rules for Composer Entry do not apply, and the recording features the Boston Pops. This means that a Performer Entry for Boston Pops is made for recordings which would otherwise have a Collection Entry.

"Viennese Night."   **EA**
Featuring the **Boston Pops**   ◉ **BOST**
Victor LSC 2548

7. *Bands as Performers*

Concert and marching bands are classed in category H, and the name of the band is used as Performer Entry provided the rules for Composer Entry do not apply.

"Trooping the Colour."   **H**
Featuring the **Grenadier** Guards   ◉ **GREN**
London 44044

"Sousa Marches."   **H**
Featuring the Grenadier Guards   ● **SOUS** (Composer Entry)
London 44103

C. How to Form Individual Performers' Names in Term Two

The following rules illustrate how to abbreviate the names of *individual* performers to form Term Two. Paragraph 206-D contains the rules for abbreviating names of *performing groups* to form Term Two.

(For rules and explanations regarding transliterated names, spelling and pseudonyms, see section II-217, 218.)

1. *Basic Rule*
Use the first four consecutive letters of the performer's surname to form Term Two.

Gorme **GORM**

2. *Three Letter Surnames*
In the case of three letter surnames, three letters may be used to form Term Two instead of the standard four.

Lee **LEE**

3. *Similar Surnames*
To distinguish between surnames in which the first four letters are identical, apply rule 206-C4, following, for identical surnames.

4. *Identical Surnames*
To distinguish between surnames which are identical, or between names in which the first four letters are identical, use the first four consecutive letters of the surname followed by a hyphen and the initial of the first name.

Franchi, Sergio **FRAN-S**
Francis, Connie **FRAN-C**

Gould, Morton **GOUL-M**
Goulet, Robert **GOUL-R**

Williams, Andy **WILL-A**
Williams, Roger **WILL-R**

5. *Identical First Name Initials*
If the initials of the first names are identical, as well as the first four letters of the surname, use the first two letters of the first name following the hyphen.

Smith, Jimmy **SMIT-JI**
Smith, Johnny **SMIT-JO**

6. *Performing Families*
If several members of a family follow the same profession, use the simplest abbreviation for the name of the most well known individual (at the time of classication), or the name of the oldest if they are of equal preeminence. Add initials for the other members of the family.

Sinatra, Frank **SINA**
Sinatra, Frank Jr. **SINA-F**
Sinatra, Nancy **SINA-N**

Kipnis, Alexander **KIPN**
Kipnis, Igor **KIPN-I**

7. *Authority File on Performers' Names*

The rapidity of change and shifts in popularity suggest that in popular music (where Performer Entry is used predominantly) part of the collection will be more ephemeral and subject to discard, like fiction in the book collection. For this reason, rules for Performer Entry are simplified and a list of performers' names has not been supplied. In establishing abbreviations for performers' names, differentiate only within a category; it is not necessary to have a unique abbreviation for a performer for all categories (unlike the names of composers). An authority file should be kept so that abbreviations no longer used may be withdrawn and reassigned to new artists. The simplest four-letter abbreviations should be assigned to performers whose work has endured over a period of time and therefore will be established in the collection for some time to come.

> Armstrong, Louis   **ARMS**
> Davis, Sammy, Jr.   **DAVI**
> Liberace   **LIBE**
> Crosby, Bing   **CROS**
> Arnold, Eddy   **ARNO**
> Ellington, Duke   **ELLI**

(Differentiation between names is made only within a category; therefore the abbreviation DAVI can serve for Sammy Davis, Jr. in the MA category, and the same abbreviation, DAVI, can serve for Miles Davis in MJ category.)

D. How to Form Performing Groups' Names in Term Two

The following rules explain in detail how to abbreviate the names of performing groups in Term Two. For rules and explanations regarding transliterated names, spelling and pseudonyms, see sections II-217, 218.

1. *Basic Rule*

Use the first four consecutive letters of the first word of the corporate name of the performing group. (Disregard articles.)

> The Beatles   **BEAT**
> Jefferson Airplane   **JEFF**

2. *Two and Three Letter Words*

If the first word of a corporate group name has less than four letters, add as many letters of the second word of the group name as necessary to make four letters.

> In Crowd Singers   **INCR**
> Ink Spots   **INKS**

3. *Similar and Identical First Words*

To distinguish between group names in which the first four letters of the first word are identical, use the first four consecutive letters followed by a hyphen and the first letter of the second word in the group name. (Disregard conjunctions and prepositions.)

Peter and Gordon	**PETE-G**
Peter, Paul and Mary	**PETE-P**
Living Brass	**LIVI-B**
Living Strings	**LIVI-S**
Musikkorps Lubeck	**MUSI-L**
Musikkorps Berlin	**MUSI-B**
Kingsmen	**KING**
Kingston Trio	**KING-T**
Schola des Peres du Saint Esprit	**SCHO-P**
Schola of Sisters of Saint Benedict	**SCHO-S**

4. *Identical First and Second Words*

If the first and second words of two group names are identical, use the initials of the third or fourth words of the group name as necessary to differentiate.

Paulist Choir, Chicago	**PAUL-C**
Paulist Choir, New York	**PAUL-N**

5. *Saints' Names*

In dealing with group names which incorporate the name of a saint, use the abbreviation "S" for saint.

St. John Singers   **SJOH**

6. *Names of Individuals*

If a group performs under the name of an individual, use the surname of the individual to form Term Two.

Robert Shaw Chorale	**SHAW**
Guy Lombardo and his orchestra	**LOMB**

7. *Popular Names*

If a performing group is best known by its popular name rather than its official name, use the popular name to form Term Two.

Salt Lake Mormon Tabernacle Choir, commonly
 known as the Mormon Tabernacle Choir:
 enter under **MORM**

207. TITLE ENTRY

A. Definition

Title Entry refers to the use of the first four letters of the first word of an album title to form Term Two, so that the recordings within a category will be arranged alphabetically by title.

B. When to Use a Title Entry

When it has been determined into which category a recording is properly classed, refer to the general rules of that category to see if the use of Title Entry is allowed. If Title Entry may be used within the category, examine the content of the recording to see if the following rule applies.

1. *General Description of a Title Entry*

Title Entry is used when the album title is the quickest and most satisfactory tool in retrieving the desired recording. It is used primarily in categories K, L and W for recordings of musical shows, motion pictures, television shows and documentaries; i.e., works which are more commonly identified by title, rather than composer, author or performer. The Title Entry is also required in category A in place of the Collections Entry because a disproportionate number of recordings in this category are collections, and the effectiveness of Collections Entry would be diminished through excessive use.

"The History of Broadcasting" (documentary) Folkways 9171	**W** ● **HIST**
"Gentlemen Prefer Blondes" (musical show) Columbia OS 2310	**K** ● **GENT**
"Divorce Italian Style" (motion picture) United Artists 5106	**L** ● **DIVO**
"Beverly Hillbillies" (television show) Harmony 11269	**L** ● **BEVE**
"Plainsong to Polyphony" (music anthology) Everest 3174	**A** ● **PLAI**

C. How to Form Titles in Term Two

The following rules illustrate how to abbreviate the words of titles to form Term Two. For rules and explanations regarding transliterations and spelling, see sections II-217, 218.

1. *Basic Rule*

Use the first four consecutive letters of the first word of the title of the album to form Term Two. (Disregard articles.)

> "Flying Saucers." **FLYI**
> "From Russia with Love." **FROM**
> "The Train." **TRAI**

2. *Two and Three Letter Words*

If the first word of the title has less than four letters, add as many letters of the second and third words as necessary to make four letters.

> "G.I. Blues." **GIBL**
> "On the Beach." **ONBE**

3. *Similar and Identical Words*

If the first word or words of two titles are identical, or the first four letters are identical, no differentiation is made in the entries.

"Funny Girl." **FUNN**
"A Funny Thing Happened
   on the Way to the Forum." **FUNN**

4. *Series Titles*

If the recording is one of a distinctive series, use the series title in Term Two. (See section III-303-C on the formation of Term Three.)

Jazz—vol. 1: "The South."   **MJ**
Folkways 2801   ● **JAZZ**

Jazz—vol. 2: "The Blues."   **MJ**
Folkways 2802   ● **JAZZ**

208. COLLECTIONS ENTRY

A. Definition

Collections Entry refers to the use of the abbreviation COLL indicating "collections" in Term Two so that recordings of the collections type will be arranged together within the category.

B. When to Use the Collections Entry

When it has been determined into which category a recording is properly classed, refer to the general rules of that category to see if the use of Collections Entry is allowed. If Collections Entry may be used within the category, examine the content of the recording to see if the following rule applies.

1. *General Description of a Collections Entry*

Collections Entry is used for recordings which contain a number of works by different composers or authors, and in which the purpose of the recording is to feature the type of material selected, rather than the special talents of individuals such as composers, performers, etc. Therefore, Collections Entry may be used only when the rules for Composer, Author or Performer Entry do not apply, and if the rules for Title Entry or any of the eight subject entries do not take precedence.

"Night at the Grand Ole Opry."   **MC**
Harmony 11169   ● **COLL**

"Great Prima Donnas."   **D**
Bel Canto 205.208   ● **COLL**

"International Piano Festival."   **GP**
Everest 3128   ● **COLL**

"Treasury of Music—Symphony."   **ES**
Victor LE 6005   ● **COLL**

C. How to Form the Collections Entry in Term Two

Always use the abbreviation COLL for the Collections Entry. Any names or words used in Term Two with the same first four letters (COLL) must have additional letters added to them in order not to be confused with the Collections Entry.

Collins, Judy **COLL-J**

209. BIBLE ENTRY (a subject entry)

A. Definition

Bible Entry refers to the use of the word "BIBLE" in Term Two so that recordings of readings from the Bible will be arranged together within the category.

B. When to Use the Bible Entry

Bible Entry is used only in category V, and applies to readings of both prose and poetry from the Bible.

"Life and Passion of Our Lord."
(read by Charlton Heston.)
Vanguard 9080

"Psalms and Ecclesiastes."
(read by Abba Eban.)
Spoken Arts 757

C. How to Form the Bible Entry in Term Two

Always use the full word "BIBLE" in Term Two.

"Life and Passion of Our Lord."	V
Vanguard 9080	● BIBLE
"Poetry and Prophesy of the Old Testament."	V
Theodore Bikel, reader.	● BIBLE

210. ETHNIC ENTRY (a subject entry)

A. Definition

Ethnic Entry refers to the use of the abbreviated name of an ethnic group to form Term Two so that all recordings of music of an ethnic group will be arranged together within the category.

B. Use and Formation of Ethnic Entry

Ethnic Entry is used in category P only. Instructions on use and formation of this entry are provided under category P.

211. GEOGRAPHIC ENTRY (a subject entry)

A. Definition

Geographic Entry refers to the use in Term Two of the abbreviated name of a country, or broad geographic area, or particular style of music, so that recordings are arranged together by geographic origin or style within the category.

B. Use and Formation of Geographic Entry

Geographic Entry is used in category Q only. Instructions on use and formation of this entry are provided under category Q.

212. GREGORIAN ENTRY (a subject entry)

A. Definition

Gregorian Entry refers to the use of the abbreviation GREG in Term Two so that recordings of collections of Gregorian chants will be arranged together within the category.

B. When to Use the Gregorian Entry

Gregorian Entry is used in category A only, and applies to recordings of Gregorian and other chants developed for use in religious services of the early Christian Church.

Mass on the Feast of the Assumption	**A**
of the Blessed Virgin Mary.	● **GREG**
Holy Week Chants.	**A**
	● **GREG**

C. How to Form the Gregorian Entry in Term Two

Always use the abbreviation GREG for the Gregorian Entry. Any names or words used in Term Two with the same first four letters (GREG) must have additional letters added to them in order not to be confused with the Gregorian Entry. (This applies only to Term Two entries in category A.)

213. INSTRUCTIONAL SUBJECT ENTRY (a subject entry)

A. Definition

Instructional Subject Entry refers to the use in Term Two of abbreviations for subjects treated by instructional recordings, so that all recordings dealing with a particular skill or subject will be arranged together within the category.

B. Use and Formation of Instructional Subject Entry

Instructional Subject Entry is used only in category X, and instructions on use and formation of this entry are provided under category X.

214. LANGUAGE ENTRY (a subject entry)

A. Definition

Language Entry refers to the use in Term Two of an abbreviation representing the name of a language, so that all recordings of literature from that language will be arranged together within the category.

B. When to Use the Language Entry

When it has been determined into which category a recording is properly classed, refer to the general rules of that category to see if the use of Language Entry is allowed. If Language Entry may be used within the category, examine the content of the recording to see if one of the following rules applies.

1. *Single Language Literature by More Than One Author*
If the recording contains works of prose and/or poetry by two or more authors, and all the authors wrote in the same language, use the name of that language to form Term Two.

"Early English Poetry."	**U**
Read by Dunn.	● **ENGL**
Folkways 9851	

"Golden Treasury of	**V**
French Prose."	● **FREN**
(Excerpts of Montaigne,	
Pascal, Sevigné, Fenelon,	
etc.) Read by Le Marchand	
and Riquier.	
Spoken Arts 795	

2. *Anonymous Authors*
Use the Language Entry for anonymous works. If the recording contains works from more than one language, use the Collections Entry.

"Beowulf and Other Poetry in	**U**
Old English."	● **ENGL**
Caedmon 1161	

3. *Translations*
If the recording contains works of prose and/or poetry by two or more authors, and all the authors wrote in the same language, but the readings on the recordings are in translation, use the name of the original language to form Term Two.

"Anthology of French Poetry."	**U**
Read in English by Guilloton.	● **FREN**
Caedmon 1184	

4. *Two or More Languages*
If the selections on the recording are taken from the literature of more than one language, use the abbreviation COLL indicating "collection" in Term Two. (Do not apply this rule in the case of National Literature —see section II-214-B4.)

"Jean Vilar: Ses Grands Roles."	**T**
(Scenes from Corneille, Moliere,	● **COLL**
Gide, and Pirandello.)	
Spoken Arts 924	

5. *National Literature*

Literature of the nation in which the class scheme is being used is grouped separately by a Geographic Entry rather than a Language Entry. For example, libraries in the United States will use the Term Two abbreviation AMER for American literature, thereby separating the national literature from the general grouping of English language literature (ENGL). Libraries in Canada will use the Term Two abbreviation CANA for Canadian literature, thereby separating the national literature from the general grouping of English language literature (ENGL) and French language literature (FREN).

Libraries in the United States	**U**
"Anthology of Contemporary American Poetry."	● **AMER**
Read by Abbe, Ciardi, Roethke, etc.	
Folkways 9735	
"Six Toronto Poets."	**U**
Read by Ross, Wilkinson, etc.	● **ENGL**
Folkways 9806	
Libraries in Canada	**U**
"Anthology of Contemporary American Poetry."	● **ENGL**
Read by Abbe, Ciardi, Roethke, etc.	
Folkways 9735	
"Six Toronto Poets."	**U**
Read by Ross, Wilkinson, etc.	● **CANA**
Folkways 9806	

C. How to Form the Language Entry in Term Two

Use the following Basic Rule when abbreviating names of languages for Term Two. A table of language abbreviations is also provided based on currently available recorded material and should be consulted first when establishing Term Two Language Entry.

1. *Basic Rule*

Use the first four consecutive letters of the name of the language to form Term Two.

    Chinese   **CHIN**

Add a fifth letter if it is necessary to differentiate between similar abbreviations.

2. *National Literature Abbreviations*

The Term Two abbreviation representing a national literature is based upon the name of the country in which the ANSCR scheme is being used, but the exact form of the abbreviated name will depend entirely upon the judgment of the classifier. Only the usage to be followed in the United States and in Canada has been established herein. It is suggested, however, that in establishing the entry for his particular country, the classifier should avoid an abbreviation which resembles a Language Entry. For example, libraries in England should not use ENGL (language abbreviation) as the Term Two entry designating their national literature. If classifiers outside the United States or Canada feel it would be desirable to place recordings of their national literature in a specific place within each category (such as at the beginning or at the end) they may establish any arbitrary combination of letters for Term Two from "AAAA" to "ZZZZ."

3. *Table of Abbreviations*

Name of Language	Term Two Abbreviation
Armenian	**ARME**
Arabic	**ARAB**
Aztec	**AZTEC**
Catalan	**CATA**
Chinese	**CHIN**
Corsican	**CORS**
Danish	**DANI**
Dutch	**DUTCH**
English	**ENGL**
French	**FREN**
Finnish	**FINN**
Flemish	**FLEM**
German	**GERM**
Greek	**GREEK**
Hebrew	**HEBR**
Hungarian	**HUNG**
Irish **(Gaelic)**	**IRISH**
Italian	**ITAL**
Icelandic	**ICEL**
Japanese	**JAPA**
Korean	**KORE**
Latin	**LATIN**
Norwegian	**NORW**
Persian	**PERS**
Polish	**POLI**
Portuguese	**PORT**
Russian	**RUSS**
Sanskrit	**SANS**
Scottish **(Gaelic)**	**SCOT**
Serbian	**SERB**
Slovakian	**SLOV**
Slavonic	**SLAV**
Spanish	**SPAN**
Tagalog	**TAGA**
Ukrainian	**UKRA**
Welsh	**WELSH**
Yiddish	**YIDD**
Yugoslavian	**YUGO**

For American Literature collections in libraries in the United States, use **AMER**

For Canadian Literature collections in libraries in Canada, use **CANA**

215. PERSON-AS-SUBJECT ENTRY (a subject entry)

A. Definition

Person-As-Subject Entry refers to the use of the abbreviated name of an individual to form Term Two so that all recordings about that individual will be arranged together within the category.

B. When to Use the Person-As-Subject Entry

When it has been determined into which category a recording is properly classed, refer to the general rules of that category to see if the use of Person-As-Subject Entry is allowed. If Person-As-Subject Entry may be used within the category, examine the content of the recording to see if one of the following rules applies.

1. *One Individual*

If the recording documents, discusses or commemorates the life, works, influence or significance of one individual, then use the name of that individual to form Term Two.

> "That Was the Week That Was."   **W**
> (Documentary of John F. Kennedy.)   ● **KENN**
> Decca 79116

2. *Two or More Individuals*

If the recording documents, discusses or commemorates the life, works, influence or significance of two or more individuals do not use the Person-As-Subject Entry: see the specific category in which the recording is classed to determine the appropriate entry. (An exception to this rule may be made if the subject individuals are related by blood ties and bear the same surname; in this case Person-As-Subject Entry may be made under that common surname.)

C. How to Form Person-As-Subject Entry in Term Two

The following rules explain in detail how to abbreviate the names of individuals treated as subjects, and the use of those abbreviations to form Term Two. (For rules and explanations regarding transliterated names, spelling and pseudonyms, see sections II-217, 218.)

1. *Basic Rule*

Use the first four consecutive letters of the surname of the individual to form Term Two.

> "Life and Legend of General   **W**
>   Douglas MacArthur."   ● **MACA**
> MGM 4245

2. *Three Letter Surnames*

In the case of three letter surnames, three letters may be used in Term Two instead of the standard four.

> Robert E. Lee   **Lee**

3. *Similar and Identical Surnames*

Always use the first four consecutive letters of the surname to form Term Two. Do not differentiate between similar or identical names.

> John F. Kennedy   **KENN**
> Robert F. Kennedy   **KENN**

4. *Prefixes on Surnames*

If the surname has a separately written prefix such as an article, a preposition, or a combination of these two, treat the name in Term Two according to established usage.

> Charles De Gaulle   **DEGA**

216. SOUND ENTRY (a subject entry)

A. Definition

Sound Entry refers to the use in Term Two of the abbreviation for the name of a sound so that recordings of particular sounds will be arranged together within the category.

B. Use and Formation of Sounds Entry

Sounds Entry is used only in category Y. Instructions on use and formation of this entry are provided under category Y.

217. SPELLINGS AND TRANSLITERATIONS OF NAMES

A. Spellings

1. *Basic Rule*

Use the spelling preferred by the artist as indicated on works published during his lifetime.

2. *Contemporary Spelling*

If changes have occurred over the years in the spelling of names of artists long deceased, and these changes, whether from error or intent, have become established and accepted contemporary usage, then use that modern form of the name. As a guide to contemporary usage, consult the spellings preferred most frequently in current books, journals, periodicals, television and film documentaries, and recording jackets and labels produced and printed in the United States. (Adapt this rule according to the country in which the classification scheme is used.)

B. Transliterations (record collections in the U.S.A.)

1. *Basic Rule*

Use the American English transliteration of names which come from languages with non-Roman alphabets (such as Chinese, Russian and Arabic).

Mussorgsky, not Moussorgsky (French transliteration)

2. *Phonetics and Diacritical Marks*

Do not use phonetic transcriptions or employ diacritical marks which run counter to the general patterns of use and recognition in the English language.

Prokofiev, not Prokof'ev

3. *Variant Transliterations*

If several transliterations of a name are in use, select the one most commonly found in contemporary printed and recorded media, and the one most frequently used by major American record companies.

Scriabin, not Skriabin
Tchaikovsky, not Tschaikowsky or Chaikovskii
Chekov, not Tchekov

4. *Artists' Transliterations*

If the artist is alive and his work is currently published in the United States, use the spelling on the record label: assume this is the spelling preferred by the artist.

Shostakovich
Yevtushenko

If the artist is no longer living, but during his lifetime he was active artistically in the United States, use the transliteration he chose to use for his name, even if it is not American English usage.

Rachmaninoff
Koussevitsky

5. *Authority for Transliterations*

It is suggested that record classifiers consult the *Schwann Long Playing Record Catalog* when determining which transliterations are most commonly used in contemporary media. The Schwann entries are based on the principle of American English transliteration and contemporary usage. *Baker's Biographical Dictionary of Musicians** and *Thompson's Cyclopedia of Music and Musicians** should also be consulted, as well as other standard biographical dictionaries and sources. In case of serious disagreement between authorities, it should be pointed out that the *Schwann Catalog* usually indicates the usage most commonly employed and recognized by the public and the major recording companies, and this is the ruling guideline in this classification scheme. (For * see the bibliography.)

218. PROFESSIONAL NAMES AND PSEUDONYMS

A. Professional Names (stage names)

1. *Basic Rule*

Use the name which the artist has selected to be known by in his profession, as indicated on the label of the disc. Do not attempt to determine original or "real" names, and do not substitute more formal names for nicknames.

> **Andy Williams** not Andrew Williams
> **Bing Crosby** not Harry Lillis Crosby
> **Jan Peerce** not Jacob Perelmuth
> **Bruno Walter** not B. W. Schlesinger

2. *Multiple Professional Names*

Rarely does a performer achieve wide recognition under two different stage names; frequently, however, he may adopt several stage names in the course of his career until he becomes successful. Use the stage name by which the performer has gained widest recognition.

> **Tiny Tim** not Herbert Khaury (real name)
> or former stage names: Emmett
> Swink, Rollie Dell, Darry Dover,
> or Larry Love the Singing Canary.

B. Pseudonyms (noms de plume)

1. *Basic Rule*

Use the name which the artist has selected to be signed to his published works. Do not attempt to determine original or "real" names, and do not substitute more formal names for nicknames.

> **Peter Menin** not Peter Menini
> **Peter Warlock** not Philip Heseltine
> **Mark Twain** not Samuel Clemens

2. *Multiple Pseudonyms*

Composers and authors may publish any number of works under any number of pseudonyms. Use the pseudonym which appears on the recording since this indicated the artist's intent that these works be publicly identified by the pseudonym. Do not attempt to determine original or "real" names for individuals with numerous pseudonyms: any attempt to draw these together should be done through the catalog and not through the classification scheme.

219. TABLE OF COMPOSERS' NAMES

Abaco, Evaristo Felice Dall'	**ABAC**	Austin, Larry	**AUST**
Abramson, Robert	**ABRA**	Avni, Tzvi	**AVNI**
Adam, Adolphe-Charles	**ADAM**	Avshalomov, Aaron	**AVSH-A**
Adam de la Halle	**ADAMD**	Avshalomov, Jacob	**AVSH**
Adaskin, Murray	**ADAS**	Ayala, Daniel	**AYAL**
Addinsell, Richard	**ADDI**	Azzaiolo, Filippo	**AZZA**
Adler, Samuel	**ADLE**		
Adolphus, Milton	**ADOL**	Babadzhanian, Arnold	**BABA**
Akutagawa, Yasushi	**AKUT**	Babits (Patrick), Linda	**BABI**
Albéniz, Isaac	**ALBE**	Babbitt, Milton	**BABB**
D'Albert, Eugene	**ALBER**	Bacewicz, Grazyna	**BACE**
Alberti, Giuseppe Matteo	**ALBERT**	Bach, Carl Philipp Emanuel	**BACH-C**
Albicastro, Henricus	**ALBI**	Bach, Johann Christian	**BACH-J**
Albinoni, Tomaso	**ALBIN**	Bach, Johann Christoph	**BACH-JC**
Albrechtsberger, Joh. Georg	**ALBR**	Bach, Joh. Christoph Friedrich	
Alfidi, Joey	**ALFI**		**BACH-JF**
Alfonso El Sabio	**ALFO**	Bach, Johann Sebastian	**BACH**
Alfven, Hugo	**ALFV**	Bach, Wilhelm Friedemann	**BACH-W**
Alkan, Charles-Henri	**ALKA**	Bacon, Ernst	**BACO**
Allende-Blin, Juan	**ALLE**	Badings, Henk	**BADI**
Almand, Claude	**ALMA**	Baird, Tadeusz	**BAIR**
Altenburg, Johann Ernst	**ALTE**	Balada, Leonardo	**BALAD**
Amirov, Fikret	**AMIR**	Balakirev, Mily	**BALAK**
Amram, David	**AMRA**	Balasanyan, Sergei	**BALAS**
Amy, Gilbert	**AMY**	Balazs, Frederic	**BALAZ**
Anderson, Garland	**ANDE-G**	Balbastre, Claude	**BALB**
Anderson, Leroy	**ANDE**	Ballou, Esther Williamson	**BALL**
Andriessen, Hendrik	**ANDR**	Balfe, Michael William	**BALF**
Anerio, Giovanni Francesco	**ANER**	Banchieri, Adriano	**BANC**
D'Anglebert, Jean-Henri	**ANGL**	Banfield, Raffaello De	**BANF**
Anhalt, Istvan	**ANHA**	Banks, Don	**BANK**
Antes, John	**ANTE**	Barati, George	**BARA**
Antheil, George	**ANTH**	Barber, Samuel	**BARB**
Antill, John Henry	**ANTI**	Barlow, Samuel	**BARL**
Arbeau, Thoinot	**ARBE**	Barlow, Wayne	**BARL-W**
Arcadelt, Jacob	**ARCA**	Barsanti, Francesco	**BARS**
Archangelsky, Alexander	**ARCH**	Bartók, Béla	**BART**
Arel, Bülent	**AREL**	Bassani, Giovanni Battista	**BASS**
Arensky, Anton	**AREN**	Bassett, Leslie	**BASSE**
Ariosti, Attilio	**ARIO**	Baston, John	**BAST**
Arkas, Nikolai	**ARKA**	Bateson, Thomas	**BATE**
Arne, Thomas	**ARNE**	Bath, Hubert	**BATH**
Arnold, Malcolm	**ARNO**	Batten, Adrian	**BATT**
Arriaga, Juan Chrisostomo	**ARRI**	Bauer, Marion	**BAUE**
Arrieta, Emilio	**ARRIE**	Bavicchi, John	**BAVI**
Ashley, Robert	**ASHL**	Bayle, François	**BAYL**
Asioli, Bonifazio	**ASIO**	Bax, Arnold	**BAX**
Asplmayer, Franz	**ASPL**	Bazelon, Irwin	**BAZE**
Attaignant, Pierre	**ATTA**	Beach, Mrs. H. H. A.	**BEAC**
Auber, Daniel François	**AUBE**	Beck, Franz	**BECK**
Aubert, Jacques	**AUBER**	Becker, John J.	**BECKE**
Auffmann, Joseph Anton	**AUFF**	Beckwith, John	**BECKW**
Auric, Georges	**AURI**	Bedford, David	**BEDF**

Beecroft, Norma	BEEC	Boismortier, Joseph Bodin de	BOIS
Beeson, Jack	BEES	Boito, Arrigo	BOIT
Beethoven, Ludwig van	BEET	Bond, Capel	BOND
Beginiker, Henricus	BEGI	Bondon, Jacques	BONDO
Behrend, Siegfried	BEHR	Bononcini, Antonio Maria	BONO
Bellini, Vincenzo	BELL	Bonporti, Francesco Antonio	BONP
Bellman, Carl Mikael	BELLM	Borkovec, Pavel	BORK
Benda, Franz	BEND	Borodin, Alexander	BORO
Benda, Georg	BEND-G	Borowski, Felix	BOROW
Ben-Haim, Paul	BENH	Bortkiewicz, Sergei	BORT
Benedict, Julius	BENE	Borup-Jorgensen, Axel	BORU
Benjamin, Arthur	BENJ	Boscovich, Alexander Uriah	BOSC
Bennett, Richard Rodney	.BENN	Boucourechliev, Andre	BOUC
Bennett, Robert Russell	BENN-R	Boulanger, Lili	BOULA
Benson, Warren	BENS	Boulez, Pierre	BOUL
Bentzon, Niels Viggo	BENT	Bowles, Paul	BOWL
Berezowsky, Nicolai	BERE	Boyce, William	BOYC
Berg, Alban	BERG	Boydell, Brian	BOYD
Berger, Arthur	BERGE	Boyvin, Jacques	BOYV
Bergsma, William	BERGS	Brahms, Johannes	BRAH
Berio, Luciano	BERI	Brant, Henry	BRAN
Berkeley, Lennox	BERK	Brehm, Alvin	BREH
Berlinski, Herman	BERLI	Bress, Hyman	BRES
Berlioz, Hector	BERL	Bridge, Frank	BRID
Bernstein, Leonard	BERN	Bright, Houston	BRIG
Bertheaume, Isidore	BERT	Britten, Benjamin	BRIT
Berton, Pierre-Montan	BERTO	Brixi, Franz Xaver	BRIX
Berwald, Franz	BERW	Brons, Carel	BRON
Besard, Jean-Baptiste	BESA	Brott, Alexander	BROT
Beversdorf, Thomas	BEVE	Brown, Earle	BROW-E
Bezanson, Philip	BEZA	Brown, Rayner	BROW-R
Biber, Heinrich von	BIBE	Brubeck, David	BRUB
Billings, William	BILL	Brubeck, Howard	BRUB-H
Binchois, Gilles	BINC	Bruch, Max	BRUC
Binkerd, Gordon	BINK	Bruckner, Anton	BRUCK
Birtwistle, Harrison	BIRT	Brun, Herbert	BRUN
Bittner, Jacques	BITT	Brunetti, Gaetano	BRUNE
Bizet, Georges	BIZE	Brunswick, Mark	BRUNS
Blacher, Boris	BLAC	Brustad, Bjarne	BRUS
Blackwood, Easley	BLACK	Bubalo, Rudolph	BUBA
Blavet, Michel	BLAV	Bucchi, Valentino	BUCC
Bliss, Arthur	BLIS	Bucci, Mark	BUCCI
Blitzstein, Marc	BLIT	Bull, John	BULL
Bloch, Ernest	BLOC	Burge, David	BURG
Blomdahl, Karl-Birger	BLOM	Burgmüller,	
Blow, John	BLOW	Johann Friedrich	BURGM
Blumenfeld, Harold	BLUM	Bush, Alan	BUSH
Boatrite, Harold	BOAT	Busoni, Ferruccio	BUSO
Boccherini, Luigi	BOCC	Bussotti, Sylvano	BUSS
Boda, John	BODA	Buxtehude, Dietrich	BUXT
Bodinus, Sebastian	BODI	Byrd, William	BYRD
Bodley, Seoirse	BODL		
Boguslawski, Edward	BOGU	Caamaño, Roberto	CAAM
Böhm, Georg	BOHM	Cabanilles, Juan Bautista	CABA
Boieldieu, François	BOIE	Cabezon, Antonio De	CABE

Cacioppo, George	**CACI**	Cirri, Giovanni Battista	**CIRR**
Cadman, Charles Wakefield	**CADM**	Claflin, Avery	**CLAF**
Cage, John	**CAGE**	Clarke, Jeremiah	**CLAR-J**
Caix D'Hervelois, Louis De	**CAIX**	Clarke, Laurence	**CLAR-L**
Caldara, Antonio	**CALD**	Clementi, Muzio	**CLEM**
Califano, Arcangelo	**CALI**	Clerambault, Louis Nicolas	**CLER**
Cambini, Giovanni Giuseppe	**CAMB**	Coates, Eric	**COAT**
Campion, Thomas	**CAMP**	Coleman, Ornette	**COLE**
Campos-Parsi, Hector	**CAMPO**	Colgrass, Michael	**COLG**
Campra, André	**CAMPR**	Constant, Marius	**CONS**
Canby, Edward Tatnall	**CANB**	Conus, Julius	**CONU**
Cannabich, Christian	**CANN**	Converse, Frederick Shepherd	**CONV**
Canning, Thomas	**CANNI**	Cooley, Carlton	**COOL**
Canteloube, Joseph	**CANT**	Cooper, Paul	**COOP**
Carey, Henry	**CARE**	Copland, Aaron	**COPL**
Carissimi, Giacomo	**CARI**	Corelli, Arcangelo	**CORE**
Carlos, Walter	**CARL**	Corigliano, John, Jr.	**CORI**
Carpenter, John Alden	**CARP**	Cornelius, Peter	**CORN**
Carson, Philippe	**CARS**	Correa De Araujo, Francisco	**CORR**
Carter, Elliott	**CART**	Corrette, Michel	**CORRE**
Carulli, Ferdinando	**CARU**	Cortes, Ramiro	**CORT**
Casadesus, Robert	**CASA**	Coulthard, Jean	**COUL**
Casals, Pablo	**CASAL**	Couperin, François	**COUP**
Cascarino, Romeo	**CASC**	Couperin, Louis	**COUP-L**
Casella, Alfredo	**CASE**	Courbois, Philippe	**COUR**
Castelnuovo-Tedesco, Mario	**CAST**	Cowell, Henry	**COWE**
Castiglioni, Niccolo	**CASTI**	Cramer, Johann Baptist	**CRAM**
Castro, Juan José	**CASTR**	Crawford (Seeger), Ruth	**CRAW**
Catalani, Alfredo	**CATA**	Crecquillon, Thomas	**CREC**
Cavalli, Nicolo	**CAVA-N**	Creston, Paul	**CRES**
Cavalli, Pier Francesco	**CAVA-P**	Crumb, George	**CRUM**
Cererols, Juan	**CERE**	Cumming, Richard	**CUMM**
Cerha, Friedrich	**CERH**	Cushing, Charles	**CUSH**
Certon, Pierre	**CERT**	Cyr, Gordon	**CYR**
Chabrier, Emmanuel	**CHAB**	Czerny, Carl	**CZER**
Chadwick, George Whitefield	**CHAD**		
Chaikin, Nikolai	**CHAI**	Dahl, Ingolf	**DAHL**
Chajes, Julius	**CHAJ**	Dallapiccola, Luigi	**DALL**
Chance, John Barnes	**CHAN**	Damase, Jean-Michel	**DAMA**
Chanler, Theodore	**CHANL**	Dandrieu, Jean Francois	**DAND**
Chambonnieres, Jacques	**CHAM**	Daniels, Mabel	**DANI**
Chaminade, Cecile	**CHAMI**	Dankevitch, Konstantin	**DANK**
Champagne, Claude	**CHAMP**	Danzi, Franz	**DANZ**
Charpentier, Gustave	**CHAR**	Daquin, Louis-Claude	**DAQU**
Charpentier, Marc-Antoine	**CHAR-M**	Dargomyzhsky, Alexander	**DARG**
Chausson, Ernest	**CHAU**	Dauvergne, Antoine	**DAUV**
Chávez, Carlos	**CHAV**	Daveluy, Raymond	**DAVE**
Cheetham, John	**CHEE**	David, Gyula	**DAVI**
Cheney, Timothy	**CHEN**	Davidovsky, Mario	**DAVID**
Cherubini, Luigi	**CHER**	Davies, Henry	**DAVIE-H**
Childs, Barney	**CHIL**	Davies, Peter	**DAVIE-P**
Chopin, Frederic	**CHOP**	Dawson, William Levi	**DAWS**
Chou Wen-Chung	**CHOU**	Debussy, Claude	**DEBU**
Cilea, Francesco	**CILE**	Deering, Richard	**DEER**
Cimarosa, Domenico	**CIMA**	Delage, Maurice	**DELA**

Delibes, Léo	**DELI**	Eimert, Herbert	**EIME**
Delius, Frederick	**DELIU**	Einem, Gottfried Von	**EINE**
Dello Joio, Norman	**DELL**	Eisenstein, Alfred	**EISE**
De Luca, Edmond	**DELU**	Eisler, Hanns	**EISL**
Demantius, Christoph	**DEMA**	El-Dabh, Halim	**ELDA**
Denisov, Edison	**DENI**	Elgar, Edward	**ELGA**
Denny, William	**DENN**	Elkus, Jonathan	**ELKU**
Des Prez, Josquin	**DESP**	Eloy, Jean-Claude	**ELOY**
Dessau, Paul	**DESS**	Elwell, Herbert	**ELWE**
Devienne, François	**DEVI**	Enesco, Georges	**ENES**
Diabelli, Anton	**DIAB**	Ephros, Gershon	**EPHR**
Diamond, David	**DIAM**	Epstein, Alvin	**EPST**
Dick, Marcel	**DICK**	Erb, Donald	**ERB**
Dillon, Fannie Charles	**DILL**	Erickson, Frank	**ERIC-F**
D'Indy, Vincent	**Refer to "I"**	Erickson, Robert	**ERIC-R**
	alphabet	Erkel, Franz	**ERKE**
Dittersdorf, Karl Ditters von	**DITT**	Esplá, Oscar	**ESPL**
Dobrowolski, Andrzej	**DOBR**	Etler, Alvin	**ETLE**
Dockstader, Tod	**DOCK**	Evangelisti, Franco	**EVAN**
Dodgson, Stephen	**DODG**	Ewald, Victor	**EWAL**
Dohnányi, Ernst von	**DOHN**		
Donizetti, Gaetano	**DONI**		
Donovan, Richard	**DONO**	Falla, Manuel de	**FALL**
Dorati, Antal	**DORA**	Farberman, Harold	**FARB**
Dowland, John	**DOWL**	Farnaby, Giles	**FARN**
Downey, John	**DOWN**	Farkas, Ferenc	**FARK**
Druckman, Jacob	**DRUC**	Fasch, Johann Friedrich	**FASC**
Dubois, Theodore	**DUBO**	Fauré, Gabriel	**FAUR**
Dufay, Guillaume	**DUFA**	Fayrfax, Robert	**FAYR**
Duff, Arthur	**DUFF**	Feldman, Morton	**FELD**
Dufrene, François	**DUFR**	Fellegara, Vittorio	**FELL**
Dukas, Paul	**DUKA**	Ferguson, Howard	**FERG**
Duke, John	**DUKE-J**	Ferrari, Luc	**FERR**
Duke, Vernon	**DUKE-V**	Fesch, Willem De	**FESC**
Dunstable, John	**DUNS**	Festing, Michael Christian	**FEST**
Duparc, Henri	**DUPA**	Fetler, Paul	**FETL**
Dupre, Marcel	**DUPR**	Fickenscher, Arthur	**FICK**
Durante, Francesco	**DURA**	Field, John	**FIEL**
Durko, Zsolt	**DURK**	Filtz, Anton	**FILT**
Duruflé, Maurice	**DURU**	Fine, Irving	**FINE-I**
Dussek, Johann Ladislaus	**DUSS**	Fine, Vivian	**FINE-V**
Dutilleux, Henri	**DUTI**	Finney, Ross Lee	**FINN**
Dvorak, Antonin	**DVOR**	Finzi, Gerald	**FINZ**
Dvorkin, Judith	**DVORK**	Fiocco, Joseph-Hector	**FIOC**
		Fiorenza, Nicola	**FIOR**
Easdale, Brian	**EASD**	Fischer, Irwin	**FISC-I**
Eaton, John	**EATO**	Fischer, Johann Christian	**FISC-J**
Eckhardt-Gramatte,		Fischer, Johann Kaspar	**FISC-JK**
Sophie Carmen	**ECKH**	Flagello, Nicholas	**FLAG**
Eder, Helmut	**EDER**	Flanagan, William	**FLAN**
Edmunds, John	**EDMU**	Flotow, Friedrich von	**FLOT**
Effinger, Cecil	**EFFI**	Floyd, Carlisle	**FLOY**
Egge, Klaus	**EGGE**	Foerster, Josef Bohuslav	**FOER**
Egk, Werner	**EGK**	Foote, Arthur	**FOOT**
Eichner, Ernst	**EICH**	Foss, Lukas	**FOSS**

Foster, Dudley	**FOST-D**	Giuliani, Giovanni	**GIUL-G**
Foster, Stephen	**FOST**	Giuliani, Mauro	**GIUL-M**
Francaix, Jean	**FRANC**	Glanville-Hicks, Peggy	**GLAN**
Franchetti, Arnold	**FRANCH**	Glazounov, Alexander	**GLAZ**
Franck, César	**FRAN**	Gliére, Reinhold	**GLIE**
Franck, Melchior	**FRAN-M**	Glinka, Mikhail	**GLIN**
Franco, Johan	**FRANCO**	Globokar, Vinko	**GLOB**
Francoeur, François	**FRANCE**	Gluck, Christoph Willibald	**GLUC**
Frankel, Benjamin	**FRANK**	Gnattali, Radames	**GNAT**
Frederick II	**FRED**	Goeb, Roger	**GOEB**
Freedman, Harry	**FREE**	Goehr, Alexander	**GOEH**
Frescobaldi, Girolamo	**FRES**	Goetz, Hermann	**GOET**
Fricker, Peter Racine	**FRIC**	Goldmark, Karl	**GOLD**
Froberger, Johann Jakob	**FROB**	Gombert, Nicolas	**GOMB**
Fromm, Herbert	**FROM**	Goodenough, Forrest	**GOOD**
Fukushima, Kazuo	**FUKU**	Goodman, Joseph	**GOODM**
Fussl, Karl Heinz	**FUSS**	Goossens, Eugene	**GOOS**
Fux, Johann Joseph	**FUX**	Gordeli, Otar	**GORD**
		Gossec, François Joseph	**GOSS**
Gabrieli, Andrea	**GABR-A**	Gottschalk, Louis Moreau	**GOTT**
Gabrieli, Domenico	**GABR-D**	Gould, Morton	**GOUL**
Gabrieli, Giovanni	**GABR-G**	Gounod, Charles	**GOUN**
Gaburo, Kenneth	**GABU**	Grainger, Percy	**GRAI**
Gadbois, Rev. Charles E.	**GADB**	Granados, Enrique	**GRAN**
Gade, Niels	**GADE**	Grant, Parks	**GRANT**
Galindo, Blas	**GALI**	Grauer, Victor	**GRAU**
Galliard, Johann Ernst	**GALL**	Graun, Johann	**GRAUN-J**
Gallus, Jacobus	**GALL**	Graun, Karl	**GRAUN-K**
Galuppi, Baldassare	**GALU**	Graupner, Christoph	**GRAUP**
Galynin, Herman	**GALY**	Green, Ray	**GREE**
Garant, Serge	**GARA**	Gretry, Andre	**GRET**
Garcia-Morillo, Roberto	**GARC**	Grieg, Edvard	**GRIE**
Gardner, John	**GARD**	Griffes, Charles Tomlinson	**GRIF**
Gassmann, Florian	**GASS-F**	Griffis, Elliot	**GRIFF**
Gassmann, Remi	**GASS-R**	Grigny, Nicolas De	**GRIG**
Gaubert, Philippe	**GAUB**	Griller, Arnold	**GRIL**
Gavinies, Pierre	**GAVI**	Grofé, Ferde	**GROF**
Gay, John	**GAY**	Gross, Robert	**GROS**
Gelineau, Joseph	**GELI**	Gruenberg, Louis	**GRUE**
Geminiani, Francesco	**GEMI**	Guarnieri, Camargo	**GUAR**
Gerhard, Roberto	**GERH**	Guilain, Jean Adam	**GUIL**
German, Edward	**GERM**	Guillemain, Gabriel	**GUILL**
Gerschefski, Edwin	**GERSC**	Gulak-Artemovsky, Semyon	**GULA**
Gershwin, George	**GERS**	Gutche, Gene	**GUTC**
Gervaise, Claude	**GERV**		
Gesualdo, Don Carlo	**GESU**	Haba, Alois	**HABA**
Giannini, Vittorio	**GIAN**	Haber, Louis	**HABE**
Gibbons, Orlando	**GIBB**	Haessler, Johann W.	**HAES**
Gideon, Miriam	**GIDE**	Haieff, Alexei	**HAIE**
Gilbert, Henry	**GILB**	Haines, Edmund	**HAIN**
Gilbert and Sullivan	See Sullivan,	Halevy, Jacques	**HALE**
	Sir Arthur	Halffter, Ernesto	**HALF-E**
Ginastera, Alberto	**GINA**	Halffter, Rodolfo	**HALF-R**
Giordani, Tommaso	**GIOR**	Hall, Richard	**HALL**
Giordano, Umberto	**GIORD**	Hambraeus, Bengt	**HAMB**

Hamerik, Ebbe	**HAME**	Hubay, Jeno	**HUBA**
Hamilton, Iain	**HAMI**	Hummel, Johann N.	**HUMM**
Hamm, Charles	**HAMM**	Humperdinck, Engelbert	**HUMP**
Hammond, Don	**HAMMO**	Husa, Karel	**HUSA**
Hampton, Calvin	**HAMP**		
Handel, George Frideric	**HAND**	Ibert, Jacques	**IBER**
Hanson, Howard	**HANS**	Ichiyanagi, Toshi	**ICHI**
Harman, Carter	**HARM**	Imbrie, Andrew W.	**IMBR**
Harris, Roy	**HARR**	d'Indy, Vincent	**INDY**
Harrison, Lou	**HARRI**	Ippolitov-Ivanov, Mikhail	**IPPO**
Harsanyi, Tibor	**HARS**	Ireland, John	**IREL**
Hartley, Walter	**HART**	Isaac, Heinrich	**ISAA**
Hartmann, Karl Amadeus	**HARTM**	Isolfsson, Pall	**ISOL**
Hasse, Johann Adolph	**HASS**	Ives, Charles	**IVES**
Haubenstock-Ramati, Roman	**HAUB**	Ivey, Jean E.	**IVEY**
Haubiel, Charles	**HAUBI**		
Haufrecht, Herbert	**HAUF**	Jacobi, Frederick	**JACO**
Haydn, Joseph	**HAYD**	James, Philip	**JAME**
Haydn, Michael	**HAYD-M**	Janácek, Leos	**JANA**
Heiden, Bernhard	**HEID**	Jannequin, Clement	**JANN**
Heiller, Anton	**HEIL**	Jenkins, John	**JENK**
Heilner, Irwin	**HEILN**	Jerger, Wilhelm	**JERG**
Hellendaal, Pieter	**HELL**	Jirko, Ivan	**JIRK**
Heller, Stephen	**HELLE**	Jirovec, Vojtech	**JIRO**
Helm, Everett	**HELM**	Joaquim, Otto	**JOAQ**
Helps, Robert	**HELP**	Johann Ernst,	
Hely-Hutchinson, Victor	**HELY**	Prinz von Sachsen-Weimar	**JOHA**
Henry, Pierre	**HENR**	Johansen, Gunnar	**JOHAN**
Henze, Hans Werner	**HENZ**	Johns, Louis Edgar	**JOHN**
Herbert, Victor	**HERB**	Johnson, Hunter	**JOHNS**
Herder, Ronald	**HERD**	Johnston, Ben	**JOHNST**
Hérold, Louis J.	**HERO**	Jolivet, André	**JOLI**
Hertel, Johann W.	**HERT**	Jones, Kelsey	**JONE**
Hetu, Jacques	**HETU**	Jongen, Joseph	**JONG**
Hewitt, James	**HEWI**	Jora, Mihail	**JORA**
Hilber, Johann Baptist	**HILB**	Josquin Des Pres	**See Des Pres**
Hill, Edward B.	**HILL**	Josten, Werner	**JOST**
Hiller, Lejaren	**HILLE**	Joubert, John	**JOUB**
Hindemith, Paul	**HIND**		
Hively, Wells	**HIVE**	Kabalevsky, Dmitri	**KABA**
Hoddinott, Alun	**HODD**	Kabelac, Miloslav	**KABE**
Hoffmann, Ernst	**HOFF-E**	Kadosa, Paul	**KADO**
Hoffmann, Johann	**HOFF-J**	Kagel, Mauricio	**KAGE**
Hofmann, Josef	**HOFM**	Kahn, Erich	**KAHN**
Hoiby, Lee	**HOIB**	Kalinnikov, Vassili	**KALI**
Holborne, Antony	**HOLB**	Kaltnecker, Msgr. Maurice	**KALT**
Hollingsworth, Stanley	**HOLL**	Kapelent, Marek	**KAPE**
Holmboe, Vagn	**HOLM**	Karlowicz, Mieczyslaw	**KARL**
Holst, Gustav	**HOLS**	Kasements, Udo	**KASE**
Holzbauer, Ignaz	**HOLZ**	Kauffmann, Leo	**KAUF**
Honegger, Arthur	**HONE**	Kaufmann, Walter	**KAUFM**
Hotteterre, Jacques	**HOTT**	Kay, Hershy	**KAY-H**
Hovhaness, Alan	**HOVH**	Kay, Ulysses	**KAY-U**
Howe, Mary	**HOWE**	Keetbaas, Dirk	**KEET**
Hracek, Antonin Ignac	**HRAC**	Keiser, Reinhard	**KEIS**

Kelemen, Milko	**KELE**	Landini, Francesco	**LAND**
Keller, Homer	**KELL**	Lange-Müller, Peter	**LANG**
Kelly, Robert	**KELLY-R**	Langlais, Jean	**LANGL**
Kelly, Thomas	**KELLY-T**	Larchet, John	**LARC**
Kennan, Kent	**KENN**	Larsson, Lars-Erik	**LARS**
Kennedy-Fraser, Marjory	**KENNE**	La Rue, Pierre De	**LARU**
Kerle, Jacobus De	**KERL**	Lassus, Orlandus de	**LASS**
Kern, Jerome	**KERN**	Laszlo, Alexander	**LASZ**
Kerr, Harrison	**KERR**	Latham, William	**LATH**
Ketelbey, Albert W.	**KETE**	La Vigne, Philibert de	**LAVI**
Keyes, Nelson	**KEYE**	Lavry, Marc	**LAVR**
Khachaturian, Aram	**KHAC**	Lawes, William	**LAWE**
Khachaturian, Karen	**KHAC-K**	Layton, Billy Jim	**LAYT**
Khandoshkin, Ivan	**KHAN**	Lazarof, Henri	**LAZA**
Khrennikov, Tikhon	**KHRE**	Lebegue, Nicolas-Antoine	**LEBE**
Kielland, Olav	**KIEL**	Lechner, Leonhard	**LECH**
Kirchner, Leon	**KIRC**	Leclair, Jean Marie	**LECL**
Klein, Lothar	**KLEI**	Lecocq, Charles	**LECO**
Knight, Morris	**KNIG**	Lecuona, Ernesto	**LECU**
Knipper, Lev	**KNIP**	Lee, Dai-Keong	**LEE-D**
Knüpfer, Sebastian	**KNUP**	Lee, Noël	**LEE-N**
Koch, John	**KOCH**	Lees, Benjamin	**LEES**
Kodály, Zoltán	**KODA**	Leeuw, Ton De	**LEEU**
Koechlin, Charles	**KOEC**	Lefebvre, Charles Edouard	**LEFE**
Kohaut, Karl	**KOHA**	Le Gallienne, Dorian	**LEGA**
Kohs, Ellis	**KOHS**	Legrenzi, Giovanni	**LEGR**
Kokai, Rezso	**KOKA**	Lehar, Franz	**LEHA**
Kolz, Ernst	**KOLZ**	Lehmann, Hans	**LEHM**
Kolinski, Mieczyslaw	**KOLI**	Leifs, Jon	**LEIF**
Korn, Peter	**KORN**	Le Jeune, Claude	**LEJE**
Korngold, Erich	**KORNG**	Lekeu, Guillaume	**LEKE**
Kotonski, Wlodzimierz	**KOTO**	Lendvay, Kamillo	**LEND**
Koutzen, Boris	**KOUT**	Lentz, Nicola	**LENT**
Kraft, William	**KRAF**	Leo, Leonardo	**LEO**
Kraus, Joseph	**KRAU**	Leoncavallo, Ruggiero	**LEON**
Krebs, Johann	**KREB**	Leonin	**LEONI**
Kreisler, Fritz	**KREI**	Le Roux, Gaspard	**LERO**
Krenek, Ernst	**KREN**	Lessard, John	**LESS**
Krommer, Franz	**KROM**	Lesur, Daniel	**LESU**
Krumlovsky, Jan	**KRUM**	Letelier, Alfonso	**LETE**
Krumpholtz, Johann	**KRUMP**	Lewin-Richter, Andres	**LEWI**
Kubik, Gail	**KUBI**	Liadov, Anatol	**LIAD**
Kuhlau, Friedrich	**KUHL**	Liebermann, Rolf	**LIEB**
Kuhnau, Johann	**KUHN**	Lieberson, Goddard	**LIEBE**
Künneke, Eduard	**KUNN**	Ligeti, György	**LIGE**
Kupferman, Meyer	**KUPF**	Lindberg, Oskar Fredrik	**LIND**
Kurka, Robert	**KURK**	Lipatti, Dinu	**LIPA**
		List, Kurt	**LIST**
La Barre, Michel De	**LABA**	Liszt, Franz	**LISZ**
Laderman, Ezra	**LADE**	Locatelli, Pietro	**LOCA**
La Guerre, Elizabeth De	**LAGU**	Locke, Matthew	**LOCK**
Lajtha, Laszlo	**LAJT**	Lockwood, Normand	**LOCKW**
Lalande, Michel-Richard de	**LALA**	Loeffler, Charles M.	**LOEF**
Lalo, Edouard	**LALO**	Loeillet, Jacques	**LOEI**
LaMontaine, John	**LAMO**	Loeillet, Jean Baptiste	**LOEI-J**

Loeillet, John	**LOEI-JO**	Massenet, Jules	**MASSE**
Loewe, Karl	**LOEW**	Mather, Bruce	**MATH**
Lopatnikoff, Nicolai	**LOPA**	Matsudaira, Yoritsune	**MATS**
Lo Presti, Ronald	**LOPR**	Mattheson, Johann	**MATT**
Lora, Antonio	**LORA**	Maurice, Paule	**MAUR**
Lorenziti, Bernard	**LORE**	Maxfield, Richard	**MAXF**
Lortzing, Albert	**LORT**	May, Frederic	**MAY**
Lothar, Mark	**LOTH**	Mayer, William	**MAYE**
Lotti, Antonio	**LOTT**	Mayuzumi, Toshiro	**MAYU**
Louis XIII	**LOUI**	Mazzocchi, Domenico	**MAZZ**
Louis Ferdinand	**LOUIS**	McBride, Robert	**MCBR**
Lübeck, Vincentius	**LUBE**	McGrath, Joseph J.	**MCGR**
Lucchinetti, Giovanni B.	**LUCC**	McKenzie, Jack H.	**MCKE**
Lucier, Alvin	**LUCI**	McPhee, Colin	**MCPH**
Luening, Otto	**LUEN**	Meek, Kenneth	**MEEK**
Luke, Ray	**LUKE**	Mellnas, Arne	**MELL**
Lully, Jean-Baptiste	**LULL**	Menasce, Jacques de	**MENA**
Lumbye, Hans Christian	**LUMB**	Mendelssohn, Felix	**MEND**
Lutoslawski, Witold	**LUTO**	Mennin, Peter	**MENN**
Lutyens, Elizabeth	**LUTY**	Menotti, Gian Carlo	**MENO**
Lybbert, Donald	**LYBB**	Mercure, Pierre	**MERC**
Lysenko, Mykola	**LYSE**	Messiaen, Olivier	**MESS**
		Meyerbeer, Giacomo	**MEYE**
MacDowell, Edward	**MACD**	Miaskovsky, Nikolai	**MIAS**
Mace, Thomas	**MACE**	Mieg, Peter	**MIEG**
Macero, Teo	**MACER**	Mihaly, Andras	**MIHA**
Machaut, Guillaume	**MACH**	Milhaud, Darius	**MILH**
MacMillan, Ernest	**MACM**	Millet, Luis	**MILL**
Maconchy, Elizabeth	**MACO**	Mills, Charles	**MILLS**
Maderna, Bruno	**MADE**	Millöcker, Karl	**MILLO**
Mahler, Gustav	**MAHL**	Mimaroglu, Ilhan	**MIMA**
Malawski, Artur	**MALA**	Miyagi, Michio	**MIYA**
Malcolm, George	**MALC**	Miyoshi, Akira	**MIYO**
Maldere, Pierre Van	**MALD**	Moevs, Robert	**MOEV**
Malec, Ivo	**MALE**	Mohaupt, Richard	**MOHA**
Malipiero, Gian F.	**MALI**	Molter, Johann Melchior	**MOLT**
Mamlok, Ursula	**MAML**	Mompou, Federico	**MOMP**
Manevich, Alexander	**MANE**	Moncayo, Pablo	**MONC**
Manfredini, Francesco	**MANF**	Mondonville, Jean-Joseph	**MOND**
Mann, Robert	**MANN**	Moniuszko, Stanislaw	**MONI**
Marais, Marin	**MARA**	Monn, Georg M.	**MONN**
Marcello, Alessandro	**MARC-A**	Monte, Philippe De	**MONT**
Marcello, Benedetto	**MARC-B**	Monteclair, Michel P. de	**MONTE**
Marenzio, Luca	**MARE**	Montemezzi, Italo	**MONTEM**
Maros, Rudolf	**MARO**	Monteverdi, Claudio	**MONTEV**
Marti, José	**MARTI**	Montsalvatge, Xavier	**MONTS**
Martin, David	**MART-D**	Moor, Emanuel	**MOOR**
Martin, Frank	**MART-F**	Moore, Douglas	**MOORE**
Martino, Donald	**MARTIN**	Morales, Cristobal de	**MORA**
Martinon, Jean	**MARTIO**	Morawetz, Oscar	**MORAW**
Martinu, Bohuslav	**MARTIU**	Morel, François	**MOREL**
Martirano, Salvatore	**MARTIR**	Moreno Torroba, Federico	**MOREN**
Mascagni, Pietro	**MASC**	Morin, Jean Baptiste	**MORI**
Mason, Daniel	**MASO**	Moritz, Edvard	**MORIT**
Massana, Antonio	**MASS**	Morley, Thomas	**MORL**

Moross, Jerome	**MORO**	Obrecht, Jacob	**OBRE**
Morris, Franklin	**MORR-F**	Ockeghem, Johannes	**OCKE**
Morris, Harold	**MORR-H**	Offenbach, Jacques	**OFFE**
Moscheles, Ignaz	**MOSC**	Ohana, Maurice	**OHAN**
Mosonyi, Mihaly	**MOSO**	Oliveros, Pauline	**OLIV**
Moss, Lawrence	**MOSS**	Orbon, Julian	**ORBO**
Mossolov, Alexander	**MOSSO**	Orff, Carl	**ORFF**
Moszkowski, Moritz	**MOSZ**	Orr, Robin	**ORR**
Mourant, Walter	**MOUR**	Orrego Salas, Juan	**ORRE**
Mouret, Jean J.	**MOURE**	Overton, Hall	**OVER**
Moussorgsky	**See Mussorgsky**		
Mouton, Charles	**MOUT**	Pachelbel, Johann	**PACH**
Mozart, Leopold	**MOZA-L**	Paderewski, Ignace Jan	**PADE**
Mozart, Wolfgang Amadeus	**MOZA**	Paganini, Niccolo	**PAGA**
Muczynski, Robert	**MUCZ**	Paine, John	**PAIN**
Mudge, Richard	**MUDG**	Paisiello, Giovanni	**PAIS**
Muffat, Georg	**MUFF**	Pakhmutova, Alexandra	**PAKH**
Müller, Paul	**MULL**	Palau, Manuel	**PALA**
Mumma, Gordon	**MUMM**	Palestrina, Giovanni	**PALE**
Murray, Bain	**MURR-B**	Palmer, Robert	**PALM**
Murray, Dom Gregory	**MURR-D**	Panufnik, Andrzej	**PANU**
Musgrave, Thea	**MUSG**	Papineau-Couture, Jean	**PAPI**
Mussorgsky, Modest	**MUSS**	Papp, Lajos	**PAPP**
Müthel, Johann	**MUTH**	Parker, Horatio	**PARK**
Mysliveczek, Joseph	**MYSL**	Parris, Robert	**PARR**
		Partch, Harry	**PART**
Nabokov, Nicolas	**NABO**	Partos, Oedoen	**PARTO**
Nagel, Robert	**NAGE**	Pasquini, Bernardo	**PASQ**
Napravnik, Eduard	**NAPR**	Peeters, Flor	**PEET**
Nancarrow, Carlo	**NANC**	Peloquin, C. Alexander	**PELO**
Nardini, Pietro	**NARD**	Penderecki, Krzystof	**PEND**
Naudot, Jean Jacques	**NAUD**	Pentland, Barbara	**PENT**
Naumann, Johann G.	**NAUM**	Pepin, Clermont	**PEPI**
Naylor, Bernard	**NAYL**	Pepping, Ernst	**PEPP**
Negrea, Martian	**NEGR**	Pepusch, John C.	**PEPU**
Nelhybel, Vaclav	**NELH**	Peragallo, Mario	**PERA**
Nelson, Ron	**NELS**	Pergolesi, Giovanni B.	**PERG**
Nepomuceno, Alberto	**NEPO**	Peri, Jacopo	**PERI**
Nero, Peter	**NERO**	Perkins, John M.	**PERK**
Neubaur, Franz C.	**NEUB**	Perkowski, Piotr	**PERKO**
Newlin, Dika	**NEWL**	Perle, George	**PERL**
Nicode, Jean-Louis	**NICO**	Perotin	**PERO**
Nicolai, Otto	**NICOL**	Perry, Julia	**PERR**
Nieland, Jan	**NIELA**	Persichetti, Vincent	**PERS**
Nielsen, Carl	**NIEL**	Pescetti, Giovanni Battista	**PESC**
Nigg, Serge	**NIGG**	Peter, Johann F.	**PETE**
Nixon, Roger	**NIXO**	Petrassi, Goffredo	**PETR**
Nono, Luigi	**NONO**	Petrini, Franz	**PETRI**
Nordoff, Paul	**NORD**	Petrovics, Emil	**PETRO**
Norgaard, Per	**NORG**	Peyrot, Fernande	**PEYR**
North, Alex	**NORT**	Pezel, Johann C.	**PEZE**
Norton, Spencer	**NORTO**	Pfeiffer, John	**PFEI**
Noskowski, Sigismund	**NOSK**	Pfitzner, Hans	**PFIT**
Novak, Vitezslav	**NOVA**	Philidor, Anne D.	**PHILID**
Nunlist, Juli	**NUN**	Philippot, Michel	**PHILIP**

Phillips, Burrill	PHIL-B	Reichert, James A.	REICHR
Phillips, Peter	PHIL-P	Reif, Paul	REIF
Piazza, Gaetano	PIAZ	Reinecke, Carl	REIN
Pichl, Wenzel	PICH	Respighi, Ottorino	RESP
Pick, Richard	PICK	Reubke, Julius	REUB
Pierné, Gabriel	PIER	Revueltas, Silvestre	REVU
Pijper, Willem	PIJP	Reznicek, Emil Nikolaus	REZN
Pinkham, Daniel	PINK	Rheinberger, Joseph	RHEI
Pisendel, Johann G.	PISE	Ricciotti, Carlo	RICC
Pisk, Paul A.	PISK	Richter, Franz X.	RICH
Piston, Walter	PIST	Riegger, Wallingford	RIEG
Pizzetti, Ildebrando	PIZE	Rieti, Vittorio	RIET
Pleyel, Ignaz	PLEY	Rigai, Amiram	RIGA
Pokorny, Franz X.	POKO	Riisager, Knudage	RIIS
Ponce, Manuel	PONC	Riley, Terry	RILE
Ponchielli, Amilcare	PONCH	Rimsky-Korsakov, Nicolai	RIMS
Porpora, Nicola	PORP	Rinaldo Di Capua	RINA
Porter, Quincy	PORT	Rivier, Jean	RIVI
Potter, Archibald	POTT	Robb, John B.	ROBB
Poulenc, Francis	POUL	Robinson, Earl	ROBI
Pousseur, Henri	POUS	Rochberg, George	ROCH
Powell, John	POWE-J	Rodrigo, Joaquin	RODR
Powell, Mel	POWE-M	Rogalski, Theodor	ROGA
Pozdro, John	POZD	Rogers, Bernard	ROGE-B
Praetorius, Michael	PRAE	Rogers, William	ROGE-W
Prince, Robert	PRIN	Rohe, Robert K.	ROHE
Procter, Leland	PROC	Roldan, Amadeo	ROLD
Prokofiev, Serge	PROK	Roman, Johan H.	ROMA
Puccini, Domenico	PUCC-D	Ropartz, Guy	ROPA
Puccini, Giacomo	PUCC	Rorem, Ned	RORE
Pugnani, Gaetano	PUGN	Roseingrave, Thomas	ROSE
Purcell, Henry	PURC	Rosen, Jerome	ROSEN
Purvis, Richard	PURV	Rosenberg, Hilding	ROSENB
		Rosenmüller, Johann	ROSENM
Quantz, Johann J.	QUAN	Rosetti, Francesco A.	ROSET
Quentin, Jean-Baptiste	QUEN	Rossi, Luigi	ROSSI
		Rossini, Gioacchino	ROSS
Raaijmakers, Dick	RAAI	Rousseau, Jean Jacques	ROUS-J
Rachmaninoff, Sergei	RACH	Rousseau, Marcel	ROUS-M
Rainer, Priaulx	RAIN	Roussel, Albert	ROUSS
Raison, Andre	RAIS	Roy, Klaus G.	ROY
Rakov, Nicolas	RAKO	Rozsa, Miklos	ROZS
Rameau, Jean-Philippe	RAME	Rozycki, Ludomir	ROZY
Rangström, Ture	RANG	Rubbra, Edmund	RUBB
Ranki, Gyorgy	RANK	Rubinstein, Anton	RUBI
Rathaus, Karol	RATH	Rudin, Andrew	RUDI
Ratner, Leonard	RATN	Rudzinski, Zbigniew	RUDZ
Ravel, Maurice	RAVE	Ruger, Morris H.	RUGE
Rawsthorne, Alan	RAWS	Ruggieri, Giovanni	RUGG
Read, Gardner	READ	Ruggles, Carl	RUGGL
Reed, H. Owen	REED	Russell, William	RUSS
Reger, Max	REGE	Russo, William	RUSSO
Reich, Steve	REIC		
Reicha, Anton	REICH	Saar, Mart	SAAR
Reichel, Bernard	REICHL	Saboly, Nicolas	SABO

Sachs, Hans	SACH	Seiber, Matyas	SEIB
Saeverud, Harald	SAEV	Semmler, Alexander	SEMM
Saint-Saëns, Camille	SAIN	Senfl, Ludwig	SENF
Sala, Oskar	SALA	Serebrier, José	SERE
Salieri, Antonio	SALI	Serocki, Kazimierz	SERO
Salomon, Karel	SALO	Sessions, Roger	SESS
Salzedo, Carlos	SALZ	Sgrizzi, Luciano	SGRI
Sammartini,		Shahan, Paul	SHAH
Giovanni Battista	SAMM	Shankar, Ravi	SHAN
Sammartini, Giuseppe	SAMM-G	Shapero, Harold	SHAP
Sanders, Robert L.	SAND	Shapey, Ralph	SHAPE
Sandi, Luis	SANDI	Shaporin, Yuri	SHAPO
Sanjuan, Pedro	SANJ	Shchedrin, Rodion	SHCH
Sarai, Tibor	SARA	Shebalin, Vissarion	SHEB
Sarasate, Pablo de	SARAS	Sherman, Robert W.	SHER
Sarközy, Istvan	SARK	Shield, William	SHIE
Sarro, Domenico	SARR	Shifrin, Seymour	SHIF
Sarti, Giuseppe	SART	Shimizu, Osamu	SHIM
Satie, Erik	SATI	Shishakov, Yuri	SHIS
Sas, Andres	SAS	Shostakovich, Dmitri	SHOS
Sauguet, Henri	SAUG	Sibelius, Jean	SIBE
Scarlatti, Alessandro	SCAR-A	Siegmeister, Elie	SIEG
Scarlatti, Domenico	SCAR	Silcher, Friedrich	SILC
Scavarda, Donald	SCAV	Silva, Giulio	SILV
Schaeffer, Pierre	SCHA	Sims, Ezra	SIMS
Schafer, Murray	SCHAF	Sinding, Christian	SIND
Schat, Peter	SCHAT	Skalkottas, Nikos	SKAL
Scheidt, Samuel	SCHE	Smetana, Bedrich	SMET
Schein, Johann H.	SCHEI	Smith, Hale	SMIT-H
Schibler, Armin	SCHI	Smith, Leland	SMIT-L
Schifrin, Boris (Lalo)	SCHIF	Smith, Russell	SMIT-R
Schlick, Arnolt	SCHL-A	Smith, William O.	SMIT-W
Schlick, Johann Conrad	SCHL-J	Smith-Brindle, Reginald	SMIT-RE
Schmelzer, Johann Heinrich	SCHM	Soler, Padre Antonio	SOLE
Schmidt, Franz	SCHMI-F	Sollberger, Harvey	SOLL
Schmidt, William	SCHMI-W	Somers, Harry S.	SOME
Schnabel, Artur	SCHN	Soproni, Jozsef	SOPR
Schoeck, Othmar	SCHOE	Sor, Fernando	SOR
Schoenberg, Arnold	SCHO	Sowerby, Leo	SOWE
Schoenfield, Paul	SCHOEN	Speer, Daniel	SPEE
Schubel, Max	SCHUBL	Spohr, Ludwig	SPOH
Schubert, Franz	SCHUB	Spontini, Gasparo	SPON
Schule, Bernard	SCHULE	Stainer, John	STAI
Schulhoff, Erwin	SCHULH	Stamitz, Johann	STAM-J
Schuller, Gunther	SCHULL	Stamitz, Karl	STAM
Schultze, Johann C.	SCHULT	Starer, Robert	STAR
Schuman, William	SCHUM-W	Stein, Leon	STEI
Schumann, Clara	SCHUM-C	Stenhammar, Wilhelm	STEN
Schumann, Robert	SCHUM	Stevens, Halsey	STEV
Schürmann, Gerard	SCHUR	Stich, Jan V.	STIC
Schütz, Heinrich	SCHUT	Stockhausen, Karlheinz	STOC
Schwartz, Paul	SCHW	Stoltzer, Thomas	STOL
Scott, Tom	SCOT	Stölzel, Gottfried H.	STOLZ
Scriabin, Alexander	SCRI	Stout, Alan	STOU
Sculthorpe, Peter	SCUL	Stradella, Alessandro	STRAD

Straight, Willard	**STRAI**	Titelouze, Jean	**TITE**
Strang, Gerald	**STRAN**	Toch, Ernst	**TOCH**
Straus, Oscar	**STRAU-O**	Tomasi, Henri	**TOMA**
Strauss, Franz	**STRAU-F**	Tomkins, Thomas	**TOMK**
Strauss, Johann	**STRAU**	Torelli, Giuseppe	**TORE**
Strauss, Johann, Sr.	**STRAU-S**	Tosar, Hector	**TOSA**
Strauss, Josef	**STRAU-J**	Tosti, Francesco	**TOST**
Strauss, Richard	**STRAU-R**	Tournemire, Charles	**TOUR**
Stravinsky, Igor	**STRAV**	Tovey, Donald	**TOVE**
Subotnick, Morton	**SUBO**	Toyama, (Françoise) Michiko	**TOYA**
Suk, Josef	**SUK**	Trabaci, Giovanni	**TRAB**
Sullivan, Sir Arthur	**SULL**	Tremblay, George	**TREM**
Suppé, Franz von	**SUPP**	Trimble, Lester	**TRIM**
Surinach, Carlos	**SURI**	Trogan, Roland	**TROG**
Susato, Tielman	**SUSA**	Trythall, Gilbert	**TRYT**
Süssmayr, Franz	**SUSS**	Tsintsadze, Sulkhan	**TSIN**
Swanson, Howard	**SWAN**	Turina, Joaquín	**TURI**
Sweelinck, Jan P.	**SWEE**	Turner, Charles	**TURN**
Swing, Raymond G.	**SWIN**	Tuthill, Burnet	**TUTH**
Sydeman, William	**SYDE**		
Szabelski, Boleslaw	**SZAB**	Uhl, Alfred	**UHL**
Szabo, Ferenc	**SZABO**	Urbanner, Erich	**URBA**
Szalowski, Antoni	**SZAL**	Ussachevsky, Vladimir	**USSA**
Szeligowski, Tadeusz	**SZEL**	Uttini, Francesco	**UTTI**
Szervansky, Endre	**SZER**		
Szokolay, Sandor	**SZOK**	Vainberg, Moysey	**VAIN**
Szymanowski, Karol	**SZYM**	Valentine, Robert	**VALE**
		Valentini, Giuseppe	**VALEN**
		Vallerand, Jean	**VALL**
Taffanel, Paul	**TAFF**	Van Hulse, Camil	**VANH**
Tailleferre, Germaine	**TAIL**	Van Vactor, David	**VANV**
Takata, Saburo	**TAKA**	Vandelle, Romuald	**VAND**
Takemitsu, Toru	**TAKE**	Vandor, Sandor	**VANDO**
Tallis, Thomas	**TALL**	Vanhal, Jan K.	**VANH**
Talma, Louise	**TALM**	Varèse, Edgar	**VARE**
Tanenbaum, Elias	**TANE**	Varga, Ruben	**VARG**
Taneyev, Sergei	**TANEY**	Vassilenko, Sergey	**VASS**
Tansman, Alexandre	**TANS**	Vaughan Williams, Ralph	**VAUG**
Tardos, Bela	**TARD**	Vecchi, Orazio	**VECC**
Tartini, Giuseppe	**TART**	Vejvanovsky, Pavel	**VEJV**
Tate, Phyllis	**TATE**	Veracini, Francesco	**VERA**
Taverner, John	**TAVE**	Verdi, Giuseppe	**VERD**
Taylor, Deems	**TAYL**	Verrall, John	**VERR**
Tchaikovsky, Peter Ilyitch	**TCHA**	Viadana, Lodovico	**VIAD**
Tcherepnin, Alexander	**TCHE**	Victoria, Tomas Luis de	**VICT**
Telemann, Georg Philipp	**TELE**	Vierne, Louis	**VIER**
Templeton, Alec	**TEMP**	Vieuxtemps, Henri	**VIEU**
Terreni, Bonaventura	**TERR**	Villa-Lobos, Heitor	**VILL**
Thomas, Ambroise	**THOM**	Vincent, John	**VINC**
Thompson, Randall	**THOMP**	Vincze, Imre	**VINCZ**
Thomson, Virgil	**THOMS**	Viotti, Giovanni B.	**VIOT**
Thorne, Francis	**THOR**	Visee, Robert de	**VISE**
Tigranian, Armen	**TIGR**	Viski, Janos	**VISK**
Tinctoris, Johannes	**TINC**	Vitali, Tommaso A.	**VITA**
Tippett, Michael	**TIPP**	Vivaldi, Antonio	**VIVA**
Tischhauser, Franz	**TISC**	Vorisek, Jan V.	**VORI**

Wagenaar, Bernard	**WAGE**	Wilder, Alec	**WILD**
Wagenseil, Georg C.	**WAGEN**	Wilding-White, Raymond	**WILDI**
Wagner, Josef F.	**WAGN-J**	Wilhelmine,	
Wagner, Richard	**WAGN**	Markgrafin von Bayreuth	**WILH**
Waldteufel, Emil	**WALD**	Willaert, Adrian	**WILLA**
Wallace, William V.	**WALL**	Williams, Clifton	**WILL**
Walther, Johann G.	**WALTH**	Williamson, Malcolm	**WILLI**
Walton, William	**WALT**	Wilton, Charles H.	**WILT**
Wanhal	**See Vanhal**	Wimberger, Gerhard	**WIMB**
Ward, Robert	**WARD-R**	Winter, Peter	**WINT**
Ward-Steinman, David	**WARD-D**	Wiren, Dag	**WIRE**
Warlock, Peter	**WARL**	Wissmer, Pierre	**WISS**
Warren, Elinor R.	**WARR**	Wolf, Hugo	**WOLF**
Waxman, Ernest	**WAXM**	Wolf-Ferrari, Ermanno	**WOLF-F**
Weber, Ben	**WEBE-B**	Wolff, Christian	**WOLF-C**
Weber, Carl Maria von	**WEBE**	Wolff, Erich	**WOLF-E**
Webern, Anton	**WEBER**	Wolpe, Stefan	**WOLP**
Weelkes, Thomas	**WEEL**	Wood, Joseph	**WOOD**
Weill, Kurt	**WEIL**	Woodcock, Robert	**WOODC**
Weinberger, Jaromir	**WEIN**	Work, Julian C.	**WORK**
Weiner, Leo	**WEINE**	Wuorinen, Charles	**WUOR**
Weinzweig, John	**WEINZ**	Wykes, Robert	**WYKE**
Weis, Flemming	**WEIS-F**	Wyner, Yehudi	**WYNE**
Weisgall, Hugo	**WEISG**		
Weiss, Adolph	**WEIS-A**	Xenakis, Yannis	**XENA**
Weiss, Sylvius	**WEIS-S**		
Wellesz, Egon	**WELL**	Yardumian, Richard	**YARD**
Werner, Gregor	**WERN**	Ysaye, Eugene	**YSAY**
Wesley, Samuel S.	**WESL**	Yun, Isang	**YUN**
Weyse, Christoph	**WEYS**		
White, Donald	**WHIT-D**	Zachau, Friedrich W.	**ZACH**
White, Ruth	**WHIT-R**	Zador, Eugen	**ZADO**
Whitney, Robert	**WHITN**	Zandonai, Riccardo	**ZAND**
Whittaker, Howard	**WHITT**	Zanetti, Gasparo	**ZANE**
Whittenberg, Charles	**WHITTE**	Zaninelli, Luigi	**ZANI**
Widmann, Erasmus	**WIDM**	Zbinden, Julien-François	**ZBIN**
Widor, Charles Marie	**WIDO**	Zeisl, Eric	**ZEIS**
Wieniawski, Henryk	**WIEN**	Zelenski, Wladislaw	**ZELE**
Wigglesworth, Frank	**WIGG**	Zelenka, Jan D.	**ZELEN**
Wilbye, John	**WILB**		

CHAPTER III

CHAPTER III

BASIC RULES FOR TERM THREE

RULES ON THE USE AND FORMATION OF TERM THREE

300. DEFINITION

Term Three is the third part of the class number. Its function is to indicate a title.

301. PHYSICAL FORMATION OF TERM THREE

Term Three is placed directly under Term Two, and may be composed of two or three capital letters, a number or series of numbers, or a combination of capital letters and numbers.

ES	(Term One: Symphonies)
BRAH	(Term Two: Brahms)
2	(Term Three: Symphony no. **2**)
F	(Term One: Chamber Music)
BEET	(Term Two: Beethoven)
SER	(Term Three: **Serenade**)
GP	(Term One: Music for Solo Piano)
MOZA	(Term Two: Mozart)
SON 10	(Term Three: **Sonata no. 10**)

302. TYPES OF TITLES

Two types of titles may be used to form Term Three: *album titles* and *work titles*. The following rules define each type, and indicate their proper use.

303. ALBUM TITLES

A. Definition

An album title is the name given a recording by the record company; such a title may mention the composer, the author, a work of literature, a work of music or a performer, or it may be a wholly fanciful name.

"Louise Bogan Reads Her Own Works." Decca 9132
"Sousa Forever." Victor LSC 2569
"Pennario Plays Concert Encores." Capitol P 8338
"Meet the Beatles." Capitol T 2047
"Music of the High Renaissance in England." Turnabout 4017
"Rhapsody Under the Stars." Capitol SP 8494

B. When to Use an Album Title

Use the album title to form Term Three when one of these forms of entry are used in Term Two:

PERFORMER ENTRY	COLLECTIONS ENTRY
TITLE ENTRY	ALL SUBJECT ENTRIES

"An Evening with Belafonte."	**MA**
Featuring Harry **Bela**fonte.	● **BELA** (Performer Entry)
Victor LSP 1402	● **EB** (Album Title)

If a Composer Entry or an Author Entry is used in Term Two, use the album title to form Term Three if the first work on the recording does not occupy one-third or more of side one.

Sousa: "Sousa Forever."	**H**
Morton Gould and his	● **SOUS** (Composer Entry)
Symphonic Band.	● **SF** (Album Title)
Victor LSC 2569	
Dickens: "Dickens Duets."	**V**
Excerpts from various works	● **DICK** (Author Entry)
read by Frank Pettigell.	● **DD** (Album Title)
Spoken Arts 741	

C. Albums in a Series

In the rules on Title Entry in chapter II, rule II-207-c4 indicates that if a recording is part of a special series, and Title Entry is to be used in Term Two, the series title is used, and not the title of the individual album. [Series titles may be used to form Term Two when necessary, even if the specific rules of a category do not allow for the use of Title Entry.] In cases when a series title has been used to form Term Two, the name of the individual album is used in Term Three.

Jazz: vol. 1, "The **South**."	**MJ**
Folkways 2801	**JAZZ** (Series Title)
	● **SOU** (Album Title)
	F 01
Jazz: vol. 2, "The **Blues**."	**MJ**
Folkways 2802	**JAZZ** (Series Title)
	● **BLU** (Album Title)
	F 02

D. How to Abbreviate an Album Title for Use in Term Three

The following rules describe how to abbreviate an album title for use in Term Three. (For rules and explanations regarding transliterated titles, translated titles, and spellings, see section III-308.)

1. *Basic Rule*

Use the initial of each consecutive key word in the album title, up to a total of three letters. A key word is one which is not a preposition or an article.

"**Pennario Plays Concert** Encores." **PPC**
"**Melodies** of the **Masters**." **MM**

2. *Titles Beginning With a Preposition*

If an album title begins with a preposition, use the initial of that preposition as part of Term Three.

"**By** the **Time I Get** to Phoenix." **BTI**

3. *Titles in Foreign Languages*

If an album title is in German or one of the romance languages, observe the same rules as for English titles: use the initial of each consecutive key word up to a total of three letters, and ignore articles and prepositions, unless the title begins with a preposition. For titles in other languages (especially transliterated titles), use the initial of each consecutive word (including articles and prepositions) up to a total of three letters.

> "Le Temps des Guitares." (Tino Rossi)   **TG**
> "Det Sjunger Nagonting Inom Mej." (Macs Olsson)   **DSN**

4. *One-Word Titles*

If the title of an album is composed of only one word, use the first three consecutive letters of that word. (In determining one-word titles, do not count articles.)

> "Revolver." (Beatles)   **REV**

5. *Performer's Name in the Album Title*

Many album titles include the name of the featured performer. When Performer Entry is used in Term Two, and the album title begins with the FULL name of the performer, do not use his name as part of the title in forming Term Three, but start with the first word following his name.

> "Mahalia Jackson in Concert."   **IC**
> "Johnny Cash at Folsom Prison."   **AFP**

If only part of the performer's name is used, or if it appears somewhere other than in the beginning of the title, include the name as part of the title.

> "Johnny's Greatest Hits."   **JGH**
> "Uniquely Mancini."   **UM**

304. WORK TITLES

A. Definition

Work titles are the names given to specific works of music or literature by their composers or authors.

> Shakespeare: "A Midsummer Night's Dream."
> Bergsma: "Carol on Twelfth Night."
> Lalo: "Concerto in D Major for Cello and Orchestra."

B. When to Use Work Titles

Use the work title to form Term Three when Composer Entry or Author Entry has been used in Term Two, provided that the first work on the recording occupies one-third or more of side one.

Verdi: "Rigoletto."	**B**
Berger, Peerce, Warren, etc.	**VERD** (Composer Entry)
Victor LM 6021	◉ **RIG** (Work Title)
Wilde: "Picture of Dorian Gray."	**V**
Caedmon 1095	**WILD** (Author Entry)
	◉ **PDG** (Work Title)

C. How to Abbreviate Work Titles in Term Three

Because of special problems in the field of music regarding titles, the rules for work titles in literature and music are listed separately. (See sections III-305, 306 following.) For rules and explanations regarding transliterations, translations, and spellings, see section III-307.

305. ABBREVIATION OF WORK TITLES: LITERATURE

A. Initials of Key Words

To form Term Three, use the initial of each consecutive key word of the work title, up to a total of three letters. A key word is one which is not a preposition or an article.

"Taming of the Shrew." **TS**

B. Titles Beginning With a Preposition

If a work title begins with a preposition, use the initial of that preposition as part of Term Three.

"At the Hawk's Well." **AHW**

C. Titles in Foreign Languages

If a work title is in German or one of the romance languages, observe the same rules as for English titles: use the initial of each consecutive key word up to a total of three letters, and ignore articles and prepositions, unless the title begins with a preposition. For titles in other languages (especially transliterated titles), use the initial of each consecutive word (including articles and prepositions) up to a total of three letters.

"Jeu de l'Amour et du Hasard." **JAH**

D. One-Word Titles

If the work title is composed of only one word, use the first three consecutive letters of that word to form Term Three. (In determining one-word titles, do not count articles.)

"Hair." **HAI**

306. ABBREVIATION OF WORK TITLES: MUSIC

There are two types of work titles used for works of music: *distinctive titles* and *non-distinctive titles*. It is necessary to understand clearly the difference between these two in order to make the proper entry in Term Three.

A. Distinctive Titles

1. *Definition*

A distinctive work title is a unique, descriptive name which the composer has chosen for a specific composition. This name may indicate the musical form and/or the medium for which the work was composed, or the title may be completely fanciful; it will be unique, however, in that it cannot be confused with any other title by the same composer.

> Stravinsky: "Le Baiser de la Fee."
> Tansman: "Triptych for String Orchestra."
> Ives: "Three Page Sonata for Piano."
> Cage: "Amores for Prepared Piano and Percussion."
> Purcell: "Music for the Funeral of Queen Mary."

2. *Popular Titles*

The distinctive title should not be confused with the "popular" title. Whereas distinctive titles are those selected by the composer, "popular" titles are descriptive names or phrases added by others, such as critics, publishers, musicologists, etc., and which have come to be associated with a particular work over a period of time. These names are *not* used in the classification number.

> Beethoven: "Concerto No. 5, **The Emperor.**"
> Mozart: "Symphony No. 41, **Jupiter.**"

3. *Abbreviation of Distinctive Titles for Use in Term Three*

The rules for the abbreviation of distinctive work titles are identical to those for the abbreviation of Work Titles of Literature. (See section III-305.)

B. Non-Distinctive Titles

1. *Definition*

A non-distinctive work title is one which merely indicates the musical form of the composition, and/or the medium for which it was composed. These titles are considered non-distinctive because a composer may write any number of compositions in the same form or for the same medium, and it is necessary to add identifying information, such as the musical key or a number, in order to distinguish one work from another.

Piano Sonata   **Piano Sonata No. 14**
Mass   **Mass in B Minor**
Symphony   **Symphony No. 2, Op. 42**
Quartet   **Quartet No. 4, Op. 3, No. 1**

"Sonata," "symphony," "quartet," etc., are actually musical form words. If a musical form word is used with a descriptive adjective or phrase, it becomes part of a distinctive title.

"Symphony on a French Mountain Air."

Thus the presence of a musical form word does not mean automatically that one is dealing with a non-distinctive title. However, a phrase indicating the MEDIUM for which the work is written *does not* make the title distinctive.

Sonata for Violin and Piano.
Suite for Violin, Viola and Cello.

The addition of a unique, descriptive word DOES make a title distinctive.

"Dahomey Suite for Oboe and Piano."

2. *Formation of Non-Distinctive Titles for Use in Term Three*
Use the abbreviation of the musical form word to form Term Three. The abbreviation is composed of the first three letters of the musical form word in most cases. The following table is a *partial listing* of musical form words and their Term Three abbreviation. (See 306D-B3 for important exceptions to this rule.)

Serenade for Violin and Piano   **SER**

TABLE OF ABBREVIATIONS OF MUSICAL FORMS

adagio	**ADA**	nonet	**NON**
andante	**AND**	octet	**OCT**
allemande	**ALL**	pastorale	**PAS**
bagatelle	**BAG**	polonaise	**POL**
ballade	**BAL**	prelude	**PRE**
canon	**CAN**	quartet	**QUA**
cantata*	**CAN**	quartet (string)*	**QS**
cassation	**CAS**	quintet	**QUI**
concerto*	**CON**	requiem	**REQ**
concertone	**CON**	rhapsody	**RHA**
divertimento	**DIV**	romance	**ROM**
duet	**DUE**	rondino	**RON**
duo	**DUO**	rondo	**RON**
fantasia	**FAN**	scherzo	**SCH**
(also fantasy, phantasie, etc.)		septet	**SEP**
fugue	**FUG**	serenade	**SER**
impromptu	**IMP**	sextet	**SEX**
magnificat	**MAG**	sinfonia	**SIN**
mass*	**MAS**	sinfonia concertante	**SC**
(also missa brevis &		sonata*	**SON**
missa solemnis)		suite	**SUI**
mazurka	**MAZ**	trio	**TRI**
motet	**MOT**	variation	**VAR**
nocturne	**NOC**	waltz	**WAL**

*Use these abbreviations only after consulting the following special rules

3. *Exceptions in the Term Three Formation of Non-Distinctive Title Abbreviations*

Exceptions to the standard rules for Term Three entry formation are provided for certain musical works. These special rules are given because the peculiar structure of some categories dictate a variant entry, or because the exceptional length, quantity, or popularity of some types of works require a more detailed shelving organization.

NOTE: *In the following rules there are repeated references to music numbers; a full description of music numbers is found in section III-307.*

a. Cantatas

The entry for a cantata in Term Three is the abbreviation CAN followed by a *form* number.

> Bach: "Cantata No. 80. Ein feste
> Burg ist unser Gott."   **CAN-80**

If there is no *form* number, use the distinctive title to form Term Three.

b. Concertos

The Term Three entry for a concerto in category EC is the abbreviation for the solo instrument plus the *form* number. (Complete rules are given in category EC for the Term Three entry.) If a work is called "concerto," but is not classed in category EC because it is not actually a work for solo instrument and orchestra, use the abbreviation CON in Term Three.

| Prokofiev: "Concerto No. **3**, for Piano and Orchestra." | EC
PROK
● **P-3** |
| Soler: "**Con**certi for Two Organs." | GO
SOLE
● **CON** |

c. Masses

The Term Three entry for a "mass" is the abbreviation MAS followed by a *form* number. This abbreviation applies to the terms "missa brevis" and "missa solemnis," but not to "requiem mass." (See the Table of Abbreviations in section III-306-B2 to determine the entry for "requiem.") If there is no *form* number, use the *opus* number, or the *thematic catalog* number, in that order of preference.

Mozart: "Mass in C Minor, K.427." **MAS-427**
Beethoven: "Missa Solemnis in
D Major, Op. 123." **MAS-123**

If there are no music numbers available, but a distinctive title exists, then the distinctive title may be used in Term Three.

Palestrina: "Missa Aeterna Christi Munera." **MAC**

d. Piano and Other Solo Instrument Sonatas

The Term Three entry for a sonata is the abbreviation SON followed by a *form* number. If there is no *form* number available, use the *opus* number or the *thematic catalog* number, in that order of preference. If no music number is available, use only the abbreviation SON.

Dello Joio: "**Son**ata No. **3** for Piano." **SON-3**

Schubert: "**Son**ata in A for Piano,
Op. **120**, D.664." **SON-120**

Liszt: "**Son**ata in B for Piano." **SON**

e. String Quartets

The Term Three entry for a string quartet is the abbreviation QS followed by a *form* number. If there is no *form* number available, use the *opus* number or the *thematic catalog* number, in that order of preference. If no music number is available, use only the abbreviation QS.

> Janacek: "Quartet No. 2."   **QS-2**
> Haydn: "Quartet, Op. 42."   **QS-42**

All other types of quartets, such as "wind quartet," "guitar and strings quartet," "percussion quartet," etc., are entered solely as the abbreviation QUA in Term Three.

> Paganini: "Quartet in A for Guitar and Strings."   **F**
> **PAGA**
> ● **QUA**

> Beethoven: "Quartet in E Flat for Piano and   **F**
> Strings, Op. 16."   **BEET**
> ● **QUA**

f. Symphonies

The Term Three entry for a symphony in category ES is the *form* number. (Complete rules are given in category ES for the Term Three entry.) The word "symphony" is sometimes used in distinctive titles, and then is treated as part of the distinctive title.

> Mendelssohn: "Symphony No. **3**."   **ES**
> **MEND**
> ● **3**

> Stravinsky: "Symphony of Psalms."   **C**
> **STRAV**
> ● **SP**

307. MUSIC NUMBERS

A. Explanation of Music Numbers

Four different types of numbers are used to identify works of music: Form Numbers, Opus Numbers, Sub-Opus Numbers, and Thematic Catalog Numbers. Each has a specific function, and a single work of music may have one, several, all or none of these numbers assigned to it.

1. *Opus Numbers*

Opus numbers are those assigned consecutively to all works written by a composer, usually by chronological order of composition. These numbers are assigned either by the composer or by the original publisher. (In the case of early music publishers, the opus numbers often represent the order of publication rather than the order of composition.) The term Opus is usually abbreviated Op. when used as part of a title.

> Prokofiev: "Sonata for Cello and Piano, **Op. 119**."
> Chausson: "Symphony in B Flat, **Op. 20**."

2. *Sub-Opus Numbers*

Sub-opus numbers are used as a means of individual identification when several works have been published simultaneously and assigned the same opus number.

> Beethoven: "Piano Trio in E Flat, Op. 1, **No. 1**."
> "Piano Trio in G, Op. 1, **No. 2**."
> "Piano Trio in C Minor, Op. 1, **No. 3**."

3. *Form Numbers*

Form numbers are those assigned to all works written in one musical form by a composer; usually the numbering is by chronological order of composition.

> Rachmaninoff: "Piano Concerto **No. 1**, Op. 1."
> "Piano Concerto **No. 2**, Op. 18."
> "Piano Concerto **No. 3**, Op. 30."
> "Piano Concerto **No. 4**, Op. 40."

NOTE: Some authorities use the term "serial number" rather than "form number." The term "form number" is preferred in this publication because it describes the particular music number and differentiates it from the other types of music numbers (all of which are variations of serial numbers).

4. *Thematic Catalog Number (Musicologist's Number)*

In the case of certain prolific composers whose works had no opus numbers, or where such numbering was inconsistent and faulty, individual musicologists have compiled catalogs of all of a composer's known works, arranged them in chronological order of composition (insofar as possible), and numbered them in that order. Three such numbering schemes are the Kochel listings for Mozart, Schmieder for Bach, and Deutsch for Schubert.

> Mozart: "Fantasia in C Minor, **K**. 475."
> Bach: "Concerto in A Minor for Flute, Violin
> and Harpsichord, **S**. 1044."
> Schubert: "Sonata for Arpeggione and Piano, **D**. 821."

5. *Numbers in Combination*

Since each type of number serves a specific function, a single work may have several such numbers, and it is not impossible, though not usual, for one work to have all four types of numbers.

> Schubert: "Quartet, **No. 10**, **Op. 125**, **No. 1**, **D.87**."

6. *Accuracy and Use*

The numbers used for musical works are simply a device for identification. There is nothing sacred about these numbers, and the accuracy of many of them is often brought into question, especially when chance or scholarship unearths new information or unpublished compositions. Occasionally it becomes necessary to change the numbering of a composer's works (the Dvorak symphonies are a notable example). When new numberings are established, and these are subsequently adopted and used by recording companies, the classifier should make the necessary changes in the classification.

B. Music Numbers in Term Three

Music numbers are used in Term Three with some non-distinctive title entries. (See III-306-B.) (Music numbers are never used with distinctive titles.) When the rules permit the use of several different types of music numbers, always select the number to be used by the following order of preference:

1. Form Number
2. Opus Number
3. Thematic Catalog Number

Note that the sub-opus number is *never* used in Term Three.

308. SPELLINGS, TRANSLATIONS AND TRANSLITERATIONS

A. Basic Rule

Titles of musical works may appear in several variant forms and in languages translated from the original.

    Le Nozze di Figaro
    Le Mariage de Figaro
    Marriage of Figaro

When using a musical work title to form Term Three, use the version of the title which has most popular use in current books, journals, periodicals, documentaries of motion pictures or television, and concert program notes. Especially useful is title information found on the labels and jackets of recordings produced and printed in the United States or Canada. (See also 308-E.)

Since the objective of the ANSCR class number is to arrange recorded materials for ease of use by the general public, the musical work title used to form Term Three must be the one of most popular use and must take precedence over the original language title or other variations unless, of course, the original language title is the title of most popular use. Once the popular use title of a work is established, this title should be used as the authority for determining the class numbers for all future recordings of that work. (See 308-B below.)

This emphasis on the use of common or popular title in the class number may mean that the language or spelling of the title used to form

Term Three and the language or spelling of the title used for cataloging will not correspond. These differences are intended and will not affect the usefulness of either.

Title Used for Class Number
Marriage of Figaro (title most popularly used)

Catalog Uniform Title
Le Nozze di Figaro (title of scholarly use)

B. Consistent Use of Title

Always use the musical work title of popular use to form Term Three, and establish that title as the authority for all future classification, regardless of the language variations found on various recordings, or of the language of the title used in cataloging.

C. Transliterated Titles

Use the English or romance language translations whenever possible in preference to transliterated titles.

The Fair at Sorochinsk, not Sorochinskaia iarmarka.

Transliterated titles are used when the work is best known by its transliteration.

Boris Godunov (transliteration of the Russian)

D. Spellings

The spellings of transliterated titles used in Term Three do not pose special problems as a rule, since only the first letter of key words are used (except in the case of one-word titles, where the first three consecutive letters are used to form Term Three). The American English transliteration is preferred in cases of doubt.

E. Authorities on Title Translations and Transliterations

Rule 308-A states that when there are several variations in spelling or language, the selection of the correct form of a title is based upon the most common or popular usage. If there is difficulty in determining common usage, the classifier is advised to consult current tools such as the *Schwann Long Playing Record Catalog*. Such publications attempt to reflect common usage and have the additional advantage of being readily available to the public to orient the record user's approach.

CHAPTER
IV

CHAPTER IV

BASIC RULES FOR TERM FOUR

RULES ON THE USE AND FORMATION OF TERM FOUR

400. DEFINITION

Term Four is the fourth part of the class number. Its function is to identify specific recordings by giving each a version number. The ANSCR scheme is not designed to class works of music and literature, but to class recorded performances of such works. The addition of Term Four to the other three terms of the class number results in a unique class number for each recorded performance (*i.e.*, version) of a work.

401. PHYSICAL FORMATION OF TERM FOUR

Term Four is placed directly under Term Three, and is composed of one capital letter which is called the alpha symbol followed by one space and two numbers. The alpha symbol is the initial of a name connected with the actual performance on the recording, and the two numbers are the last two digits of the commercial record number.

ES	(TERM ONE, indicating the category "Symphonies")
BEET	(TERM TWO, indicating the composer "Beethoven")
9	(TERM THREE, indicating the title "Symphony No. 9")
O 16	(TERM FOUR, indicating the Ormandy version of Beethoven's "Symphony No. 9," available on the Columbia recording MS-7016.)

402. HOW TO DETERMINE THE ALPHA SYMBOL FOR USE IN TERM FOUR

The alpha symbol (capital letter) used in Term Four is the initial of the name of a performer who is "featured" on the recording. If the featured performer is an individual, the initial letter of his surname is used. If the featured performer is a group, the initial letter of the first word in the corporate group name is used.

Horowitz   **H**
Amadeus Quartet   **A**

403. HOW TO DETERMINE A "FEATURED" PERFORMER

The following rules indicate how to determine which names on the recording are those of "featured" performers and may be considered for use in Term Four. The word "performer" is used to define both an individual and a corporate group.

A. Performer Entry in Term Two

None of the rules in this section applies if Term Two of the class number is a Performer Entry. By establishing a Performer Entry for a recording (according to the rules in section II-206), the classifier has already determined the featured performer, and the initial letter of that performer's surname or corporate name is also used in Term Four. It is important to keep this rule in mind because some of the following rules would be inconsistent or contradictory if applied to recordings with the Performer Entry in Term Two. It should be remembered also that Performer Entry is the principal form of entry in a number of categories, particularly in the areas of popular and folk music; therefore, most of the rules concerning music recordings in this section apply to recordings of classical music.

B. Names on the Album Cover

To be considered a "featured" performer, the performer's name must appear on the album front cover. A performer's name is displayed on the album cover because he has a major or important role in the performance on the recording, or because he is very well known and his name will help identify and sell the recording, even if his part in the recording is small. Where there are performers featured on the album cover, those performers whose names appear only in the program notes or on the disc label are not considered "featured" performers.

C. When There Are No Names on the Album Cover

If no performers' names are featured on the album's front cover, then the program notes or other descriptive materials on the album cover are examined to see which names are given prominence (by means of bolder or larger type, by format and layout, etc.). Do not consider as "featured" performers those persons whose names are found only on the disc label.

D. When There Are No Prominent Names

If no names are given prominence through large or bold type and all the names are listed in a specific arrangement, such as alphabetical order, order of appearance, etc., the classifier must reason that those artists with the longest or most important parts on the recording are the featured performers. In this case, if a well-known artist has a bit part, he will not be considered a "featured" performer, since no attempt has been made to advertise his presence on the recording. (This type of problem usually occurs with recordings with a cast of characters, such as operas, plays and oratorios.)

E. When There Are No Names at All

If there are no performers' names available anywhere on the cover, then it is necessary to use the initial letter of the record company's name in place of a performer's initial. (Do not use the names of performers which appear only on the disc label.)

F. Collections

If the recording is a collection of individual performances by many different performers, then use the initial letter of the record company's name to form the alpha symbol of Term Four.

G. Music and Non-Music Recordings

The above rules apply to all types of recordings; detailed rules are provided in the following sections for music recordings and non-music recordings.

404. MUSIC RECORDINGS — TYPES OF PERFORMERS

There are three types of performers to be considered in music recordings: the soloist, either vocal or instrumental, the performing group, either vocal or instrumental, and the conductor.

A. The Soloist

If a soloist is featured on the recording, use the initial letter of his surname in Term Four.

Schumann: "Frauenliebe und Lieben."	**D**
Sung by Kathleen Ferrier.	**SCHUM**
London 5020	**FL**
	● **F 20**
Brahms: "Concerto No. 2 for Piano."	**EC**
Van Cliburn, pianist, with the Chicago	**BRAH**
Symphony, Fritz Reiner conducting.	**P-2**
RCA Victor LSC 2581	● **C 81**
Britten: "Young Person's Guide to the Orchestra."	**EA**
Conducted and narrated by the composer (Britten).	**BRIT**
London 6398	**YPG**
	● **B 98**

(See detailed rules in sections IV-405, 406.)

B. The Performing Group

If one performing group is featured on the recording, use the initial letter of the first word of the group name in Term Four. (A symphony orchestra is not treated as a performing group.)

Debussy: "Quartet in G Minor, Op. 10."	**F**
Played by the Budapest String Quartet.	**DEBU**
Columbia MS 6015	**QS-10**
	● **B 15**
Palestrina: "Magnificat."	**C**
Sung by the Strasbourg Choral Society.	**PALE**
Period 513	**MAG**
	● **S 13**

(See detailed rules in section IV-407, 408.)

184

C. The Conductor

If the work or works on the recording are for orchestra, without soloists or performing groups, then the initial letter of the orchestra conductor's name is used in Term Four. (A symphony orchestra is not treated as a performing group.)

Tchaikovsky: "Sleeping Beauty."   **EB**
Ansermet conducting the Suisse Romande Orchestra.   **TCHA**
London 2304   **SB**
        ● **A 04**

(See detailed rules in section IV-409.)

D. Order of Precedence

Various types and combinations of performers may be featured on a recording and pose a problem as to which name should be used to form Term Four. There are two basic rules of precedence in selecting names. They are as follows and IN THIS ORDER:

1. Individuals (not including conductors) take
   precedence over groups.
2. Voices take precedence over instruments.

Therefore, to select the proper initial for Term Four, proceed in the following order:

1. Singer/narrator
2. Instrumentalist
3. Vocal group
4. Instrumental group (not including
   symphony orchestras)
5. Conductor

(Detailed instructions on the use and selection of these types of performers' names are provided in sections IV-405, 406, 407, 408, 409.)

405. SINGERS

This section provides detailed rules on the use and selection of singers' names in Term Four.

A. Categories in Which Names of Singers Are Used

The names of singers may be used in Term Four on recordings classed in the following categories:

A MUSIC APPRECIATION
B OPERAS: COMPLETE AND HIGHLIGHTS
C CHORAL MUSIC
D VOCAL MUSIC
K through **R**

(The classifier is reminded that these rules do not apply when Term Two is a Performer Entry—see section IV-403.)

185

B. When to Use the Name of a Singer

If a singer is featured on the recording, use the initial of the singer's surname in Term Four.

Schubert: "Die Schone Mullerin."	**D**
Sung by Dietrich **Fischer-Dieskau.**	**SCHUB**
Angel S 3628	**SM**
	● **F 28**

C. More Than One Singer

If more than one singer is featured on the recording, use the surname of the singer in the highest voice register to form Term Four.

Mahler: "Das Lied von der Erde."	**D**
Sung by Elsa **Cavelti**, soprano,	**MAHL**
and Anton Dermota, tenor.	**LE**
Vox VBX 115	● **C 15**

D. Collections of Singers

If the recording is a collection of individual performances by many different singers, then use the initial of the record company's name in Term Four.

"Royal Family of Opera."	**D**
London RFO-S-1	**COLL**
	RFO
	● **L 1**

E. Singers in the Same Voice Register

If two singers who are featured on a recording sing in the same voice register, use the name which comes first in alphabetical order in Term Four.

Strauss, J.: "Die Fledermaus."	**B**
Sung by Wilma Lipp and Hilde	**STRAU**
Gueden, sopranos; Anton	**FLE**
Dermota and Julius Patzak,	● **G 06**
tenors; Clemens Kraus	
conducting the Vienna	
Philharmonic Orchestra.	
Richmond 62006	

F. Singers and Vocal Groups

If a singer and a vocal group are featured on the recording, use the name of the singer to form Term Four. (A member of the vocal group who sings a solo is not considered a featured singer.)

Handel: "Messiah."	**C**
Sung by Adele **Addison**, soprano;	**HAND**
Russell Oberlin, counter-tenor;	**MES**
David Lloyd, tenor; William	● **A 03**
Warfield, baritone; the West-	
minister Choir, and the New York	
Philharmonic, Leonard Bernstein	
conducting.	
Columbia M2S 603	

G. Singers and Instrumentalists or Instrumental Groups

If a singer and an instrumentalist or instrumental group are featured on a recording, use the name of the singer to form Term Four.

Brahms: "Songs for Alto, Viola, and Piano."	**D**
Sung by Helen **Watts,** contralto, with	**BRAH**
Cecil Aronowitz, viola, and Geoffrey	**SAV**
Parsons, piano.	● **W 68**
Oiseau S 268	

Barber: "Dover Beach."	**D**
Sung by Dietrich **Fischer-Dieskau,**	**BARB**
with the Juilliard Quartet.	**DB**
Columbia KS 7131	● **F 31**

406. INSTRUMENTALISTS

This section provides detailed rules on the use and selection of instrumentalists' names in Term Four.

A. Categories in Which Names of Instrumentalists Are Used

The names of instrumentalists may be used in Term Four on recordings classed in the following categories:

A   MUSIC APPRECIATION
EC CONCERTOS
F   CHAMBER MUSIC
G   SOLO INSTRUMENTAL MUSIC
K through **R**

(The classifier is reminded that these rules do not apply when Term Two is a Performer Entry—see section IV-403.)

B. When to Use the Name of an Instrumentalist

If an instrumentalist is featured on the recording, use the initial letter of the instrumentalists' surname to form Term Four.

Mozart: "Concerto No. 21 for Piano."	**EC**
Robert **Casadesus,** pianist, with the	**MOZA**
Cleveland Orchestra, Szell conducting.	**P-21**
Columbia MS 6695	● **C 95**

C. More Than One Instrumentalist

If more than one instrumentalist is featured on the recording, use the initial letter of the surname of the artist who performs on the instrument named first in the title of the work.

> Haydn's "Quartet for Lute, Violin, Viola and Cello:" use the name of the lute player to form Term Four.
> Saint-Saens' "Sonata for Clarinet and Piano, Op. 167:" use the name of the clarinetist to form Term Four.

If the musical instruments are not named in the title of the work, use the instrumentalists' name which is first in alphabetical order to form

Term Four. (Do not include accompanists; accompanists are never considered featured performers.)

Dohnanyi: "Serenade in C, Op. 10."	F
Played by Heifetz, violin; Primrose,	DOHN
viola, and **Feuermann,** cello.	SER
Victor LVT 1017	● F 17

D. Collections of Instrumentalists

If the recording is a collection of individual performances by many different instrumentalists, then use the initial letter of the record company's name to form Term Four.

"Treasury of Music: The Concerto."	EC
RCA 2-Victor LE 6001	COLL
	TMC
	● R 01

E. Works for Identical Instruments

If the work title lists two identical instruments, use the initial letter of the instrumentalist's name which is first in alphabetical order to form Term Four.

Mozart: "Concerto No. 7 for Two Pianos."	EC
Badura-Skoda and Gianoli, pianists.	MOZA
Westminster 18546	P-7
	● B 46

F. Instrumentalists and Vocal Groups

If an instrumentalist and a vocal group are featured on the recording, use the initial of the name of the instrumentalist to form Term Four. (Do not include accompanists; accompanists are never considered featured performers.) Rule 406-f does not apply for recordings classed in category C.

Gabrieli: "Intonazioni d'Organo and Motets."	GO
Biggs, organ, Greg Smith Singers, Texas Boys Choir	GABR
and the Tarr Brass Ensemble.	IO
Columbia MS 7071	● B 71

G. Instrumentalists and Instrumental Groups

If an instrumentalist and an instrumental group are both featured on a recording, use the initial of the name of the instrumentalist to form Term Four. (Never use the individual names of members of a performing group.)

Schubert: "Quintet in A, Op. 114."	F
Curzon, pianist, with members of	SCHUB
the Vienna Octet.	QUI
London 6090	● C 90

H. Instrumentalists and Singers

If an instrumentalist and singer are featured on a recording, use the initial of the name of the singer to form Term Four.

Britten: "Serenade for Tenor, Horn & Strings."	**D**
Peter **Pears,** tenor; Barry Tuckwell, horn,	**BRIT**
and the London Symphony.	**SER**
London 6398	● **P 98**

407. VOCAL GROUPS

This section provides detailed rules on the use and selection of names of vocal groups in Term Four.

A. Categories in Which Names of Vocal Groups Are Used

The names of vocal groups may be used in Term Four on recordings classed in the following categories:

    A MUSIC APPRECIATION
    C CHORAL MUSIC
    K through **R**

(The classifier is reminded that these rules do not apply when Term Two is a Performer Entry—see section IV-403.)

B. When to Use the Name of a Vocal Group

If a vocal group is featured on the recording, use the initial of the name of the group to form Term Four.

Gabrieli: "Sacrarum Symphoniarum	**C**
Continuato (9 Motets)."	**GABR**
Sung by the **Munich** Capella Antiqua.	**SSC**
Conducted by Ruhland.	● **M 56**
Telefunken S 9456	

Bach: "Cantata No. 18."	**C**
Monteverdi Choir and	**BACH**
Leonhardt Consort.	**CAN-18**
Telefunken S 9442	● **M 42**

C. More Than One Vocal Group

If more than one vocal group is featured on the recording, use the initial of the group name which is first in alphabetical order to form Term Four.

Thomson: "Alleluia."	**C**
Harvard Glee Club and Radcliffe Choral	**THOMS**
Society, Woodworth conducting.	**ALL**
Cambridge 403	● **H 03**

189

D. Collections of Vocal Groups

If the recording is a collection of individual performances by many different vocal groups, then use the initial of the record company's name to form Term Four.

"First International University	C
Choral Festival."	COLL
RCA Victor LSC 7043	FIU
	● R 43

E. Vocal Group and Singers

If a vocal group and a singer are featured on the recording, use the initial of the name of the singer to form Term Four. (A member of a vocal group who sings a solo is not considered a featured singer.)

Verdi: "Requiem."	
Sung by **Nelli,** soprano; Barbieri,	
mezzo-soprano; Di Stefano, tenor;	C
Siepi, bass-baritone; the Robert	VERD
Shaw Chorale and the NBC Symphony	REQ
conducted by Toscanini.	● N 18
RCA Victor LM 6018	

F. Vocal Group and Instrumentalists

If a vocal group and an instrumentalist are featured on the recording, use the initial of the name of the instrumentalist to form Term Four. (Do not include accompanists; accompanists are never considered featured performers.) Rule 407-f does not apply for recordings classed in category C.

Gabrieli: "Intonazioni d'Organo and Motets."	GO
Biggs, organ; Greg Smith Singers, Texas	GABR
Boys Choir, Tarr Brass Ensemble.	IO
Columbia MS 7071	● B 71

G. Vocal Group and Instrumental Group

If a vocal group and an instrumental group are both featured on the recording, use the initial of the name of the vocal group to form Term Four.

Bach: "Cantata No. 18."	C
Monteverdi Choir and the	BACH
Leonhardt Consort.	CAN-18
Telefunken S 9442	● M 42

408. INSTRUMENTAL GROUPS

This section provides detailed rules on the use and selection of names of instrumental groups in Term Four.

A. Categories in Which Names of Instrumental Groups Are Used

The names of instrumental groups may be used to form Term Four for recordings classed in the following categories. (A symphony orchestra is not treated as a performing group.)

A MUSIC APPRECIATION
F CHAMBER MUSIC
H BAND MUSIC
K through **R**

(The classifier is reminded that these rules do not apply when Term Two is a Performer Entry—see section IV-403.)

B. When to Use the Name of an Instrumental Group

If an instrumental group is featured on the recording, use the initial of the first word of the group's corporate name to form Term Four.

Beethoven: "Quartet No. 5, Op. 18, No. 5."	**F**
Claremont Quartet.	**BEET**
Nonesuch 71152	**QS-5**
	● **C 52**

C. More Than One Instrumental Group

If more than one instrumental group is featured on the recording, use the initial of the group name which is first in alphabetical order to form Term Four.

Hindemith: "Octet."	**F**
Fine Arts Quartet, and members	**HIND**
of the N.Y. Woodwind Quintet.	**OCT**
Concert-Disc 218	● **F 18**

D. Collections of Instrumental Groups

If the recording is a collection of individual performances by many different instrumental groups, then use the initial of the record company's name to form Term Four.

"Heart of the March."	**H**
Featuring three concert bands	**COLL**
in separate performances.	**HM**
Mercury SR-2-9131	● **M 31**

E. Instrumental Group and Singers

If an instrumental group and a singer are featured on the recording, use the initial of the name of the singer to form Term Four.

Barber: "Dover Beach."	**D**
Sung by Dietrich **Fischer-Dieskau**	**BARB**
with the Juilliard Quartet.	**DB**
Columbia KS 7131	● **F 31**

F. Instrumental Group and Instrumentalist

If an instrumental group and an instrumentalist are featured on the recording, use the initial of the name of the instrumentalist to form Term Four. (Never use the individual names of members of an instrumental group.)

Schumann: "Quintet in E Flat for Piano and Strings, Op. 44."	**F**
	SCHUM
Leonard **Bernstein,** pianist, and the Juilliard Quartet.	**QUI**
Columbia MS 6929	● **B 29**

G. Instrumental Group and Vocal Group

If an instrumental group and a vocal group are featured on the same recording, use the initial of the name of the vocal group to form Term Four.

Bach: "Cantata No. 18."	**C**
Monteverdi Choir and the Leonhardt Consort.	**BACH**
Telefunken S 9442	**CAN-18**
	● **M 42**

409. CONDUCTORS

This section provides detailed rules on the use of conductors' names in Term Four.

A. Categories in Which Names of Conductors Are Used

The names of conductors may be used to form Term Four for recordings classed in the following categories:

A MUSIC APPRECIATION
EA GENERAL ORCHESTRAL MUSIC
EB BALLET MUSIC
ES SYMPHONIES
J ELECTRONIC AND MECHANICAL MUSIC
K through **R**

(The classifier is reminded that these rules do not apply when Term Two is a Performer Entry—see section IV-403.)

B. When to Use the Name of a Conductor

If there are no featured singers, narrators, instrumentalists, vocal groups, or instrumental groups on the recording, use the initial of the name of the conductor of the orchestra or chamber orchestra to form Term Four. (Symphony orchestras are not treated as instrumental groups. See section IV-404-B.)

Holst: "The Planets."	**EA**
Adrian **Boult** and the Vienna State Opera Orchestra	**HOLS**
	PLA
Westminster 14067	● **B 67**

C. More Than One Conductor

If more than one conductor is featured on the recording, and classification is by composer and *work title* (i.e., Composer Entry in Term Two and work title in Term Three) use the initial of the name of the conductor who conducts the first work on side one of the recording to form Term Four.

<pre>
Ives: "Symphony No. 1."   ES
Recording contains four Ives symphonies.   IVES
   Ormandy conducts no. 1, Bernstein   1
   nos. 2 and 3, Stokowski no. 4.   ● O 83
   Columbia D3S 783
</pre>

If more than one conductor is featured on the recording, and the recording is classed as a collection (i.e., Title, Subject or Collection Entry in Term Two), use the initial of the name of the conductor which is first in alphabetical order.

<pre>
"Evening at the Ballet Russe."   EB
   Dorati and the London Symphony,   COLL
   Fennell and the Eastman-Rochester   EBR
   Orchestra, and Skrowaczewski and   ● D 95
   the Minneapolis Symphony.
   Mercury 18095
</pre>

D. Collections of Conductors

If the recording is a collection of individual performances by different conductors and none is featured on the album cover, then use the initial of the record company's name to form Term Four.

<pre>
"Melodies of the Masters."   EA
   Capitol SP 8563   COLL
                                               MM
                                            ● C 63
</pre>

410. NARRATORS IN MUSICAL WORKS AS PERFORMERS

In some works of music, the part of solo performer is written for a speaking voice rather than a singing voice. Use the unitial of the name of the person who narrates or recites to form the alpha symbol in Term Four. If there is more than one speaker, use the initial of the name which is first in alphabetical order.

<pre>
Prokofiev: "Peter and the Wolf."   EA
   Ustinov, narrator, with Von   PROK
   Karajan and the Philharmonia Orchestra.   PW
   Angel S 35638   ● U 38
</pre>

411. NON-MUSIC RECORDINGS

Two types of non-music recordings are provided for in this scheme: spoken recordings and recordings of sounds.

A. Spoken Recordings

Categories S through X, ZI and ZS are designated for spoken record-ings. The following rules apply to all spoken recordings except for those classed in categories X, ZI and ZS. (Specific rules for category X are found in section I-Xd and for categories ZI and ZS in section I-Z.)

1. *Alphabetical Order*

Determine the featured performers on the recording according to the rules outlined in section II-403, and then use the initial of the surname which is first in alphabetical order to form Term Four.

Coleridge: "Rhyme of the Ancient Mariner."	**U**
Read by Christopher **Casson,** John	**COLE**
Franklyn and William Styles.	**RAM**
Spoken Arts 910	● **C 10**

2. *Performing Group*

If a performing group is featured on the recording, use the initial of the first word of the group name to form Term Four.

Goldsmith: "She Stoops to Conquer."	**T**
Performed by the **Swan** Theatre	**GOLD**
Players of Dublin.	**SSC**
Spoken Arts 958	● **S 58**

3. *Individual and Performing Group*

If an individual and a performing group are both featured on the recording, use the initial of the name of the individual to form Term Four. (Do not use the names of members of a performing group.)

Shakespeare: "Rape of Lucrece."	**T**
Tony **Church** and the Cambridge	**SHAK**
University Marlowe Dramatic Society.	**RL**
Argo 139/41	● **C 39**

4. *No Performers' Names Featured*

If no names are featured on the recording, use the initial of the record company's name to form Term Four.

Shakespeare: "Julius Caesar."	**T**
Recorded in performance by	**SHAK**
the Shakespeare for Students Company.	**JC**
Folkways 9614	● **F 14**

5. *Documentary Recordings*

In the case of documentary recordings, use the initial of the name of narrator to form Term Four. (If there is more than one narrator, use the name which is first in alphabetical order.)

"Blitzkrieg."	**W**
Narrated by Walter **Cronkite.**	**BLIT**
Columbia ML 5511	**BLI**
	● **C 11**

If there is no narrator, and the names of the editor, producer, writer, director, or speakers are featured on the recording, use the initial of the name which is first in alphabetical order to form Term Four.

<table>
<tr><td>"The Mormon Pioneers."</td><td>**W**</td></tr>
<tr><td>Produced by Goddard **Lieberson.**</td><td>MORM</td></tr>
<tr><td>Columbia LS-1025</td><td>MP</td></tr>
<tr><td></td><td>● **L 25**</td></tr>
</table>

If no one's name is featured, use the initial of the record company's name to form Term Four.

B. Sounds Recordings

If the recording features the name of the individual who has made the recording, use the initial of his surname to form Term Four. (If there is more than one individual, use the name which is first in alphabetical order.)

<table>
<tr><td>"Sounds of Sea Animals."</td><td>**Y**</td></tr>
<tr><td>Recorded and narrated by W. N. **Kellogg.**</td><td>NATURE</td></tr>
<tr><td>Folkways 6125</td><td>SSA</td></tr>
<tr><td></td><td>● **K 25**</td></tr>
</table>

If no one's name is featured, use the initial of the record company's name to form Term Four.

<table>
<tr><td>"Authentic Sound Effects."</td><td>**Y**</td></tr>
<tr><td>**Electra** 7313/4</td><td>SOUNDS</td></tr>
<tr><td></td><td>ASE</td></tr>
<tr><td></td><td>● **E 13**</td></tr>
</table>

APPENDIX
ADAPTATION OF THE ANSCR SYSTEM
IN OTHER COUNTRIES

Although the ANSCR system was developed by American authors with experience in library systems in the United States, the scheme itself has no specific national orientation. In point of fact, a number of provisions have been built into the scheme so that it can be used effectively in any country which employs the Roman alphabet.

First of all, no mnemonic relationship exists between the letter representing a category and the heading for the material classed in the category. Therefore, no adjustment of the letters is needed; only the headings need be translated into the appropriate language.

Secondly, certain categories are designed so that the special interests of a country may be served. Category P, for example, is entitled *Folk and Ethnic Music, National*. The examples provided within this category relate to the United States, but this category should always contain the folk music of the country in which the scheme is used. Therefore, the country's name is to be substituted for "United States" wherever indicated. The ethnic divisions provided in this category refer of course to those in the United States, and it is expected that appropriate ones will be substituted according to the needs of individual countries.

Thirdly, the sub-categories of category M reflect popular music interests in the United States, particularly category MC for country and western music. Those sub-categories which are not useful may be dropped and others more pertinent to a country's popular music interests established in their place, using any letters in combination with M which are most convenient.

Other adjustments which may be made in the matter of Language Entry and Geographic Entry in Term Two are explained in detail in the rules for these forms of entry. (See sections II-211, 214.)

The rules in this first edition regarding spellings, translations, and transliterations are based upon American English usage. When using ANSCR in a country other than the United States, these rules may be modified to reflect the usage common to that country.

BIBLIOGRAPHY

The American Record Guide. New York: American Record Guide Inc. Monthly.

Anglo-American Cataloging Rules. Chicago: American Library Association, 1967.

Apel, Willi. *Harvard Dictionary of Music*. Cambridge, Massachusetts: Harvard University Press, 1967.

Baker, Theodore. *Biographical Dictionary of Musicians* with 1965 supplement. 5th edition, revised and enlarged by Nicolas Slonimsky. New York: G. Schirmer, 1958.

Berkowitz, Freda Pastor. *Popular Titles and Subtitles of Musical Compositions*. New York: The Scarecrow Press, Incorporated, 1962.

Ewen, David. *Encyclopedia of the Opera*. New York: Hill and Wang, 1963. 2nd edition.

Feather, Leonard. *The Encyclopedia of Jazz*. Revised edition. New York: Horizon, 1960.

Grants, Parks. *Handbook of Music Terms*. Metuchen, New Jersey: The Scarecrow Press, 1967.

Grove, Sir George. *Dictionary of Music and Musicians*. 5th edition, edited by Eric Blom. London: Macmillan, 1954. 9 volumes. 1961 supplement.

High Fidelity. Great Barrington, Massachusetts: Billboard Publications.

Lawless, Ray M. *Folksingers and Folksongs in America*. 2nd edition. New York: Duell, Sloan and Pearce, 1965.

Lubbock, Mark. *The Complete Book of Light Opera*. London: Putnam, 1962.

Mann, Margaret. *Introduction to Cataloging and the Classification of Books*. Chicago: American Library Association. 2nd edition, 1943.

The New Records. Philadelphia: H. Royer Smith Co. Monthly.

Pearson, Mary D. *Recordings in the Public Library*. Chicago: American Library Association, 1963.

Rules for Descriptive Cataloging in the Library of Congress. Washington: Library of Congress, 1949.

Scholes, Perey Alfred. *The Oxford Companion to Music.* 9th edition revised. London: Oxford University Press. 1955.

Stereo Review. Chicago: Ziff-Davis Publishing Company. Monthly.

Thompson, Oscar, editor. *The International Cyclopedia of Music and Musicians.* 8th edition, revised and edited by Nicolas Slonimsky. New York: Dodd, 1958.

World Almanac and Book of Facts. New York: Newspaper Enterprise Association, Inc., 1968.

INDEX

INDEX

INDEX

Entries in this index are arranged letter by letter as they are spelled. A typical index entry contains the following information:

Ballet instruction X-2B1b, 117

| Subject | Paragraph Citation | Page Number |

Entries in all capital letters refer to specific category headings:

CHAMBER MUSIC—CATEGORY F

200

Country and western music MC-1, *91*;
see also Cowboy music, Gospel music,
Frontier songs
COUNTRY AND WESTERN
MUSIC—CATEGORY MC
formation of class number MC-2, *91*
types of recordings MC-1, *91*
Cowboy music P-1C, *95*; MC-1, *91*
Creative writing, instruction X-2B1b,
117
Criticism
literary V-1, *111*; T-1, *106;*
U-1, *108*
music A-1, *44*

Dance bands H-1A, *80*
Dance instruction X-2, *116*
Dance music, popular MA, *90*
Dictation X-1, *116*
Dieting X-2B1c, *118; see also Reducing*
exercises
Disc recordings, basic rule of
classification 100, *43*
Distinctive titles
definition 306-A1, *172*
"popular titles" 306-A2, *172*
rules for abbreviating 305, *171;*
306-A3, *172*
Dixieland music MJ, *93*
Documentaries
for children ZI-1, *123*
dramatized biographies W-1, *114*
of historical events W-1, *114*
memoirs (read or related by the person) W-1, *114*
on music, lives of musicians, etc.
A-1, *44*
of popular music and musicians
M-2C, *90*; A-1B, *45*
reenactments W-1, *114*
on society and social problems W-1,
114
speeches, "live" W-1, *114*
DOCUMENTARY: HISTORY AND
COMMENTARY—CATEGORY W
formation of class number W-2, *115*
types of recordings W-1, *114*
Double-bass, solo GS-1, *73*
also categories L through R
Drag racing sounds Y-2B1, *120*
Drama *see Plays*
Duets D-1B, *52*; B-1B5, *47*
also categories K through R
Duets, instrumental *see Duos*
Duos GG-1B, *68*; GO-1B, *70*; GP-1B,
71; GS-1B, *73*; GV-1B, *75*; GW-1B,
77; GX-1B, *78*

also categories L through R
Duos, vocal *see Duets*

Easter carols R-1, *104*
ELECTRONIC AND MECHANI-
CAL MUSIC—CATEGORY J
formation of class number J-2, *82*
types of recordings J-1, *82*
Electronic music J-1, *82*
English language instruction X-2B1b,
117; X-2C1, *118*
Ensembles
string F-1A, *65*
wind F-1B, *65*; H-1B, *80*
Eskimo music (U.S.) P-1E, *95*;
P-2B2, *96*
Essays V-1, *111*
Ethnic entry
definition 210-A, *145;* P-2B2a, *96*
use & formation 210-B, *145;*
P-2B2b, *96*
Ethnic dances and rituals P-1, *94;*
Q-1, *97*
Ethnic music, outside U.S. Q-1, *97*
Ethnic music, U.S. P-1, *94*
Cajun music P-1E, *95*; P-2B2, *96*
Eskimo music P-1E, *95*; P-2B2, *96*
Hawaiian music P-1E, *95*;
P-2B2, *96*
Indian music, American P-1E, *95*;
P-2B2, *96*
Exercises, physical X-1, *116*;
X-2B1b, *117*

Fairytales ZS-1, *126*
Fife and drum music H-1, *80*
Film music L-1, *85*
Film soundtrack music L-1, *85*
Flute, solo GW-1, *76*
also categories L through R
FOLK AND ETHNIC MUSIC:
INTERNATIONAL—
CATEGORY Q
formation of class number Q-2, *97*
types of recordings Q-1, *97*
use of ANSCR outside U.S., *196*
FOLK AND ETHNIC MUSIC:
NATIONAL—CATEGORY P
formation of class number P-2, *95*
types of recordings P-1, *94*
use of ANSCR outside U.S., *196*
Folk dance instruction X-2B1b, *117*
Folk dance music *see Folk music, U.S.,*
and *Folk music, outside the U.S.*
Folk music, outside the U.S. Q-1, *97*;
C-1B, *49*; C-1D, *50*; D-1E, *53*

Folk music, U.S. P-1, *94*
  Afro-American P-1A, *94*
  anthologies A-1A, *44*
  bluegrass P-1, *94*
  contemporary P-1B, *94*
  cowboy and frontier P-1C, *95*
  gospel D-1E, *53*; P-1D, *95*; MC-1,
    91
  hymns C-1D, *50*; P-1E, *95*; D-1E,
    53
  indigenous ethnic P-1E, *95*
  spirituals D-1E, *53*; P-1A, *94*
Folksongs *see Folk music, U.S., and
  Folk music, outside the U.S.*
Forest sounds Y-2B1, *120*
Form numbers *see Music numbers*
French language instruction X-2C3,
  119; X-2B1b, *117*
Frontier songs P-1C, *95*

Geographic entry
  abbreviations, table of, *101*
  colonies, status of Q-3B, *99*
  countries
    abbreviation, rules for Q-3C, *100*
    definition Q-3A, *99*
    when to use Q-2B1c, *98*
  cultural styles Q-2B1e, *98*
  definition 211, *145*; Q-2B1a, *97*
  geographic areas Q-2B1d, *98*
  how to form Q-2B1b, *98*; Q-3C, *100*
German language instruction X-2B1b,
  117; X-2C3, *119*
Gilbert & Sullivan operettas K-1, *83*
Glass harmonica music GX-1, *78*
Glockenspiel GX-1, *78*
Gospel music P-1D, *95*; D-1E, *53*;
  MC-1, *91*
Grammar instruction X-2B1b, *117*
Gregorian chants A-1C, *45*
Gregorian entry
  definition 212-A, *146*
  how to form 212-C, *146*; A-2B2, *46*
  when to use 212-B, *146*; A-2B2, *46*
Group names *see Performers' names*
Guitar music
  concertos GG-1A, *68*; EC-1, *59*
  duos GG-1B, *68*
  "how-to" play X-1, *116*
  solo GG-1, *68*
  sonatas 306-B3d, *175*
  also categories L through R
GUITAR, MUSIC FOR SOLO—
  CATEGORY GG
  formation of class number GG-2, *68*
  types of recordings GG-1, *68*
Gypsy music Q-2B1e, *98*

Harmonica GW-1, *76*
  also categories L through R
Harmonica, glass, music GX-1, *78*
Harp, solo GS-1, *73*
  also categories L through R
Harpsichord music
  concertos GP-1A, *71*; EC-1, *59*
  duos GP-1B, *71*
  solo GP-1, *71*
  sonatas 306-B3d, *175*
  also categories L through R
Hawaiian music P-1E, *95*; P-2B2, *96*
  also categories L through R
History
  for children ZI-1, *123*
  documentary W-1, *114*
  of literature & authors V-1, *111*
  of music A-1 *44*
  of plays & playwrights T-1, *106*
  of poetry & poets U-1, *108*
Holiday music
  Christian R-1, *104*
  Christmas music R-1, *104*
  classical music used for holidays
    R-1A, 1B, *104*
  Jewish R-1, *104*
  national R-1, *104*
  also category Q, *97*
HOLIDAY MUSIC—CATEGORY R
  formation of class number R-2, *104*
  types of recordings R-1, *104*
Holidays, national, music for R-1, *104*
Holy days, music for, *see Holiday music*
Horn, solo GW-1, *76*
  also categories L through R
"How-to" recordings X-1, *116*
  for children ZI-1, *123*
Humanities
  lectures, essays V-1, *111*
  study courses in X-1, *116*
Humor *see Varieties and Humor—
  Category S*
Hymns
  choral C-1D, *50*
  Christmas R-1, *104*
  concert solo voice D-1E, *53*
  folk or ethnic P-1, *94*; Q-1, *97*
  by pop performers MA, *90*; MC, *91*;
    MJ, *93*

Indian music, American P-1E, *95*;
  P-2B2, *96*
INSTRUCTIONAL RECORDINGS—
  CATEGORY X
  formation of class number X-2, *116*
  types of recordings X-1, *116*

203

INSTRUCTIONAL RECORDINGS
    FOR CHILDREN—CATEGORY ZI
    formation of class number ZI-2, *123*
    treatment of non-children's record-
        ings ZI-3, *123*
    types of recordings ZI-1, *123*
Instructional subject entry
    basic instructional skills X-2B1b, *117*
    definition 213-A, *146*; X-2B1a, *117*
    key names of skills X-2B1c, *118*
    use & formation 213-B, *146*;
        X-2B1b, *117*
Instrumental choirs, grouping by
    G-1B, *67*
INSTRUMENTAL MUSIC, SOLO—
    CATEGORY G
    guide to classification G-2, *67*
    structure G-1, *67*
        scope G-1A, *67*
        sub-categories G-1B, *67*
Instrumentalists (groups), use of
    names in Term Four
    collections of groups 408-D, *191*
    instrumental group and instrumen-
        talists 408-F, *192*
    instrumental group and singer
        408-E, *191*
    instrumental group and vocal group
        408-G, *192*
    more than one group 40-8C, *191*
    when to use 408-A,B, *191*
Instrumentalists (groups), use of
    names in Term Two 206-B, *137*
Instrumentalists (soloists), use of
    names in Term Four
    collections of instrumentalists 406-D,
        188
    identical instruments 406-E, *188*
    instrumentalists and instrumental
        groups 406-G, *188*
    instrumentalists and singers 406-H,
        189
    instrumentalists and vocal groups
        406-F, *188*
    more than one instrumentalist
        406-C, *187*
    when to use 406-A,B, *187*
Instrumentalists (soloists), use of
    names in Term Two 206-C, *139*
Instruments, musical
    abbreviations for EC-2C2, *60*
    history or description of A-1, *44*
    "how-to" play X-1A, *116*
Instruments, solo, with orchestra
    EC-1, *59*
Interview W-1, *114*
Islands, name abbreviations for, *102*

Japanese language instruction
    X-2B1b, *117*; X-2C3, *119*
Japanese Noh plays T-2B3, *107*
Jazz bands H-1A, *80*; MJ-1, *93*
Jazz music MJ-1, *93*
    blues MJ-1, *93*; P-1A, *94*; MA-1, *90*
    dixieland music MJ-1, *93*
JAZZ MUSIC—CATEGORY MJ
    formation of class number MJ-2, *93*
    types of recordings MJ-1, *93*
Jewish cantorial music D-1, *52*
Jewish holiday music R-1, *104*
Jug bands H-1A, *80*

Language entry
    definition 214-A, *146*
    how to form 214-C, *148*
    when to use 214-B, *147*
        anonymous works 214-B2, *147*
        multiple languages 214-B4, *147*
        national literature 214-B5, *148*
        single language, multiple authors
            214-B1, *147*
        translated works 214-B3, *147*
Language instruction X-1, *116*;
    X-2B1b, *117*; X-2C3, *119*
Languages, names of in Term Three
    X-2C3, *119*
Languages, names of in Term Two
    how to form 214-C, *148*
        abbreviations
            in national literature 214-C2,
                148
            table of 214-C3, *149*
        basic rule 214-C1, *148*
Lectures
    on humanities, sciences, arts, etc.
        V-1, *111*
    on music A-1, *44*
    on plays & playwrights T-1, *106*
    on poets & poetry U-1, *108*
    on prose, literature, and writers
        V-1, *111*
    to teach specific skills X-1, *116*
Literary criticism
    general works V-1, *111*
    plays T-1, *106*
    poetry U-1, *108*
    prose V-1, *111*
Literary history *see History*
Literature
    American 214-B5, *148*; 214-C2, *148*
    anonymous works 214-B2, *147*
    Canadian 214-B5, *148*; 214-C2, *148*
    for children ZI-1, *123*; ZS-1, *126*
    foreign 214-C3, *149*

performers' names (individuals)—
  Term Two
performers' names—Term Four
performers' names—Term Three
person-as-subject names
professional names
pseudonyms
spellings
stage names
transliterations
Narrators' names
  in Term Four 410, *193*
  in Term Two A-2B1, *45*; W-2B1, *115*
Nature sounds Y-1, *120*
Negro music *see Afro-American music*
Negro spirituals *see Spirituals*
Nickelodeon music Y-1, *120*
Nightclub acts S-1, *105*
Noh plays T-2B3, *107*
Non-distinctive titles
  abbreviating, rules for 306-B2, *173*
  abbreviating—exceptions 306B3, *174*
    cantatas 306-B3a, *174*
    concertos 306-B3b, *175*;
      EC-2C1, *60*
    masses 306-B3c, *175*
    sonatas 306-B3d, *175*
    string quartets 306-B3e, *174*
    symphonies 306-B, *172*;
      ES-2C1, *64*
  definition 306-B1, *172*
  musical forms, table of abbreviations
    306-B2, *174*
Novels V-1, *111*
Numbering of musical works
  see Music numbers
Nursery rhymes ZS-1, *126*; ZM-1, *124*

Oboe, solo GW-1, *76*
  also categories L through R
Opera
  arias B-1B1, *47*; D-1A, *52*
  ballet music from B-1B2, *47*;
    EB-1B, *57*
  choruses B-1B3, *47*; C-1F, *50*
  complete, highlights, selections
    B-1A, *47*
  orchestral excerpts and arrange-
    ments B-1B4, *47*; EA-1B, *55*
  overtures EA-1B, *55*
  television productions of L-1D, *86*
  vocal combinations, operatic B-1B5,
    47; D-1B, *52*
OPERAS: COMPLETE AND
  HIGHLIGHTS—CATEGORY B
  formation of class number B-2, *48*
  types of recordings B-1, *46*

Operettas
  ballet music from EB-1C, *58*
  complete & excerpts K-1, *83*
  orchestral collections K-1B, *83*
  television productions of L-1D, *86*
  vocal collections K-1A, *83*
Opus numbers 307-A1, *176*
Oratorios C-1, *49*; L-1D, *86*
Orchestral music
  ballet suites and arrangements
    EA-1A, *55*; EB-1B, *57*
  with chorus C-1G, *50*
  concertos EC-1, *59*
  general works (excluding concertos,
    ballet music and symphonies)
    EA-1, *55*
  incidental music EA-1, *55*
  opera excerpts and arrangements
    EA-1B, *55*
  overtures EA-1, *55*
  sinfonias and sinfonia concertantes
    EA-1C, *56*
  suites EA-1, *55*
  symphonies ES-1, *62*
  tone poems EA-1, *55*
ORCHESTRAL MUSIC—
  CATEGORY E
  guide to classification E-2, *55*
  structure E-1, *55*
  sub-categories E-1, *55*
ORCHESTRAL MUSIC, GENERAL
  —CATEGORY EA
  formation of class number EA-2, *56*
  types of recordings EA-1, *55*
Orchestras as performers, in Term
  Two 206-B5, *139*
Orchestras, chamber F-1A, *65*; E-1, *55*
Organ music
  concertos GO-1A, *69*; EC-1, *59*
  duos GO-1B, *70*
  solo GO-1, *69*
  sonatas 306-B3d, *175*
  also categories L through R
ORGAN, MUSIC FOR SOLO—
  CATEGORY GO
  formation of class numbers GO-2, *70*
  types of recordings GO-1, *69*
Overtures, operatic EA-1B, *55*
Overtures, orchestral EA-1B, *55*

Part songs C-1, *49*; D-1B, *52*
PERCUSSION AND UNUSUAL
  INSTRUMENTS—
  CATEGORY GX
  formation of class number GX-2, *79*
  types of recordings GX-1, *78*

Viola, solo GS-1, *73*
Violin music
  concertos GV-1A, *75*
  duos GV-1B, *75*
  solo GV-1, *75*
  sonatas 306-B3d, *175*
  also categories L through R
VIOLIN, MUSIC FOR SOLO—
  CATEGORY GV
  formation of class number GV-2, *75*
  types of recordings GV-1, *75*
Violoncello *see Cello*
Vocal combinations, operatic B-1B5, *47*
Vocal groups
  choruses C-1, *49*
  duets, trios, quartets, etc. D-1B, *52*;
    from opera B-1B5, *47*
  popular groups—categories K
    through R, *83-105*
Vocal groups, use of names in
  Term Four
  collections of vocal groups, 407-D,
    190
  more than one vocal group 407-C,
    189
  vocal groups and instrumentalists
    407-F,G, *190*
  vocal groups and singers 407-E, *190*
  when to use 407-A,B, *189*
Vocal music
  arias D-1A, *52*; B-1B1, *47*
  art songs D-1, *52*
  blues MJ-1, *93*; MA-1, *90*; P-1A, *94*
  carols R-1, *104*
  children's songs ZM-1, *124*; ZI-1,
    123
  chorales C-1, *49*
  choruses C-1, *49*
  Christmas music R-1, *104*
  cowboy music P-1C, *95*; MC-1, *91*
  duets, trios, quartets, etc. B-1B5, *47*;
    D-1B, *52*
  ethnic music P-1, *94*; Q-1, *97*
  folk music P-1, *94*; Q-1, *97*
  frontier songs P-1C, *95*
  gospel music P-1D, *95*; D-1E, *53*;
    MC-1, *91*
  Gregorian chants A-1C, *45*; 212, *146*
  holiday music R-1, *104*
  jazz music MJ-1, *93*
  lieder D-1, *52*
  madrigals C-1, *49*; D-1B, *52*
  masses C-1, *49*; 306-B3c, *175*
  musical shows K-1, *83*
  operas B-1, *46*
  operettas K-1, *83*
  oratorios C-1, *49*

part songs C-1, *49*; D-1B, *52*
plainsong A-1, *44*; C-1, *49*
pop music MA-1, *90*; MC-1, *91*;
  MJ-1, *93*; Q-1, *97*
pop music, foreign Q-1A, *97*; MA-1,
  90
requiems C-1, *49*; 306-B2, *173*
song cycles D-1, *52*; D-2B1, *54*
spirituals P-1A, *94*; D-1E, *53*
work songs P-1, *94*
VOCAL MUSIC—CATEGORY D
  formation of class number D-2, *53*
  types of recordings D-1, *52*
Voice register, in Term Four 405-E,
  186; B-2D, *48*; 405-C, *186*; K-2D, *85*
Voice training and instruction
  X-2B1b, *117*; X-2C4, *119*

Wind ensembles F-1B, *65*; H-1B, *80*
Wind instrument music
  concertos GW-1A, *76*
  duos GW-1B, *77*
  solo GW-1, *76*
  also categories L through R
WIND INSTRUMENTS, MUSIC
  FOR SOLO—CATEGORY GW
  formation of class number GW-2, *77*
  types of recordings GW-1, *76*
Woodwind instruments, solo *see Wind
  instrument music*
Work songs P-1, *94*
Work titles
  abbreviations of, in literature 305,
    171
    foreign languages 305-C, *171*
    initials of key words 305-A, *171*
    one-word titles 305-D, *171*
    prepositions 305-A, *171*;
      305-B, *171*
  abbreviations of, in music 306, *172*
    distinctive titles 305, *171*;
      306-A, *172*
    non-distinctive titles 306-B, *172*
  definition 304-A, *170*
  when to use 304-B, *171*
Writing, creative, instruction X-2B1b,
  117

Xylophone, solo GX-1, *78*
  also categories L through R

Yiddish music Q-2B1e, *98*

Zarzuelas K-1, *83*

212